Why the Catholic Church Must Change

Why the Catholic Church Must Change

A Necessary Conversation

Margaret Nutting Ralph

ROWMAN & LITTLEFIELD PUBLISHERS, INC.
Lanham • Boulder • New York • Toronto • Plymouth, UK

Published by Rowman & Littlefield Publishers, Inc.
A wholly owned subsidiary of The Rowman & Littlefield Publishing Group, Inc.
4501 Forbes Boulevard, Suite 200, Lanham, Maryland 20706
www.rowman.com

10 Thornbury Road, Plymouth PL6 7PP, United Kingdom

British Library Cataloguing in Publication Information Available

Library of Congress Cataloging-in-Publication Data

Ralph, Margaret Nutting.
Why the Catholic Church Must Change : a necessary conversation / Margaret Nutting Ralph.
p. cm.
ISBN 978-1-4422-2078-2 (cloth : alk. paper)—ISBN 978-1-4422-2079-9 (electronic)
1. Church renewal—Catholic Church. I. Title.
BX1746.R33 2013
282—dc23
2012050656

♾™ The paper used in this publication meets the minimum requirements of American National Standard for Information Sciences Permanence of Paper for Printed Library Materials, ANSI/NISO Z39.48-1992.

Printed in the United States of America

This book is dedicated to two valiant, faithful Catholic educators:

Sister Helen Maher Garvey, who, with five years of persistence, asked me to write this book. Some of what she taught me is discussed in chapter 5, "Ordination and Women's Role in the Church."

Father Joseph Vest, who, in my last conversation with him before his sudden death, also asked me to write this book. Some of what he taught me is discussed in chapter 6, "Homosexuality."

This dedication comes with my love and gratitude for your faithfulness to your vocations and your love for the Catholic Church.

Come, Holy Spirit.
Fill the hearts of your faithful.
Enkindle in us the fire of your love.
Send forth your Spirit,
and we shall be created,
and you shall renew the face of the earth.

This traditional Catholic prayer expresses the Catholic belief that we are not yet finished products but are in a process of being created. As we receive the inspiration of the Spirit, as we grow and change under the Spirit's urging, we become the people we are called to be, and we participate in the renewal of the whole world.

Contents

Introduction

The title of this book, *Why the Catholic Church Must Change: A Necessary Conversation*, inevitably triggers a wide variety of reactions. Some Catholics feel immediate resistance because they believe that the Catholic Church cannot change its teaching on a moral matter (more about this later). They think that what the Catholic Church needs is less conversation and more submission of will and intellect to the Magisterium. (The word *Magisterium*, which refers to the teaching authority of the Catholic Church, has been understood differently in different centuries. In this book I use the word not to refer to the teaching role of the whole people of God or to the role of theologians, but to the role of the pope and the bishops, those who have authority by virtue of ordination and office.)

Other Catholics feel attracted to the topic. Whether they themselves are practicing Catholics (the biggest group of Christians in the United States) or fallen-away Catholics (the third-biggest group of Christians in the United States),[1] they have family members and friends who no longer worship with the Catholic Church for a variety of reasons: they do not find the worship nourishing, they disagree with some teachings, they have been marginalized by present practices, or they have been hurt by an individual person's lack of pastoral response. They want the Catholic Church to be open to change.

Some people respond with indifference. If Catholic, they may want change, but they have no desire to join the conversation because they have no hope that change will occur. Why participate in a useless exercise? If not Catholic, they may think that the "necessary conversation" is one that should take place only among Catholics. Why should anyone but a Catholic care what the Catholic Church teaches?

Still others, whether Catholic or not, respond with great interest. They long for a conversation on possible changes in some Catholic teachings. They believe in the presence and power of the Spirit, inspiring disciples of Jesus Christ to be open to new knowledge and to grow in their understanding of how to continue Christ's mission to the world. They recognize that Catholic teachings play a role in public policy and affect all of us. They believe that the conversation that needs to take place must not be limited to Catholics. The experience and wisdom of others must be taken into account.

As I wrote this book, I tried to keep all of these possible readers in mind. However, I myself am Catholic and am among those Catholics who believe that the Catholic Church is being called to change some of its teachings and some of its practices. I am also firmly convinced that the Catholic Church must be in conversation with other Christians and with the world at large in order to correctly discern where the Spirit is calling not just the Catholic Church, but all of God's people.

After all, the Catholic Church is not the whole Church, not the whole body of Christ. Since Christians are called to be one in Christ, Catholics must be in dialogue with other Christians. In addition, Christians, including Catholics, live in a pluralistic society and are called to love all of God's beloved children. Since we cannot love those whom we do not know, all of us must, by necessity, be open to conversation with people of cultures and religions different from our own, and be open to understanding God's will for God's people in a wider context than we may have previously understood.

WHY "NECESSARY"?

Cardinal Timothy Dolan, in his November 2011 presidential address to the United States Conference of Catholic Bishops (USCCB) stated very clearly why a conversation about change in the Catholic Church is absolutely necessary. Then archbishop Dolan exhorted his fellow bishops to remember that "love for Jesus and His Church must be the passion of our lives." He then went on to say:

> Perhaps, brethren, our most pressing pastoral challenge today is to reclaim that truth, to restore the luster, the credibility, the beauty of the Church "ever ancient, ever new," renewing her as the face of Jesus, just as he is the face of

God. Maybe our most urgent pastoral priority is to lead our people to see, meet, hear and embrace anew Jesus in and through His Church.

Because, as the chilling statistics we cannot ignore tell us, fewer and fewer of our beloved people—to say nothing about those outside the household of faith—are convinced that Jesus and his Church are one. [2]

Some of the "chilling statistics" to which Cardinal Dolan refers have been provided to us by the U.S. Religious Landscape Survey of the Pew Research Center's Forum on Religion and Public Life. This research tells us that one out of every three people raised Catholic in the United States no longer identifies himself or herself as Catholic. [3]

If the U.S. bishops, not to mention the whole Magisterium, want to understand and reverse the reasons for this exodus, they must be in conversation with those who have left. The credibility of the Catholic Church will not be reclaimed unless the Catholic Church opens itself up to conversation and possible change.

TRANSPARENCY: CONSIDER THE SOURCE

In both Church and civil society, transparency is valued. In fact, one of the reasons the Catholic Church has lost credibility in some peoples' eyes is that our leaders have lacked transparency. This has been particularly true in the child sex abuse scandals. It has, with some frequency, been true in monetary matters. However these are not the only areas in which the Catholic Church has lacked transparency. If our deeds cannot stand the light of day, or for a Christian, the light of Christ, they are suspect.

For this reason, as I introduce the reader to an overview of the chapters, as well as an explanation of the relationship among them, I will also, when necessary, explain my personal relationship to the events described. This information will be helpful to the reader in assessing the validity of what I have to say. Each of us, myself included, brings unrecognized or unacknowledged prejudices with us when we discuss difficult issues. That is why we need to be in dialogue with each other; we need to listen to each other. That is why we need to be open with each other. This information will help the reader consider the source and draw valid conclusions based on the reliability of the information that is offered.

I want to acknowledge these experiences in this introduction rather than in the chapters that discuss particular issues because I want the chapter discussions to be about topics, not about people. My goal is to discuss issues, not to point fingers. For this reason, except for the book's dedication, in this book I refer to individual people only to name sources from which I have quoted, not to name people with whom I have had personal experience.

AN OVERVIEW OF THE CHAPTERS

Chapters 1 through 3

The first three chapters present a sustained argument that is intended to lay the foundation for the possibility of change.

Chapter 1 is titled "The Role of the Teaching Catholic Church in Our Search to Know God and God's Will." As a person who has been Catholic all my life, I greatly value the teaching voice of the Catholic Church. I want the Catholic Church to have the same formative role in the lives of my children and grandchildren that it has had in my life. However, I have had to grow in my understanding of just what that role is. Everyone who grows into adult faith faces the same task.

The chapter begins by demonstrating that there is a biblical foundation for a teaching Church as well as for a Petrine role (Peter's preeminence among the apostles). However, it also demonstrates a biblical foundation for the importance of charismatic gifts and for the priority of love over law. Explanations of infallibility and of the priority of conscience are also included. The goal of this chapter is to help the reader balance two facts: The Catholic Church is a teaching Church, and it is also a pilgrim Church. We are people on a journey. We are not undercutting the Catholic Church's teaching role by calling for change in certain areas of that teaching.

Not only the Catholic Church, but the whole body of Christ, is a pilgrim Church, led by the Spirit to grow in understanding in the light of new knowledge from many different fields in every generation. Every statement we make about God is inadequate to the truth. All of our explanations about the mysteries we are explaining use metaphorical language, not scientific language, and they include presumptions of the time. As we grow in knowledge from a wide variety of fields, we must be willing to reimage the truths we are trying to understand so that the contemporary generation can understand them. Therefore, at the same time that we accept the Scripture-based idea of a teaching Church, we must be open to the Spirit's promptings in order to fulfill our role as a pilgrim Church: to carry on Jesus's mission to the world.

Chapter 2 is titled "The Role of Experience and the Role of Scripture in Our Search to Know God and God's Will." The role of experience and the role of Scripture are integrally connected to each other in our search to know God. We know this because there is an integral connection between peoples' experiences and the very existence of Scripture. God revealed God's self through events. At the core of Scripture are people's insights about God, based on their own experiences.

My field of study is Scripture. I have had the privilege of traveling all over the country teaching Scripture, not only to Catholics but to people of other denominations. This experience has made me very aware that many people, especially Catholics, have not been encouraged to read the Bible, as distinct from the Lectionary (the book that contains the readings taken from the Bible, proclaimed at mass to celebrate the liturgical year). In addition, many people have not been taught to place biblical passages in the context in which they appear in the Bible, including the context of literary form (my field of study), in order to understand the revelation that the inspired author is teaching.

For this reason, in chapter 2 I explain what the Catholic Church, since 1943 with the publication of *Divino Afflante Spiritu*, has taught about the correct interpretation of Scripture. This contextualist approach to Scripture is not unique to Catholics. Indeed, many Jewish and Protestant scholars employed and advocated this approach to Scripture well before the Magisterium of the Catholic Church embraced it.

Familiarity with the contextualist approach to Scripture will help the reader understand the arguments presented in later chapters. In each chapter, when a present Catholic Church teaching or practice is discussed, I address the question: What does Scripture have to say on this topic? The answer to this question is important not just to Catholics but to all Christians, because all Christians have thirty-nine books of the Old Testament in common (the Catholic Old Testament canon includes an additional seven books); all Christians have the same New Testament; and Christians believe that the teachings in the Bible, once correctly understood, have authority.

In addition, chapter 2 discusses Scripture as a living word, a word that speaks to us today. This leads to a discussion of the authority of Scripture as a living word, as well as what is *use* and what is *abuse* of Scripture.

This knowledge, too, will aid the reader in understanding the arguments presented in later chapters. It is a sad fact that even though the Magisterium teaches Catholics to be contextualists, the Magisterium does not always act as a contextualist when defending certain Catholic Church doctrines that developed later in Church history. It is an abuse of Scripture to take an out-of-context biblical passage and use it to add authority to the Magisterium's teaching on a topic if the topic being taught is not the topic that was being addressed by the original inspired author.

Chapter 3 is titled "Can Catholic Church Teaching Change?" I discuss this topic because I know from my years of working in adult education for Catholic dioceses that many devoted Catholics do not believe that the Catholic Church can change its teaching on a moral matter. Until they are persuaded otherwise, they will not be open to the possibility of change in the twenty-first century.

Why do some Catholics believe that the Catholic Church cannot change teachings that have been promulgated by the Magisterium? It is because they understand such teachings to be infallible. This opinion was expressed clearly in an article on the Catholics United for the Faith website:

> To ensure unity of faith, the Magisterium of the Church has the task of interpreting the deposit of faith and applying it to specific times and circumstances. The Magisterium of the Church sometimes offers a solemn definition on a matter pertaining to faith or morals. These definitions provide absolute certainty that the teaching belongs to the deposit of faith. In other instances, the Magisterium identifies the truth found in the deposit of faith without providing a solemn definition. In these instances, though not solemnly defined, the teaching cannot be changed because it is true. These teachings are infallible. [4]

Among the teachings that the website's author claims cannot be changed are the male-only priesthood and the intrinsic evil of contraception.

I, on the other hand, am persuaded that Catholic Church teaching can change, based both on my knowledge of Church history and on my personal experience. It seems to me undeniable that the Church's teaching on usury, that is, on charging interest on a loan, has changed. In fact, I think many readers, not to mention dioceses and the Vatican Bank, routinely participate in usury by investing money on which they hope to receive a return.

Usury: An Example That Long-Standing Moral Teachings Can Change

Examining the Church's change of teaching on usury can serve as an example of how to interpret Scripture as a contextualist, how to apply core concepts to particular social settings, and how the images that we use to explain our conclusions can change, resulting in our having new insights and drawing new conclusions. Using a historical example rather than the more recent examples from my own experience, as I do in chapter 3, may meet with less resistance.

The word *usury* refers to charging interest on a loan. Many Old Testament passages forbid it. For instance, in Exodus we read: "If you lend money to my people, to the poor among you, you shall not deal with them as a creditor; you shall not exact interest from them" (Ex 22:24). Psalm 15 starts by posing the question: "O Lord, who may abide in your tent? / Who may dwell on your holy hill?" One of the responses to that question is: those "who do not lend money at interest" (Ps 15:5a).

The New Testament presumes the knowledge that charging interest on a loan is wrong. A virtuous person would not do it. For instance, in the parable of the talents, the master who is harsh, someone to fear, someone who reaps where he does not sow, is disappointed that his servant did not invest his talent and receive interest (see Matt 25:24–27 NRSV). The reason that a virtuous person would not charge interest on a loan is because it is one way of gouging the poor.

The Catholic Church taught against usury throughout its history and as recently as the eighteenth century. For instance, the Council of Vienne (1311) taught that a person who insists that usury is not a sin should be punished as a heretic. Benedict XIV taught against usury in his encyclical *Vix Pervenit* (1745).

How could a strong teaching with such a long history change? It could change because the admonition against charging interest on a loan was understood to be an application of a core biblical teaching to a particular social setting. The core teaching is that we must love our neighbor. The particular social setting is one person's lending money to another. The core teaching will never change: We must always love our neighbor. The application of that core teaching to a particular social setting may change. One may legitimately ask whether charging interest on a loan is always an example of abusing another person. Is there any social situation in which lending money and charging interest could be interpreted as loving one's neighbor, as a just act?

The answer to this question depends some on what analogies we draw to explore the problem. If we compare money to something that is consumable, like food, it does seem unjust to charge interest. If I have more food than I need, and my neighbor is starving, it seems only just that I share what I have with my neighbor. If the neighbor is ever in a position to pay me back, that would be great, but the neighbor certainly doesn't owe me more food than I gave him.

On the other hand, if I compare money not to something that is consumable, like food, but to something that can make other things grow, like land, my thinking might change. If I have more land than I need, and my neighbor needs land to grow crops to feed his family, it seems only just that I let my neighbor use some of my land. I'm not giving the neighbor the land, just letting the neighbor use it. If, when the crop has grown, my neighbor gives me a share of the crop as payment for the use of the land, that seems just. The land, however, is still mine.

Therefore, whether lending money at interest was understood to be a loving act or a selfish act changed, depending on the social setting. It could still be gouging the poor. On the other hand, many people who borrow money at a reasonable interest to go to school, to buy a car, or to buy a home do not feel that they are being abused. Rather, they are grateful for the opportunity to borrow, given their prospects and their ability to pay back the loan.

The examples of change that are used in chapter 3 to demonstrate that the Catholic Church has changed some teachings in the past are changes that have occurred in my lifetime. One hundred years ago, had I been the person I am now—a biblical contextualist and a person who, during the week, has worshipped with my ecumenical seminary colleagues at Lexington Theological Seminary (a Disciples of Christ seminary)—my actions both as a teacher of Scripture and as a worshipper would have been condemned by the teaching voice of the Catholic Church. Now, they are accepted, even encouraged. Chapter 3 establishes the fact that, in response to the Spirit's call, the Catholic Church can and does change some of its teachings.

Chapters 4 through 6

Chapters 4 through 6 discuss three areas in which many people believe that the Catholic Church is being called to be open to a conversation regarding whether its present teaching should be changed. These three topics are the use of contraception within marriage, women's role in the Catholic Church, and the civil rights of people whose sexual orientation is homosexual.

Chapter 4, on contraception, first traces the history of the Catholic Church's teaching on this subject. Many people believe that the Catholic Church's teaching on the use of contraceptives has never budged, but this is not accurate. There has already been a growth in understanding. One step has been the Church's teaching that one purpose of marriage, equal with the purpose of procreation, is the mutual expression of love between a husband and a wife. Another step has been the acceptance of the rhythm method as a means of birth control.

After tracing this history, chapter 4 discusses what Scripture has to say on the subject and what the Catholic Church presently teaches, and then discusses what questions and concerns remain. A major concern is that the Magisterium has not presented persuasive arguments to support the present teaching. Rather, the Magisterium has based much of its argument on a limited understanding of natural law, has changed the subject from teaching on contraception to stressing the authority of the Magisterium to teach on moral matters, and has admonished priests to act in obedience to this teaching as they minister to their fellow Catholics.

The Natural Law

Since the concept of natural law consistently enters the conversation when the Magisterium teaches about moral matters, including married couples' using any method of birth control other than rhythm as well as people of homosexual orientation engaging in sexual activity, it seems wise to explain this concept before we apply the concept to particular moral matters in chapters 4 and 6. One's understanding of natural law may well determine one's openness to the possibility of change in the Catholic Church's teaching regarding what is and what is not moral behavior.

To claim that there is a natural law is to claim that an objective moral order exists that has been established by God the creator, not by human consensus. Because this order is intrinsic to nature, it can be discovered through observation and through reason. For this reason, knowledge of the natural law is available to everyone and is not dependent on a particular religious creed. Because this intrinsic moral order, this natural law, affects everyone and can be discerned by everyone, when the Catholic Church bases a teaching on the natural law, that teaching is considered applicable to everyone, not just to Catholics.

Given this understanding of the natural law, individuals may differ on whether or not a teaching based on natural law can change. Some say that the created order of nature is stable. Others say that nature is involved in an evolutionary process. In addition, our understanding of the created order may change as we grow in knowledge from many different areas of study. Therefore, people define the concept of natural law differently depending on whether they stress its stability or its openness to change in the light of new knowledge.

For instance, the theologian Richard McBrien explains in his book *Catholicism* that the natural law can be understood as "the obligation, perceived by reason, to conform to nature" or it can be understood as "the obligation, built into nature, to use reason in moral judgment."[5] In the first definition, based on Greek thought, the natural law is static. Nature is a given and we are to conform our behavior to the order that God has established in nature. It is this understanding of natural law that pervades the Catholic Church's teaching on the morality of the use of birth control and on homosexual activity.

In the second definition, based on Roman thought, natural law is dynamic. Human beings, with their ability to explore, to discover new truths about nature, and to think creatively, will come to different judgments about the morality of specific acts, depending on the knowledge presently available and on the context for the action.

The moral theologian Richard Gula, in his book *Reason Informed by Faith*, agrees with McBrien on the two strains of thought in the development of the concept of natural law. He calls the Greek emphasis on the static or biological "physicalism" and the Roman emphasis on reason or the rational "personalism."[6] Embracing both emphases, Gula defines natural law as "reason reflecting on human experience discovering moral values."[7] In this definition, Gula leaves the door open for growth in understanding just what has been and is being revealed to human beings through the natural law. As human beings reflect on their experiences, they learn more about what is real, what is reality. Therefore, human beings must be open to growth in their understanding of what is true, of what is the moral action, of what action leads to human flourishing.

Based on this understanding of natural law, one must conclude that when a teaching of the Catholic Church that has been based on a natural law argument is questioned and challenged by a vast number of people, the Magisterium must be open to conversation with those who are reflecting on their own experience as they prayerfully try to discern God's will. Obviously, the truth of the teaching is not evident to other sincere truth seekers. In such a situation, the Magisterium must also be open to new understandings and possible changes in its teaching.

Women's Ordination

In chapter 5 we note that one of the reasons that the Catholic Church is losing credibility in the eyes of our younger generations is that the Magisterium refuses to allow the ordination of women. To many, this position seems indefensible. As we will demonstrate, Scripture reveals that women did serve the early Church in the role of deacon, and Scripture also reveals that Jesus did not ordain the apostles as priests. The practice of ordination developed well after Jesus's public ministry and resurrection.

For these reasons the argument that the Catholic Church lacks the authority to ordain women because Jesus picked only men for his apostles is simply not persuasive. We can't teach our young people to be critical thinkers, to examine a claim, the reasons for the claim, and the evidence that supports the reasons in every area of their lives except Church teachings. To be persuasive, the Catholic Church must be able to give sound reasons to support conclusions.

In chapter 5 we critically examine the reasons presently given by the Magisterium to justify denying ordination to women. We also note that, no matter what the intent, our present teaching against the ordination of women results in systemic discrimination against women serving the Catholic Church, even in roles that do not require ordination. The reader should be informed that in this chapter, when I refer to five nonordained Catholic Church employees who were dismissed during a "restructuring," I am referring to my own dismissal.

The Civil Rights of Homosexual People

Chapter 6 examines the Catholic Church's teaching in regard to homosexual persons. The Catholic Church presently teaches that sexual acts between people whose sexual orientation is toward members of their own sex are intrinsically disordered. Any sexual activity for such people is immoral, even within the context of a lifelong committed relationship. At the same time, the Catholic Church teaches that it is immoral to discriminate against homosexual persons.

In this chapter we first examine the biblical passages that speak of sexual activity between those of the same sex to see what exactly the inspired biblical authors are saying. We also examine the natural law arguments that result in homosexual acts being regarded as a disorder. We then note that the Catholic Church teaches us not to discriminate against homosexuals and ask whether or not forbidding civil marriage to committed homosexual couples results in discrimination. The chapter ends by posing a number of questions that those who do not want to discriminate against homosexuals must consider.

Chapters 7 through 10

Chapters 7 through 10 call on the Catholic Church to be open to change, not in teachings, but in present practices: in the way the Catholic Church applies a teaching or in the way it attempts to implement a teaching in our multicultural society. After all, the role of a teaching Church is not to lord it over people and enforce its will. The role of a teaching Church is to spread the good news of the Gospel to all people. Counterproductive tactics do not add to the Catholic Church's ability to fulfill that mission.

The four topics that are discussed are the effectiveness of the strategies that the Catholic Church is presently using to promote its teaching against abortion, the effectiveness of the annulment process in the light of the Catholic Church's understanding of marriage as a covenant relationship, the Catholic Church's treatment of nonordained employees in the light of its teaching on social justice, and the confrontational and divisive behavior both among Catholics themselves and between Catholics and other Christians in the light of the Catholic Church's teaching about the absolute necessity for visible unity in the body of Christ.

Abortion

There are few issues that cause more division than the topic of abortion. The Catholic Church's teaching on abortion is clear: One must not take any action that results in killing a yet-to-be-born human being. A human being exists from the moment an egg and sperm meet.

Given this clear teaching, how should the Magisterium itself act, and how should it counsel Catholics to act in the public sector? Do the strategies presently in use promote or fail to promote the teaching to which the Catholic Church wants to give witness? Should the Catholic Church have as its goal persuasive teaching, or should the goal be to pass laws that impose the Catholic Church's teaching on those who do not agree with it? How does the Catholic Church's teaching on the priority of conscience fit into this picture? The goal of chapter 7 is to examine how the Catholic Church might be a more effective witness to a society that is deeply divided on the issue of abortion.

Marriage and Annulments

The topic of annulments might, at first glance, appear to be of interest to, and have an effect on, only Catholics. However, this is not the case. If a person who is not a Catholic wishes to marry a Catholic, and that person has been married before, that person must receive an annulment from the Catholic Church from the previous marriage in order to marry within the Catholic Church. If the couple marries without benefit of an annulment, the Catholic partner is no longer invited to receive communion. In fact, the annulment process is one of the reasons that many people who were raised Catholic no longer worship in the Catholic Church.

The Catholic Church has a clear teaching on marriage. Marriage is understood to be a *covenant* relationship, an unbreakable relationship of mutual love that gives witness to God's covenant love, God's unceasing love for God's people. People in the United States, where about half of all marriages end in divorce, could benefit from hearing and understanding this teaching.

At the same time, many marriages are not "made in heaven." Many marriages fail to witness God's love even to the wife, husband, or children. Some are actually abusive. An abusive situation is definitely not a witness of God's covenant love for God's people. Given this fact, chapter 8 asks whether or not the annulment process is the best response to a failed marriage. Perhaps, rather than a juridical response, a pastoral response that respects the consciences of the people involved is needed.

Justice: Teaching and Behavior

Chapter 9 is titled "Teaching Social Justice and Treating Employees Justly." It is in this chapter that I particularly caution the reader to consider the source. It is my intent to discuss this topic objectively. As is true in other chapters, this chapter begins by exploring what Scripture has to say about the just treatment of employees as well as what the Catholic Church teaches on this subject. The Catholic Church's teachings on social justice are core to the identity of the Catholic Church and are a gift to the world.

However, some of the facts I report regarding whether the Catholic Church practices what it preaches in this regard are based on my own experience. When, in this chapter, I refer to the secretary of educational ministries, I am referring to myself. As mentioned earlier, when I say that five lay employees were dismissed, I am referring to my own dismissal. Obviously, this experience has had an effect on my perceptions of the situation, so the reader has a right to know that this is the case.

At the same time, I am convinced from talking with people all over the country that the situation I describe is a systemic problem, not a local problem. The Catholic Church does a far better job of teaching social justice than it does in practicing social justice. In diocesan and parish settings, policies that protect the rights of employees are often nonexistent or unenforced. Silence in regard to the way one has been treated is a condition of receiving severance pay. This chapter is a call to bishops and pastors in the Catholic Church to practice what the Catholic Church teaches.

Unity in the Body of Christ

Chapter 10 addresses the topic of unity in the body of Christ, both unity among Christians of all denominations and unity among Catholics themselves. The Catholic Church has a very strong and prophetic teaching that visible unity within the body of Christ is absolutely necessary if Christians are to be effective witnesses of Christ to the world.

However, many Catholics are completely unaware of this fact, and when they define Catholic identity, they define how Catholics differ from other Christians rather than how Catholics follow Jesus Christ. Also, despite the Catholic Church's teaching on the necessity of visible unity, the Catholic Church does not invite other Christians to receive Eucharist in the Catholic Church.

Division exists not only between Catholics and other Christians, but within the Catholic Church itself. As we know, we are called to love one another. People who love each other do not try to silence one another. They do not misrepresent another person's thinking in order to advocate their own positions. They do not excommunicate in order to have a smaller, purer group. All of these behaviors are present in today's Catholic Church.

In order to respond to these divisions, in chapter 10 we turn once more to both Scripture and Catholic Church teaching to establish the fact that unity among Christians and within the Catholic Church is essential. We then discuss the visible sign of unity, Eucharist, and discuss both the various ways that Catholics could image the truth of Christ's presence in Eucharist and whether or not excluding other Christians from the Eucharistic table at a Catholic mass gives witness to the Catholic Church's prophetic teaching on the necessity of visible unity in the body of Christ. Finally, chapter 10 outlines a first step that we all might take to overcome our divisions: We might engage in respectful dialogue.

AN OBLIGATION TO SEEK THE TRUTH

Each chapter concludes with questions for small-group conversation. As a teacher of adults, I consider the freedom to ask questions a necessity. When it comes to questions of faith, however, not everyone would agree with me. There are some in roles of authority in today's Catholic Church who discourage questions. They prefer unquestioning obedience.

Therefore, before we discuss the topics addressed in the following chapters, we should first ask whether or not a person such as myself can ask questions that challenge present Catholic Church teaching and still be a faithful Catholic. Does the Catholic Church allow challenging questions, or not?

It is my claim that in order to be a faithful Catholic one must ask pertinent questions. To do so is not only allowed but required. Catholics are called to be truth seekers, open to the Spirit, open to further understanding. If this were not true, Catholics would not become adults in their faith.

To defend this belief, one I have acted upon in writing this book, I would like to turn to *The Code of Canon Law: A Text and Commentary*. This book contains Catholic Church law, law that was revised after the Second Vatican Council to reflect new teachings and promulgated in 1983. It also includes a commentary on the law for those of us who may not understand all the nuances, lacking a canon law background.

Canon 748 of the code says:

> All persons are bound to seek the truth in matters concerning God and God's Church; by divine law they also are obliged and have the right to embrace and to observe that truth which they have recognized. [8]

The commentary on the canon states:

> This new canon reinterprets the obligation to seek and embrace religious truth in the light of the Second Vatican Council's teachings on religious freedom; the language is that of the *Declaration on Religious Liberty* (DH1). The dignity of the human person is placed in balance with the duty to search for the truth about God. [9]

Catholics, along with all persons of every faith, are obliged to seek the truth and are obliged to embrace and observe the truth that they have perceived.

Despite this clear teaching encoded in canon law, many Catholics believe that Catholics must submit their intellect and wills to the teaching of the Magisterium on all moral matters, whether or not they agree with the teachings. Canon 752 addresses this subject:

> A religious respect of intellect and will, even if not the assent of faith, is to be paid to the teaching which the Supreme Pontiff or the college of bishops enunciate on faith or morals when they exercise the authentic magisterium even if they do not intend to proclaim it with a definitive act; therefore the Christian faithful are to take care to avoid whatever is not in harmony with that teaching. [10]

The commentary on the canon says:

> This canon describes the appropriate response of the Christian faithful to the teachings of the Church. In doing so, it carefully distinguishes this level of response from that described in canon 750, namely a respect rather than the assent of faith (*religiosum obsequium* as over against *assensus fidei*). In the language of *Lumen Gentium* 25, the canon speaks of "religious respect" as the proper response to what legitimate church authority teaches in matters of faith and morals. This is a general guideline which incorporates a healthy respect for and acceptance of sound teaching in the Church. It calls for a basic attitude of religious assent based on a presumption of truth and good judgment on the part of the teaching authority. However, since teachings are included which are not infallible and can be erroneous, the principle of the pursuit of truth and the primacy of conscience still come into play. In other words, dissent is possible because the teachers mentioned in the canon can be and de facto have been mistaken. To search for the truth is everyone's duty and right (c. 748). [11]

In this commentary, a distinction is made between the kind of response that is appropriate for noninfallible teachings, such as the ones discussed in this book, and the kind of response that is appropriate for God's word. For noninfallible teachings, "the principle of the pursuit of truth and the primacy of conscience still come into play."

In contrast to canon 752, canon 750 says:

> All that is contained in the written word of God or in tradition, that is, in the one deposit of faith entrusted to the church and also proposed as divinely revealed either by the solemn magisterium of the church or by its ordinary and

universal magisterium, must be believed with divine and catholic faith; it is manifested by the common adherence of the Christian faithful under the leadership of the sacred magisterium; therefore, all are bound to avoid any doctrines whatever which are contrary to these truths. [12]

The commentary on this canon explains:

Here is described the appropriate response of the Christian faithful to God's holy word. Those things which God has revealed about Himself are to be believed with "divine and catholic faith." The canon . . . is . . . related to the teachings of *Lumen Gentium* 25 and *Dei Verbum* 10.

Those matters to be believed with "divine and catholic faith" are (1) contained in the word of God, written or handed down, and (2) proposed as divinely revealed by the teaching authority of the Church, either by solemn judgment or by the ordinary and universal magisterium. The final part of the canon warns that believers are to shun teachings which are opposed to those which are divinely revealed. [13]

We see then, that Catholics are to accept the authority of God's word. Catholics are also to accept those teachings that, based on God's word, are proposed as divinely revealed by the teaching authority of the Church. That is why for every topic we will discuss in this book, we will address the question "What does Scripture have to say?"

The topics discussed in this book do not fall into the category of divine revelation. (We will defend this statement in chapter 5 when we discuss women's ordination.) At the same time, in religious respect, Catholics are required to pay attention to the teaching on these topics, examine them, and listen carefully and prayerfully to them. That is why for every topic in this book we will address the question "What is the present Catholic Church teaching?"

While embracing this religious respect for noninfallible teachings, Catholics' duty to pursue truth to the best of their understanding remains. As canon 748 states, all people, including Catholics, are obliged to seek truth and embrace the truth we find.

Therefore, as part of our mutual search for truth, readers are invited to ask questions, to respond to questions, and to join this "necessary conversation." The wisdom of each person is needed. Only through conversation, through respectful dialogue, can Catholics—indeed, all Christians—become the one holy, catholic, and apostolic Church that we are called to be. Only when we become that Church will we be effective witnesses of Christ's good news to the world.

Chapter One

The Role of the Teaching Catholic Church in Our Search to Know God and God's Will

[Jesus] taught them as one having authority, and not as their scribes.

—Matthew 7:29

You are Peter, and on this rock I will build my church, and the gates of Hades will not prevail against it. I will give you the keys to the kingdom of heaven, and whatever you bind on earth will be bound in heaven, and whatever you loose on earth will be loosed in heaven.

—Jesus to Peter; Matthew 16:18–19

Go therefore and make disciples of all nations, baptizing them in the name of the Father and of the Son and of the Holy Spirit, and teaching them to obey everything that I have commanded you.

—Jesus to the eleven; Matthew 28:18–20a

But as for you, continue in what you have learned and firmly believed, knowing from whom you learned it, and how from childhood you have known the sacred writings that are able to instruct you for salvation through faith in Christ Jesus.

—2 Timothy 3:14–16

But when Cephas came to Antioch, I opposed him to his face.

—Galatians 2:11

The whole body of the faithful who have an anointing that comes from the holy one . . . cannot err in matters of belief.

—Second Vatican Council, *Dogmatic Constitution of the Church*, par. 12

Man's dignity therefore requires him to act out of conscious and free choice.

—Second Vatican Council, *Pastoral Constitution on the Church in the Modern World*, par. 16

19

Christians of all denominations turn to the Church for guidance regarding how to be in right relationship with God, with ourselves, with each other, and with the world—with the people of other nations as well as with our environment, God's creation. Christians turn to the Church for guidance to discern right from wrong.

To have a teaching Church is a great gift. In fact, the teaching voice of the Church is one of the ways in which Jesus fulfills his promise to his disciples: "I will not leave you orphaned." In John, during Jesus's last meal with his disciples before he dies, Jesus says:

> If you love me, you will keep my commandments. And I will ask the Father, and he will give you another Advocate, to be with you forever. This is the Spirit of truth, whom the world cannot receive, because it neither sees him nor knows him. You know him, because he abides with you, and he will be in you. I will not leave you orphaned; I am coming to you. In a little while the world will no longer see me, but you will see me; because I live, you also will live. (John 14:15–19)

Jesus did send his Spirit to the community that had gathered around him, the community described in Luke's Gospel as being present at Pentecost. Although this community included the apostles, it was not limited to the apostles. Luke tells us, "When the day of Pentecost had come, they were all together in one place" (Acts 2:1). In addition to the apostles, the "they" who were present included "certain women, including Mary the mother of Jesus, as well as his brothers" (Acts 1:14). The group of believers "numbered about one hundred twenty persons" (Acts 1:15). The whole group was involved in the discernment process to replace Judas. At Pentecost, the tongues of fire "rested on each of them" and "all of them" were filled with the Holy Spirit (Acts 2:3b, 4a).

This community of believers, the Church, exists to carry on Jesus's mission to the world. A great deal of Jesus's mission involves teaching. It is the Church's role faithfully to teach, faithfully to echo (the word *catechesis* means "echo") to every generation the truths that Jesus revealed and to apply those truths to new contexts. Christians believe that the Church has been commissioned to teach and has not only God's authority to do so, but God's help, through God's Spirit, to do so with wisdom and fidelity.

In this chapter we will first turn to Matthew's Gospel in order to lay the biblical foundation for the belief that the Church has God-given authority to teach, and then to the pastoral Epistles to lay the biblical foundation for the belief that the Church is charged with maintaining true doctrine. We will then balance the truths taught in these passages with truths taught in other biblical passages, truths we learn through Paul's example and through John's "beloved disciple." As we examine these biblical passages, it is important to remember that the passages are Scripture for all twenty-first-century Christians, not just for Catholics. Finally, we will end with a note on infallibility and a note on the priority of conscience, topics that are a necessary part of the conversation for Catholics as they seek to know God and to do God's will.

WHAT DOES SCRIPTURE HAVE TO SAY?

The Authority to Teach

The question of authority is central to Matthew's Gospel—not just the Church's authority to teach, but Jesus's authority to teach. While the community to which Matthew was writing was primarily Jewish, there were a growing number of Gentiles in their midst. The Gentiles, of course, did not keep the Jewish law. The early Church was teaching that Christians need not keep the law to be in right relationship with God. The Jewish audience was asking, "Who gave Jesus or his followers authority to say that? Moses promulgated the law and he had God's authority. What makes these people think they can teach such a revolutionary idea?"

In response to this question Matthew presents Jesus as the new Moses with authority from God to promulgate a new law. It is because Matthew is presenting Jesus as the new Moses that he pictures him promulgating his new law from a mountain, just as Moses received the law that he promulgated on a mountain (see Ex 19–20). We often refer to the speech that Jesus gives in Matthew's Gospel as the Sermon on the Mount (see Matt 5:1; cf. Luke 6:17). In this sermon Jesus describes himself not as destroying the law and the prophets, but as fulfilling them (Matt 5:17). Jesus is building on established tradition, not simply repeating it—and certainly not ignoring it.

As the Gospel continues, Matthew regularly focuses our attention on Jesus's authority. He tells us that the crowds were astounded at Jesus's teaching, "for he taught them as one having authority, and not as their scribes" (Matt 7:29). He pictures Jesus forgiving the sins of a paralytic, something that only God can do. Knowing that some of the scribes considered his words to be blasphemous, Jesus demonstrates that he speaks with authority. Jesus says, "But so that you may know that the Son of Man has authority on earth to forgive sins . . ." (Matt 9:6a), and then Jesus tells the paralytic to stand up and walk. The paralytic does just that.

Matthew then depicts Jesus giving his authority to the twelve: "Then Jesus summoned his twelve disciples and gave them authority over unclean spirits, to cast them out, and to cure every disease and every sickness" (Matt 10:1). Peter is singled out to be given particular authority. Only in Matthew do we hear Jesus say to Peter: "You are Peter, and on this rock I will build my church, and the gates of Hades will not prevail against it. I will give you the keys of the kingdom of heaven, and whatever you bind on earth will be bound in heaven, and whatever you loose on earth will be loosed in heaven" (Matt 16:18–19).

Peter is not the only one to whom Jesus gives the authority "to bind and to loose." Later Jesus says these same words to the disciples: "Truly I tell you, whatever you bind on earth will be bound in heaven, and whatever you loose on earth will be loosed in heaven" (Matt 18:18). Scripture scholars debate just what is meant by the power "to bind and to loose." Possibilities, all of which could be simultaneously correct, are the power to exorcise, the power to legislate, and the power to excommunicate. The power "to bind and to loose" is not the power to establish the moral order. God has done that, not human beings. Nor is it the power to refuse to forgive sin. Peter is taught that he must always forgive (see Matt 18:21).

In Matthew, the question of Jesus's authority and the authority that he has duly delegated to the apostles is emphasized once more in Jesus's postresurrection appearance to them. When Jesus commissions the eleven he says: "All authority in heaven and on earth has been given to me. Go therefore and make disciples of all nations, baptizing them in the name of the Father and of the Son and of the Holy Spirit, and teaching them to obey everything that I have commanded you" (Matt 28:18–20a).

Matthew leaves no doubt that Jesus's authority exceeds that of Moses, the scribes, and the Pharisees; that Jesus has God's own authority; and that Jesus delegated that authority to the twelve, giving Peter a preeminent role. The apostles are to carry on Jesus's teaching role. They are to "make disciples of all nations" (Matt 28:19).

Sound Doctrine

The apostles and those who followed them in their teaching role could not teach just anything they chose. Rather, they were faithfully to hand on what they had received. We see the Church's concern for maintaining sound doctrine in the pastoral Epistles.

Three letters, 1 Timothy, 2 Timothy, and Titus, are referred to as the pastoral Epistles because they are addressed to individual pastors and are concerned with pastoral issues, such as sound doctrine, and with Church structures, which will ensure the teaching of sound doctrine. Although the letters claim to have been written by Paul (see the first verse of each letter), Scripture scholars believe that they are pseudonymous letters—that is, they were written by a later author and were attributed to Paul. The letters are thought to date to the turn of the first century AD.

A major concern in all three letters is the teaching of sound doctrine. As 1 Timothy begins, the author gets right to the point:

> I urge you, as I did when I was on my way to Macedonia, to remain in Ephesus so that you may instruct certain people not to teach any different doctrine, and not to occupy themselves with myths and endless genealogies that promote speculations rather than the divine training that is known by faith. But the aim of such instruction is love that comes from a pure heart, a good conscience, and sincere faith. Some people have deviated from these. (1 Tim 1:3–6a)

The author goes on to say:

> Whoever teaches otherwise and does not agree with the sound words of our Lord Jesus Christ and the teaching that is in accordance with godliness, is conceited, understanding nothing, and has a morbid craving for controversy and for disputes about words. (1 Tim 6:3–4)

The letter ends with one more plea to Timothy to guard the sound doctrine that has been entrusted to him: "Timothy, guard what has been entrusted to you. Avoid the profane chatter and contradictions of what is falsely called knowledge; by professing it some have missed the mark as regards the faith" (1 Tim 6:20–21).

The second letter to Timothy continues to be concerned about the teaching of sound doctrine. The author, purportedly Paul, says: "Hold to the standard of sound teaching that you have heard from me, in the faith and love that are in Christ Jesus. Guard the good treasure entrusted to you, with the help of the Holy Spirit living in us" (2 Tim 1:13–14).

The concern in these letters is not to prepare for the imminent coming of the Son of Man, as was true in the earlier letters that were written by Paul, but to prepare to pass on the established traditions to future generations. The author tells Timothy to "be strong in the grace that is in Christ Jesus, and what you have heard from me through many witnesses entrust to faithful people who will be able to teach others as well" (2 Tim 2:1b–2).

Timothy is to be particularly mindful to teach not only what he has learned recently, but what he and his Jewish ancestors (Timothy's mother was Jewish) have known for many years, the Scripture:

> But as for you, continue in what you have learned and firmly believed, know-
> ing from whom you learned it, and how from childhood you have known the
> sacred writings that are able to instruct you for salvation through faith in Christ
> Jesus. All scripture is inspired by God and is useful for teaching, for reproof,
> for correction, and for training in righteousness, so that everyone who belongs
> to God may be proficient, equipped for every good work. (2 Tim 3:14–17)

The insistence on sound doctrine is also present in the third pastoral Epistle, Titus. In describing the qualities that are necessary for a bishop, the author says: "He must have a firm grasp of the word that is trustworthy in accordance with the teaching, so that he may be able both to preach with sound doctrine and to refute those who contradict it" (Titus 1:9). Later, the topic comes up again when the author says: "But as for you, teach what is consistent with sound doctrine" (Titus 2:1).

We see, then, that when the Second Coming did not occur as soon as expected, the Church's attention turned to establishing structures that would ensure that sound doctrine, both the Scriptures (what we now call the Old Testament) and Jesus's teachings, would be faithfully passed on to future generations. It is the Church's responsibility, with the guidance of the Holy Spirit, to do just that.

As time went on, the Spirit-filled Church added to the Scriptures. What we now call the New Testament took form over time. By the end of the second century the four Gospels that we now consider canonical became standard, and by the end of the fourth century the New Testament canon as we now know it was, for the most part, in place and in use. Were there no teaching and worshipping Church, we would not have an agreed-upon New Testament.

What Can We Learn from Paul's Experience?

So far we have examined the scriptural foundation for Christians' belief that God has chosen to establish a Church to carry on Jesus's mission to the world. We saw that Jesus called the twelve apostles, and that Jesus gave them, especially Peter, a unique leadership role. While this is all true, this is not the whole story. One of the greatest early leaders of Christianity was not one of the twelve, did not know Jesus during Jesus's public ministry on earth, and did not receive his call or his sense of vocation from the twelve. Paul was called directly by Jesus Christ after Jesus had risen from the dead.

The story of Paul's call is repeated three times in the Acts of the Apostles (see Acts 9:1–19; 22:1–16; 26:9–18). Paul had a vision in which the risen Christ asked Paul, "Why are you persecuting me?" This experience was so profound that it changed Paul's whole life. He changed from being a persecutor of those who followed Christ to being one of the greatest Christian teachers who ever lived.

How did the charismatic Paul interact with the people who had duly delegated authority in the early Church? The question is important because today's Church, too, has duly delegated authorities, and it also has charismatic people who have received their gifts and their call to serve the Church directly from God, not through due delegation. How are such people to be regarded?

Depending on whether we read Paul's own account as it appears in Galatians (Gal 1:11–2:16), or Luke's account as it appears in Acts (Acts 26–28; 15:19–20), we get a slightly different picture. It seems fair to say that Paul was not a loose cannon. Paul respected the Church authorities in Jerusalem and did meet with them and come to an agreement with them regarding Paul's vocation. Paul says: "And when James and Cephas and John, who were acknowledged pillars, recognized the grace that had been given to me, they gave to Barnabas and me the right hand of fellowship, agreeing that we should go to the Gentiles and they to the circumcised" (Gal 2:9).

At the same time, Paul was adamant that his vocation did not come to him through those acknowledged Church leaders. Paul says, "For I want you to know, brothers and sisters, that the gospel that was proclaimed by me is not of human origins; for I did not receive it from a human source, nor was I taught it, but I received it through a revelation of Jesus Christ" (Gal 1:11–12). Paul insists on this point. Again, he says: "But when God, who had set me apart before I was born and called me through his grace, was pleased to reveal his Son to me, so that I might proclaim him among the Gentiles, I did not confer with any human being, nor did I go up to Jerusalem to those who were already apostles before me, but I went away at once into Arabia"

(Gal 1:15–17a; notice that Paul, although not one of the twelve, considers himself an apostle).

While Paul respected the authority of Peter (Cephas), he did not equate Peter with God, nor abandon his own experience and understanding of God's will in his life when in conversation with Peter. Paul says:

> But when Cephas came to Antioch, I opposed him to his face, because he stood self-condemned; for until certain people came from James, he used to eat with the Gentiles. But after they came, he drew back and kept himself separate for fear of the circumcision faction. And the other Jews joined him in this hypocrisy, so that even Barnabas was led astray by their hypocrisy. But when I saw that they were not acting consistently with the truth of the gospel, I said to Cephas before them all, "If you, though a Jew, live like a Gentile and not like a Jew, how can you compel the Gentiles to live like Jews?" (Gal 2:11–14)

Based on the events that underlie these accounts, it appears evident that God, in God's wisdom, chose to work in dramatic ways both through institutional structures and through charismatic gifts. Each is to balance the other. Each is to be open to the other. The institutional Church, with its hierarchical structure and its duly delegated roles, is not the whole Church. Nor are those in duly delegated roles the gatekeepers of God's grace. Rather, the Spirit moves where the Spirit wills.

If those who hold positions in the Church's structures do not remain in respectful conversation with other Spirit-filled people and open to their insights, the Church as a whole, the body of Christ, will suffer. God has chosen to give us both people in duly delegated institutional roles and charismatic leaders. Each has gifts to offer the other. The bone cannot say to the skin, "I do not need you."

What Can We Learn from John's "Beloved Disciple"?

The "beloved disciple" is a character we read about only in John's Gospel. He does not appear during Jesus's public ministry. We first meet him at the last meal that Jesus has with his disciples (see John 13:23–26). He is most probably the unnamed person in the high priest's courtyard next to Peter (John 18:15–18). After that, we see him at the foot of the cross (see John 19:26–27). The beloved disciple is with Peter when Mary Magdalene tells him and Peter that someone has taken Jesus's body from the tomb (John 20:1–10), and at Jesus's postresurrection appearance at the Sea of Tiberius (21:1–14).

Many people never ask themselves the significance of the beloved disciple, or why he remains unnamed. Because the beloved disciple is said to be the source of John's Gospel (see John 21:24), and because, in the late second century, St. Irenaeus attributed the Gospel to the apostle John, many have concluded that the beloved disciple is the apostle John. Many Scripture scholars disagree with this conclusion.

The bulk of the Gospel attributed to John was written late in the first century AD. It was written by someone who belonged to what Scripture scholars call the Johannine community. Scripture scholars surmise that the oral tradition behind the Gospel is of Palestinian origin and dates back to the teachings of an original disciple, not one of the twelve, who is called the beloved disciple. The members of this Palestinian community, because they insisted on the divinity of Christ, were expelled from the synagogue and so moved, probably to Ephesus.

After the community moved, most of the Gospel was written. Then, a painful schism took place in the community. Some insisted on the divinity of Christ to the exclusion of Christ's humanity and to the exclusion of the importance of living according to Christ's teachings. After the community split, additions and insertions were made to the Gospel, and the three letters that are also attributed to John were written. These writings reflect what was learned because of the painful schism.

Why does the beloved disciple go unnamed? Scripture scholars surmise that this is a literary device to invite the reader to see the beloved disciple not only as a person in the story, but as a symbol. The beloved disciple is not the only person who goes unnamed in the Gospel. Jesus's mother, Mary, also goes unnamed, and in addition to being herself, her character functions as a symbol for the Church. The beloved disciple is a symbol for the priority of love in one's relationship with Jesus Christ.

In John's Gospel, in three of the scenes in which the beloved disciple appears, he is matched up with Peter. Peter, of course, represents authority. In every scene, the beloved disciple is described as being closer to Jesus and closer to the truth than is Peter. In other words, when it comes to discipleship, love takes priority over authority or law.

In the first scene in which the two appear together, Peter wants to know what Jesus meant by something he said and asks the beloved disciple to find out (John 13:23–26). In the second scene, the beloved disciple and Peter rush to Jesus's tomb. The beloved disciple gets there first, waits respectfully for Peter to arrive, and is the first to believe (John 20:1–10). In fact, the beloved disciple is the only person to believe in the resurrection without a postresur-rection appearance. In all of these scenes the beloved disciple, the figure who represents love, is closer to Jesus and quicker to arrive at the truth than is the figure who represents authority.

Finally, the beloved disciple is with Peter when Jesus appears to the disciples at the Sea of Tiberius. Peter asks Jesus a question about the beloved disciple and Jesus responds, "If it is my will that he remain until I come, what is that to you? Follow me!" (John 21:21–22). In other words, love is not made accountable to authority in all things.

Scripture scholars surmise that those in the Johannine community origi-nally emphasized love and charismatic gifts so much that they did not give enough importance to legitimate authority. Without legitimate authority there was no one to call those in the community who drifted into heresy back to true doctrine. The community lacked those kinds of structures. After the painful schism, those who remained in the community recognized the need to continue to teach the priority of love and the importance of charismatic gifts, but at the same time, they recognized the need to cooperate with legitimate authority.

It was after the community reached this insight that the story of Jesus and Peter on the shore of Tiberius was added (John 21:15–19). In this story Jesus asks Peter three times, "Do you love me?" Each time, Peter says that he does. Each time, Jesus responds with a commissioning: "Feed my lambs." "Tend my sheep." "Feed my sheep."

Jesus is giving Peter the opportunity to declare his love as often as Peter had previously denied Jesus. Jesus gives Peter a particular responsibility in relation to Jesus's "sheep," Jesus's disciples, the Church. Notice that the sheep (the Church) do not become Peter's. Peter is not to feed Peter's sheep, but Jesus's sheep. He can do this only if he makes his love of Jesus, not his own ego or his own authority, his absolute top priority.

The conclusion of the Johannine community seems to have been that because authority is necessary, Jesus delegated authority to Peter. However, authority is to put love first, and authority is to feed, rather than to lord it over, Jesus's sheep, the Church. Authority is in service to the unity of the community and to true doctrine. However, authority can never take the place of love, nor consider itself more important than love.

WHAT DOES THE CATHOLIC CHURCH HAVE TO SAY?

A Note on Infallibility

The idea that the Church is infallible—that is, immune from error—does not appear in the Bible. The teaching on infallibility did not become a dogma for the Catholic Church until very recently: at the First Vatican Council in 1870. The truth behind the teaching is that God protects the whole Church from error when it solemnly defines and receives its teachings. As we said earlier, because we have a teaching Church, we are not left orphans. The Spirit of God is with us, leading and guiding us. However, the word *infallible* is evidently a misleading word to use to teach such a truth, as evidenced by the fact that it is often misunderstood both by Catholics and by other Christians.

Infallibility does not rest in one person; it rests in the whole Church. The Second Vatican Council made this clear when it expanded the teaching of the First Vatican Council, which had come to a premature close because of invading military forces. In its document *Dogmatic Constitution on the Church*, the Second Vatican Council explains various dimensions of infallibility.

In regard to the "holy People of God," the document states:

> The whole body of the faithful who have an anointing that comes from the holy one (cf. 1 John 2:20 and 27) cannot err in matters of belief. This characteristic is shown in the supernatural appreciation of the faith (*sensus fidei*) of the whole people, when "from the bishops to the last of the faithful" they manifest a universal consent in matters of faith and morals. [1]

Within this context, the document states:

> The Roman Pontiff, head of the college of bishops, enjoys this infallibility in virtue of his office, when, as supreme pastor and teacher of all the faithful—who confirms his brethren in the faith (cf. Luke 22:32)—he proclaims in an absolute decision a doctrine pertaining to faith or morals. . . . For in such a case the Roman Pontiff does not utter a pronouncement as a private person, but rather does he expound and defend the teaching of the Catholic faith as the supreme teacher of the universal Church, in whom the Church's charism of infallibility is present in a singular way. [2]

In regard to the bishops, the document says:

> The infallibility promised to the Church is also present in the body of bishops when, together with Peter's successor, they exercise the supreme teaching office. Now, the assent of the Church can never be lacking to such definitions on account of the same Holy Spirit's influence, through which Christ's whole flock is maintained in the unity of the faith and makes progress in it.[3]

Since 1870, when infallibility was first narrowly defined and officially claimed, only one papal pronouncement has been issued fulfilling the conditions necessary for a dogma to be considered to have been taught infallibly: Mary's assumption into heaven (1954). These conditions are:

- The pope is defining a doctrine of faith or morals.
- The pope is speaking *ex cathedra*—that is, as head of the Church.
- The pope has the intention of binding the whole Church.

None of our teachings on morality have been presented as infallible dogmas.

Even in the case of an infallible dogma, the expression of that dogma can change. This is evident from the fact that the dogma of infallibility itself was broadened at the Second Vatican Council when infallibility was understood to belong to the whole Church and so was explained within the contexts of the *sensus fidei* and the pope's collegial relationship with the bishops of the world, not simply in relation to the role of the pope himself.

The document *Mysterium Ecclesiae*, issued by the Sacred Congregation for the Doctrine of the Faith in 1973, explains how such dogmas can change:

> Difficulties arise also from the historical condition that affects the expression of Revelation.
>
> With regard to this historical condition, it must first be observed that the meaning of the pronouncements of faith depends partly upon the expressive power of the language used at a certain point in time and in particular circumstances. Moreover, it sometimes happens that some dogmatic truth is first expressed incompletely (but not falsely), and at a later date, when considered in a broader context of faith or human knowledge, it receives a fuller and more perfect expression.[4]

This explanation of how Catholic Church teaching can change appears in the section of the document titled "The Notion of the Church's Infallibility Not to Be Falsified." When the notion of infallibility is used to deny that the Church can and must grow in its understanding in the light of new knowledge or in the light of new historical contexts, the notion of infallibility is being falsified. We are a pilgrim Church. We must be open to growth, to new understandings, and to new formulations of the truths that have been revealed to us.

A Note on the Priority of Conscience

One of the doctrines that the Catholic Church teaches regarding faith and morals is the priority of conscience. The Vatican II document *Pastoral Constitution on the Church in the Modern World* says:

> Deep within his conscience man discovers a law which he has not laid upon himself but which he must obey. Its voice, ever calling him to love and to do what is good and to avoid evil, tells him inwardly at the right moment: do this, shun that. For man has in his heart a law inscribed by God. His dignity lies in observing this law, and by it he will be judged. [5]
>
> Man's dignity therefore requires him to act out of conscious and free choice, as moved and drawn in a personal way from within, and not by blind impulses in himself or by mere external constraint. [6]

The Catholic Church teaches not only that people have the right to act in accord with their consciences, but that they have the obligation to do so. The Catholic Church also teaches that people will be judged, not by their obedience to the law, but by their fidelity to a well-formed conscience.

In order to form a right conscience, people must be free not only to seek answers from a teaching Church but also to ask questions of that teaching Church. We established the right and duty of each person to ask challenging questions in our introduction. Now, having affirmed the teaching role of the Catholic Church, we will discuss the efficacy of asking questions. To do so is not to ignore or undercut the teaching voice of the Church. The Church plays an indispensable role in the process of forming one's conscience. To ponder teachings and ask challenging questions about them is an essential part of becoming adults in our faith.

THE VALUE OF QUESTIONING

Whether or not faithful Church members can ask challenging questions about present teaching has been a subject of disagreement over the centuries. Elaine Pagels, in her book *The Origin of Satan*, describes the reaction of Tertullian, one of the early Church Fathers (AD 180), to people who question:

To stamp out heresy, Tertullian says, church leaders must not allow people to ask questions, for it is "questions that make people heretics. . . ." The true Christian, Tertullian declares, simply determines to "know nothing . . . at variance with the truth of faith. . . . They say that we must ask questions in order to discuss, but what is there to discuss?"[7]

Catholics can be very grateful that Tertullian's view did not prevail. Nor is Tertullian's view affirmed by Scripture, which gives us a very different model in the book of Job.

The author of Job asked a question that challenged the understanding of his generation. The question was: Is all suffering punishment for sin? The author's contemporaries believed that the answer to the question was yes. The author believed that the answer to the question was no. He therefore wrote a debate in which three of the characters, Job's so-called friends, argue beautifully and persuasively that all suffering is punishment for sin. He then has God come on stage and say that the friends are wrong. By posing a question and answering it to the best of his ability, given his time in history, the author enabled his contemporaries and all future generations to grow in their understanding of the ramifications of the fact that God is love.

The character, Job, acts as a model for those whose life experiences cause them to challenge a particular teaching. Job simply does not believe that his suffering is punishment for sin. When Job's friends, who faithfully argue the beliefs of the time, insist that it is, Job challenges them for their lack of intellectual honesty. He also asks them if they think God would be pleased with their prevarication. Job says:

> If you would only keep silent,
> That would be your wisdom!
> Hear now my reasoning,
> And listen to the pleadings of my lips.
> Will you speak falsely for God,
> and speak deceitfully for him?
> Will you show partiality toward him,
> will you plead the case for God?
> Will it be well with you when he searches you out?
> Or can you deceive him, as one person deceives another?
> He will surely rebuke you
> If in secret you show partiality.
> Will not his majesty terrify you, and the dread of him fall upon you?
> Your maxims are proverbs of ashes,
> Your defenses are defenses of clay. (Job 13:5–12)

By having the courage to ask questions, Job is able to grow beyond a mistaken belief. He is also able to refrain from treating others with prejudice and cruelty as Job's friends treat him, thinking that Job is a sinner who deserves his suffering. He is able to come to a more profound understanding of the ramifications of the belief that God is love. A God who is love would not want to be defended with shallow, unreasonable answers. A God who is love is not offended when we ask questions from the heart.

THE ROLE OF THE TEACHING CHURCH

So far in this chapter we have demonstrated that there is a scriptural basis for Christians' belief in a teaching Church, an apostolic Church, that continues Jesus's mission to the world. The Church is faithfully to pass on to each generation the truths that have been revealed by Jesus Christ, truths that are core to our salvation. There is also a scriptural basis for the Petrine role.

At the same time, we have demonstrated from Scripture that the Church's foundational blocks are not limited to "the twelve," including Peter. Paul received his commission directly from the risen Christ. He respected and cooperated with legitimate authority in Jerusalem, but he did not need that authority's permission to begin the mission that he had received from Jesus Christ. All of us who are Gentiles should be very grateful that he didn't.

In addition, we have demonstrated from Scripture that authority and law, both of which are extremely necessary if unity is to be maintained, are not the be-all and end-all of the Church. Love is most important. We don't sing, "They'll know we are Christians by our orthodoxy, by our orthodoxy." We sing, "They'll know we are Christians by our love, by our love." This insight, of course, comes from the Johannine community: "By this everyone will know that you are my disciples, if you have love for one another" (John 13:35).

PASSING ON OUR GIFTS TO OUR CHILDREN

Those who have been formed by a church and love their church want to pass on this gift to their children and grandchildren, Catholics included. However, as Catholics are well aware, the teaching voice of the Catholic Church has lost its credibility for many people who were raised in the Catholic Church. What does the Catholic Church have to do, how does the Catholic Church need to change, in order to be the credible teaching voice for present and future generations that it has been for many twentieth-century Catholics? We will explore the answers to this question in future chapters.

CONTINUING THE CONVERSATION

1. What role has the Church played in your search to know God and God's will?
2. How would you describe the mission of the Church? Do you have a scriptural basis for your answer? Explain.
3. Do you think designated and recognized authority figures are necessary in the Church? What role do you understand the pope to have? Explain.
4. What role do you think those who have charismatic gifts should have in the Church?
5. What do you think is necessary for the Catholic Church to be a credible teaching voice for future generations?

Chapter Two

The Role of Experience and the Role of Scripture in Our Search to Know God and God's Will

Is the Lord among us or not?

—the Israelites' question in the desert;
Exodus 17:7

And remember, I am with you always, to the end of the age.

—Jesus's last words to the apostles
in Matthew's Gospel; Matthew 28:20b

For as the rain and the snow come down from heaven,
and do not return there until they have watered the earth,
making it bring forth and sprout,
giving seed to the sower and bread to the eater,
so shall my word be that goes out from my mouth;
it shall not return to me empty,
but it shall accomplish that which I purpose,
and succeed in the thing for which I sent it.

—Isaiah 55:10–11

Indeed, the word of God is living and active, sharper than any two-edged sword, piercing until it divides soul from spirit, joints from marrow; it is able to judge the thoughts and intentions of the heart.

—Hebrews 4:12

All Scripture is inspired by God and is useful for teaching, for reproof, for correction, and for training in righteousness, so that everyone who belongs to God may be proficient, equipped for every good work.

—2 Timothy 3:16–17

In our last chapter we discussed the role of the teaching Church in our search to know God and God's will. When discussing the priority of conscience, we noted that the teaching voice of the Catholic Church affirms that we must obey our own well-formed consciences. In this chapter we will first consider the role that experience plays in our search to know God and God's will, a topic integrally connected to our second topic of discussion: the role that Scripture plays in this same search.

As we will see, what we learn from reflection on personal experience and what we learn from correctly understanding Scripture are both indispensable sources of knowledge in our search to know God and God's will. How do we know that reflection on personal experience is indispensable? Because, throughout history, God has chosen to reveal God's self through events. It is because God revealed God's self through events that we have the Bible. It is because God continues to reveal God's self through events that reflection on experience is an indispensable component in our search for truth.

EXPERIENCE AND THE FORMATION OF THE BIBLE

Since we have inherited the Bible, we may never have asked ourselves such questions as: How did the Bible come into existence? How did certain books make it into the Bible while others did not? Why do Christians believe that biblical authors were inspired and that the Bible teaches us the truth about God, about our relationship with God, and about our relationship with each other?

Were it not for people's lived experience there would be no Bible. The Bible is the end result of a five-step process, a process that took over two thousand years. Experience played an essential role in that five-step process, from beginning to end.

Events

The first step of the process is lived experience. The core of Scripture, the skeleton of the whole Bible, involves events. These events started about 1850 BC with the call of Abraham and continued to about the middle of the second century AD. In other words, God chose to reveal God's self to God's people not through séances or dictation, but through events, events that were experienced by individuals as well as by whole communities.

From a Christian perspective, the greatest event of God's self-revelation took place through the person of Jesus Christ. Jesus was a historical person whose powerful ministry, crucifixion, death, and postresurrection appearances were events in the lives of Jesus's contemporaries.

Oral Tradition

The second step of the process that resulted in our present-day Bible is oral tradition: People talked about their lived experience. They reflected on events in order to discern and share with others what experiencing those events revealed about their relationship with God. Those who were telling the stories were not trying to teach history or science. They were trying to probe mysteries that are, to this day, partially beyond our comprehension: Who is God? Who are we in relationship to God and to each other? What would God have us do to cooperate with God's will and God's purpose rather than to thwart it?

The oral traditions that developed as people reflected on experience and probed mystery took a variety of literary forms: songs, legends, myths, parables, laws, creeds, prayers to be said during rituals, etiologies (stories about the origins of things known from experience), genealogies, love poems, and so on. Any literary form can be a vehicle for sharing insights about one's relationship with God, insights that have been learned through experience.

Written, Then Edited

In time, oral tradition began to be written down (the third step). Later generations would read what earlier generations had come to understand through experience and would reflect on these lessons in the light of their own experience. The stories and writings inherited from the ancestors were edited in the light of the later generation's experience.

For example, when we read the stories of Abraham, Sarah (1850 BC), and the other patriarchs and matriarchs, we are reading stories as they were told after the exodus (1250 BC) and in the light of the exodus. The stories that we read in Deuteronomy about the Israelites' time in the desert are told from the point of view of those who lived after the fall of the Northern Kingdom (721 BC) and in the light of that tragic and sobering event. The stories about Jesus's public ministry that we read in the Gospels are told from a postresurrection point of view. Much more was understood after the resurrection than was understood during Jesus's public ministry. Reflection on past experience in the light of subsequent experience has always been part of the process of revelation.

A Process of Coming to Knowledge

In other words, Scripture, from beginning to end, reveals a process of coming to knowledge (the fourth step). Early insights are revised in the light of subsequent experience. An example will make this point clear. During the period of the judges, the Israelites understood that God loved them, but not that God loved their enemies. Therefore, they thought that they were doing God's will when they destroyed their enemies. A later author, the author of Jonah, understood that because God made everyone, God must love everyone. He doesn't contradict the earlier insight that God loves the Israelites, but he adds to it that God loves all nations.

This deeper, expanded truth was learned through reflection on experience: A non-Israelite, Cyrus, who was Persian, had been God's instrument to save the Israelites from exile in Babylon (537 BC). The author of Jonah realized that if God could use a non-Israelite as an instrument of God's saving power, God must love that non-Israelite.

A similar process of coming to knowledge is evident in the New Testament. In Matthew's Gospel, Jesus gives his disciples instructions to go only to the lost sheep of the house of Israel, not to Samaritans or Gentiles (Matt 10:5). After the resurrection, Peter learns by reflecting on the meaning of events in his life that he is now to go out to Gentiles, too (Acts 10). By the time Matthew's Gospel was written (AD 80) Peter's postresurrection experience was well known. In Matthew's Gospel, after Jesus's resurrection, Jesus commissions his disciples to "make disciples of all nations" (Matt 28:19).

Some Works Become Canonical

Not every story based on events, passed on through oral tradition, written, and later revised in the light of subsequent events, appears in our Bible. Those that do, we call "canonical." They are part of the canon, the Bible as we now have it.

Again, experience played a role in this fifth and last step of the formation of Scripture. The canon was not decided by hierarchical dictum, but by usage. As Jews collected their writings, and as Christians collected theirs, certain books became accepted and treasured by the Spirit-filled communities who had gathered to worship, and others did not. Those books that faithfully passed on the traditions and that affirmed the beliefs and experiences of the gathered communities are the ones that eventually became accepted as canonical.

It was not until the Council of Trent in the sixteenth century that the canon was closed. At that time the council affirmed that the books that had been accepted for well over a thousand years and that had formed the self-identity of the Church would remain the accepted canon. We would not add to them nor subtract from them.

THE AUTHORITY OF SCRIPTURE

For Christians, Catholics included, Scripture has great authority. In fact, the Second Vatican Council document *Dogmatic Constitution on Divine Revelation* (*Dei Verbum*) claims that "the entire Christian religion should be nourished and ruled by sacred Scripture" (par. 21).[1]

Since God not only revealed God's self through events, but inspired those in the community to faithfully hand on what had been learned, in one sense, God is the author of Scripture. That is not to deny, of course, that God inspired human beings like us to faithfully perceive and pass on what God had chosen to reveal.

At the same time, because it is a written text, Scripture needs to be interpreted. Just as the Church, the people of God, had a role in the formation of Scripture, so does the Church have a role in the interpretation of Scripture. It is the Church's job, through the inspiration of the Holy Spirit, to make sure that Scripture does not become simply words on a page but continues to be experienced as a living word, a word proclaimed in our liturgies and taught in our catechetical settings, a word incorporated into our personal prayer lives and listened to at times of personal discernment.

The Catholic Church teaches, with great clarity, the method we are to use in order to correctly understand the revelation that Scripture contains. However, many Catholics are unaware of this teaching, partly because the Catholic Church has grown in its understanding of this topic over the years. Another word for growth is *change*. We will discuss how the Catholic Church changed its teaching on how to correctly understand the revelation that we find in Scripture in our next chapter. For now we will simply explain what we mean when we say that the Catholic Church teaches people to be contextualists.

CONTEXTUALISTS AND FUNDAMENTALISTS

To say that the Catholic Church teaches people to be contextualists is to say that people are instructed to put whatever Scripture passage they are interested in understanding into the context in which it appears in the Bible. If a person fails to consider context, that person is very likely to misunderstand the meaning (that is, the revelation) that the inspired author intended to teach.

Catholics, then, are taught not to be fundamentalists when it comes to interpreting Scripture. A fundamentalist, in the context of this discussion, is a person who does not consider context in order to determine meaning. Fundamentalists use out-of-context Scripture passages to add authority to their opinions on all kinds of subjects, without giving any thought to whether or not the inspired biblical authors were addressing the same subject. In teaching people to be contextualists, the Catholic Church is acting in union with many other Christians. The division between contextualists and fundamentalists is not a division between denominations but is quite often a division within denominations.

One of the problems that exists in the Catholic Church is that, even though the Catholic Church teaches people to be contextualists and not fundamentalists, many Catholics, including some in the Magisterium, sometimes use Scripture as a fundamentalist would: They use it to support later teachings as though the inspired biblical authors were teaching what the Catholic Church is now teaching. This is an abuse of Scripture.

In order to demonstrate the truth of these statements we will first briefly explain the contexts that Catholics are taught to consider in order to correctly understand the Bible. We will then discuss just what we mean when we say that Scripture is also a living word, that the full meaning of the text is not exhausted by the original biblical author's intent. We will then clearly name both proper use and abuse of biblical texts used as a living word.

THE CONTEXT OF LITERARY FORM

There are three contexts that must be considered in order to correctly understand what an inspired biblical author intended to teach. The first is literary form. The Bible is not a book with chapters, but a library with books. As is true of any library, those books represent many different kinds of writing, many different literary forms.

We are all completely familiar with the idea of literary form. Every time we read a newspaper we move from one kind of writing to another: A front page article is fairly objective and is responsive to topics such as who, when, and where. The function of a front page article is to inform us. The articles on the editorial page are very different. They are far from objective. Rather, the author takes a stand and tries to persuade us to his or her point of view. The author of an editorial cartoon can attribute words to a historical character that the actual person never said. Sports page articles often build up heroes, obviously not giving us "warts and all."

We adjust to this wide variety of literary forms without giving it a thought. We give each author permission to use the conventions of that type of writing in order to tell us what that author wants to tell us. Because we understand the variety of kinds of writing involved, we do not draw false conclusions based on a literal understanding, no matter what the form.

We need exactly the same ability to discern one kind of writing from another when reading the Bible. We need to recognize the literary form the writer has chosen in order to correctly understand what that author is trying to say. If there is a talking snake, we know we are not reading history. If God acts the way human beings act—walking, talking, explaining God's self—we know that we are reading words attributed to God by an author, not words the author is claiming to have heard or overheard. Any literary form can be a vehicle for revelation, and any literary form can fail to be a vehicle of revelation, depending on the intent of the author, depending on what the author intends to teach.

We can easily demonstrate the absolute importance of considering literary form with a single example. One of the literary forms present in the Bible is debate. If a person were to write a good debate, that person would have to argue two sides of an issue persuasively. This is just what the author of the book of Job has done. In Job, the characters debate whether all suffering is punishment for sin or whether an innocent person could suffer. The author believes that an innocent person can suffer. He presents Job as an innocent person and then pictures Job's friends coming to the conclusion that Job must deserve his suffering. Finally, the author has God come on stage and correct Job's friends' misunderstanding.

Because the author argues both sides of the question well, there are many beautiful passages in Job in which Job's friends mistakenly teach and defend the opposite of what the author is actually teaching. Job's friends all tell him that he must deserve his suffering. If we did not understand that this is a debate and that Job's friends are wrong, we might "comfort" those who suffer with the same false message: "Repent and then everything will be fine. Your suffering is punishment for your sins." That conclusion, in addition to being false, could be very, very harmful, especially if we present our own lack of understanding as God's own truth. Imagine what such a teaching would do to the other person's concept of God.

THE CONTEXT OF THE BELIEFS OF THE TIME

A second context to be considered is the social context of the original author and audience. In the course of teaching a universal truth, an author often says something by way of example or application that reflects the presumed beliefs of his time. We put the authority of Scripture behind the author's core truth. We do not put the authority of Scripture behind what he says in the process of teaching this core truth by way of application or example.

Again, an example will make this point clear. Imagine that on a beautiful spring day you are simply overwhelmed with the beauty of creation. You understand all this beauty to be a gift from a loving God to all of God's people, saint and sinner alike. Imagine that you want to write a story that will teach this insight. Because you live in the twenty-first century, you might begin by picturing God forming dust into a ball. However, had you lived in 450 BC, you would have begun by picturing God forming dust, flattening it out, and placing it on four posts.

From the point of view of revelation, these two stories would be identical. Each is teaching exactly the same thing about the relationship between God and God's world. From the point of view of the presumptions of the time, the stories would differ. Now, we know that the earth is round. In 450 BC everyone presumed that the earth was flat. However, the shape of the earth is irrelevant to the point you would be making—that God created the world in love.

Throughout history the Catholic Church has occasionally unwittingly persecuted someone because it failed to separate an inspired biblical author's core point from the author's presumptions. That is what happened with Galileo. When Galileo suggested that the sun, not the earth, is the center of the movement of the planets, he was silenced, put under house arrest, and forced to endure the Inquisition. However, in preparation for the Jubilee year of 2000, Pope John Paul II formally apologized for the way in which Galileo had been disciplined. The pope clarified that the Catholic Church cannot use the Bible to affirm or deny scientific hypotheses because no biblical author has addressed any scientific subject. (We will discuss Pope John Paul II's statement in more detail in chapter 3.)

Presumptions expressed by inspired biblical authors are not always about cosmology. They can also be about the social order. The author of Ephesians tells slaves to be obedient to their masters (Eph 6:5). When the United States was debating the morality of slavery as it was practiced in the United States, Christians on both sides of the issue used Scripture to support their point of view. Those who supported slavery thought of the social order in which they had always lived as God's social order. They quoted Ephesians to prove their point.

Using Scripture to support slavery was an abuse of Scripture because it was putting the authority of Scripture behind the author's application of a core truth to a particular contemporary social setting, not behind the core truth itself. The core truth that the author is teaching is that because God loves each of us, we must love each other. He then applies that core truth to the social setting of the recipients of his letter, a social setting in which both slaves and wives were property. The author did not ask if the social order was good or bad. It was what it was. Rather, he cautioned both those in power, and those not in power, to treat others with love in every situation. The core truth is universally true, the application is not.

THE CONTEXT OF A PROCESS OF REVELATION

The third context is the two-thousand-year process of revelation that Scripture represents, a process that began with Abraham and Sarah around 1850 BC and ended shortly after the end of the first century AD.

Every book in the biblical canon is there because it teaches something that later communities found profoundly true. However, some of the truths taught are partial truths, not complete answers to the questions they are addressing. Later in the two-thousand-year process, additional insights were understood and taught. These additional insights did not contradict earlier insights but complemented them, broadened them.

For instance, a mystery that we have already briefly mentioned is the one debated in the book of Job: Why do human beings suffer? This is an appropriate question for us to ask Scripture because the topic, unlike the shape of the earth or the best social order, falls within the overall topic that inspired biblical authors are addressing: Who is God? Who are we in relationship to

God and each other? What would God have us do to cooperate with the coming of God's kingdom?

The earliest answer Scripture provides to the mystery of human suffering dates to about 1000 BC. The story of the man and woman in the garden (Gen 2:5–3:24) teaches that sin causes suffering. This is certainly true, but is it the whole truth? Is all suffering due to sin? This is the very question being debated in Job. The author of Job did not deny that sin causes suffering. However, he did not believe that all suffering was due to sin. He believed that an innocent person could suffer and that the innocent person's suffering had a purpose other than punishment.

The author of Job lived about 450 BC, before the Jewish people came to a belief in life after death. While he taught something true, he, too, taught part of the truth. By the time Paul was writing his letters, some Jews did believe in life after death. In addition, an innocent person, Jesus, had suffered greatly and then risen from the dead. Paul was able to say a great deal more about the purpose of suffering than were his two inspired predecessors. What Paul had to say did not contradict the insights of the earlier authors; Paul's insights added to their insights.

People who are unaware that Scripture presents us with a two-thousand-year process of revelation are prone to make one of two errors: They claim that Scripture contradicts itself, or they use an early insight as though it represented the fullness of revelation on a topic, when, in fact, it does not.

THE CATHOLIC CHURCH'S TEACHING

Many Catholics have not been taught that the Catholic Church teaches people to be biblical contextualists and has since 1943. That this is the Catholic Church's teaching is affirmed in the most recent *Catechism of the Catholic Church* (1994) which quotes *Dei Verbum*. Paragraph 110 of the *Catechism* says:

> In order to discover *the sacred authors' intention*, the reader must take into account the conditions of their time and culture, the literary genres in use at that time, and the modes of feeling, speaking, and narrating then current. "For the fact is that truth is differently presented and expressed in the various types of historical writing, in prophetical and poetical texts, and in other forms of literary expression."[2]

SCRIPTURE AS A LIVING WORD

At the same time that the Catholic Church teaches people to be contextualists who seek to know the original inspired author's intent, the Catholic Church also understands Scripture to be a living word that speaks to people today. This is why the Catholic Church proclaims Scripture passages during worship, and why the community hears homilies that apply the readings to their lives. This is why the Catholic Church breaks open the word with candidates (baptized people preparing to come in to full communion with the Catholic Church) and catechumens (unbaptized people preparing for baptism), so that those joining the Catholic Church will hear Scripture in conversation with their own personal lives. This is why the Catholic Church encourages such practices as *lectio divina*, so that people identify with the characters in biblical stories and listen carefully to what the Spirit is telling them today. This is why Catholics sing, "Thy word is a lamp unto our feet and light unto our path" (see Ps 119:105).

However, hearing Scripture as a living word can be dangerous if the person doing it has no knowledge of what the original authors were saying. While the meaning people draw from texts they apply to their own lives need not be identical to what the original author was teaching, neither can it contradict what the author was teaching. In addition, if a person uses a passage of Scripture to address a topic different than the original author was addressing, that person cannot put the authority of Scripture behind the application to his or her own life. The person is seeking and receiving guidance, not necessarily universal truths.

One way to assure ourselves that Scripture is meant to be a living word is that in the Gospels Jesus himself is constantly pictured as using Scripture in this way. In Luke's Gospel, when Jesus is in the synagogue and reads a text from Isaiah that describes Isaiah's call, Jesus follows the reading by applying the passage to himself: "Today this scripture has been fulfilled in your hearing" (Luke 4:21b). It is Jesus who will bring good news to the poor and sight to the blind.

When Jesus is tempted in the desert, both he and the devil are constantly quoting Scripture (Matt 4:1–11). Each time Jesus is tempted, he turns to Scripture for insight and guidance. He begins his answer by acknowledging that he is quoting Scripture: "It is written . . ." and then goes on to quote various passages from Deuteronomy.

However, the devil uses the same method. He quotes Psalm 91:11–12 when he tempts Jesus to prove his identity by jumping from the pinnacle of the temple. The devil says, "He will command his angels concerning you, and 'On their hands they will bear you up'" (Matt 4:6). We could hardly have a clearer example of the truth that a person's quoting Scripture does not mean that the person is right.

In addition to using Scripture for personal guidance, Jesus is pictured as using Scripture when teaching. When the Pharisees ask Jesus whether it is "lawful for a man to divorce his wife" (Mark 10:2), Jesus responds by quoting Genesis 2:24: "For this reason a man shall leave his father and mother and be joined to his wife, and the two shall become one flesh" (Mark 10:7). Jesus uses the passage to address a completely different question than the original story is addressing.

In using Scripture this way, Jesus is not claiming that the passage originally meant what he is using it to teach. Jesus is not teaching a universal truth, as the original story is, but is using a passage from Scripture to cast light on a different subject. A passage of Scripture used in this way does not carry the same authority as does the intent of the original author. As we will discuss in chapter 8 on marriage and annulments, Jesus's words are not, even within Scripture, understood to be a universal truth rather than an application of an insight to a particular setting. As we will see, both Matthew's Gospel and Paul's letter to the Corinthians include exceptions to Jesus's teaching about divorce.

We must also note that, once more, Jesus is not the only person quoting Scripture in this discussion. The Pharisees are quoting Deuteronomy 24:1 when they say that "Moses allows a man to write a certificate of dismissal and to divorce her" (Mark 10:4). Once more we see that quoting Scripture does not necessarily mean that the person is right. It doesn't settle the issue.

MATTHEW'S FULFILLMENT THEME

As we have seen, in Jesus's time it was simply part of the way one discussed issues to bring various passages of Scripture to bear on a topic, whether or not the original inspired author was discussing the same topic. Matthew, in his Gospel, employs another common way to use Scripture when, in the course of describing events, he says, "All this took place to fulfill what had been spoken by the Lord through the prophet" (Matt 1:22). This phrase becomes a refrain in Matthew's Gospel.

In using this refrain, Matthew is not claiming that the prophets foretold inevitable future events that later took place. If that were true people would have expected the events that later took place—a virginal conception, God's own son becoming one of us, a crucified messiah. The prophets' words did not lead anyone to expect these events. Rather, when these unexpected and mysterious events occurred, the Jews turned to their Scripture to try to understand the meaning of these events. In doing this, they discovered a second level of meaning in the words of the prophets.

In other words, the prophets did not prognosticate the events; the events unlocked an additional, and until then unseen, level of meaning in the words of the prophets. For Matthew, this was evidence that the events had been part of God's plan all along.

Again, an example will make this point clear. After the angel announces Jesus's conception to Joseph, Matthew comments: "All this took place to fulfill what had been spoken by the Lord through the prophet: 'Look, the virgin shall conceive and bear a son, and they shall name him Emmanuel'" (Matt 1:22–23).

When the prophet Isaiah said these words, he was talking to King Ahaz (see Is 7:14). He was assuring the king that God would be faithful to God's promises to the house of David. Isaiah would have a son, and this son would be a much better king than Ahaz was being. God would be with this son as God had been with faithful leaders in the past.

Isaiah's words did not lead anyone to expect that a woman would conceive without having intercourse. Nor did it lead people to expect the incarnation—God's choosing to become one of us. However, in the light of these mysterious events, an additional level of meaning was seen in the words. "A virgin shall conceive" was understood to mean that a woman had conceived a child without there being a human father. "Emmanuel," "God is with us," was understood to mean that God actually took on human flesh and lived among us.

The prophet's words actually meant more than either the prophet or his contemporaries understood. There had been a hidden meaning all along, one that was understood only in the light of subsequent events. Therefore, God's mysterious plans and purposes were understood to have been revealed both through events and through the words of the prophets.

The Catholic Church embraces this interpretation of Scripture. For instance, during the Advent season the Catholic Church proclaims Isaiah's great and glorious king prophecies and hears them as referring to Jesus.

During Lent the Catholic Church proclaims 2 Isaiah's (Is 40–55) suffering servant songs and hears them as referring to Jesus. The Catholic Church agrees that the meaning of the words of Scripture is not exhausted by the intent of the original author.

PAUL AND THE USE OF ALLEGORY

Another way in which Scripture is understood and used as a living word within Scripture itself is by allegorizing stories. Once again, when a later author allegorizes an earlier author's story, the later author is using the story to teach something different than the original author was teaching. The later author is not claiming that the original author intended to say what the later author is using the text to teach.

Paul makes use of this method when teaching the Galatians that they are saved, not by obedience to the law but through faith. After reminding the Galatians that "Abraham had two sons, one by a slave woman and the other by a free woman" (Gal 4:22), he goes on to say: "Now this is an allegory: these women are two covenants" (Gal 4:24a). He then proceeds to illustrate his point by allegorizing the story of Abraham and the two women. Paul's point has nothing to do with the original author's intent.

THE USE AND ABUSE OF SCRIPTURE

Having established that the Catholic Church teaches people to be contextualists in their understanding of the revelation that Scripture contains, and also that the Catholic Church affirms that Scripture is a living word by which the whole Christian religion should be nourished and ruled, we are left with the question: What is legitimate use of Scripture, and what is abuse of Scripture?

Spirit-Filled Use of Scripture

The most basic use of Scripture is to seek to understand what the original author intended to teach by putting that author's words in the contexts of literary form, the beliefs of the time, and the two-thousand-year process of revelation that this library of books contains. The Catholic Church puts the authority of Scripture behind the author's intent.

In addition, it is a good and Spirit-filled activity to hear Scripture as a living word, to hear it address modern-day issues in the life of the whole community, as well as issues in the life of individual people. We are hearing Scripture in this way in homilies, in spiritual reflections, and in our personal prayer lives.

However, the meaning we hear in these settings does not have the same universal authority that we give to the original intent of the author. These insights are often applications of core truths to new social settings. A different social setting might call for a different conclusion. We have discussed an example of the distinction between a core truth and an application of that core truth to a particular social setting in the introduction in regard to usury and in this chapter in regard to slavery. We will explore this insight further, with specific examples, in future chapters.

At the same time, we must constantly ask ourselves if the conclusions we are drawing are compatible with what Scripture itself teaches. We know from reading stories of Jesus's controversies with various adversaries that using Scripture as a living word can lead to truth, but it can also lead to error. In Scripture, both the devil and some of the Pharisees are pictured as quoting Scripture to prove a point or to manipulate and mislead another person.

Abuse of Scripture

It is an abuse of Scripture to claim that "the Bible teaches," and by implication, that God has revealed, definitive answers to questions that no biblical author has addressed. This abuse is often practiced by those who take a single sentence out of its biblical context and present it as though it is God's answer to a question posed by another generation. This abuse is taking place when the Bible is used to answer questions that, when answered, will be answered by scientists and not by theologians. (We will discuss this insight in more detail in chapter 3 in regard to the story of the man and woman in the garden.)

It is an abuse of Scripture to use out-of-context passages to proof text that Catholic teachings are right and others are wrong in regard to beliefs and practices that developed later in Church history. For instance, when a person says something like "Jesus ordained only men," that person is abusing Scripture. Jesus did not establish the priesthood or ordain his apostles during his public ministry or at the Last Supper. These Christian practices developed later. (We will discuss this example in more detail in chapter 5.)

That a practice is not contemporary with Jesus's public ministry does not mean that it is illegitimate. Christians believe in the ongoing presence and guidance of the Holy Spirit in the Church. However, we abuse Scripture if we try to add authority to later developments by attributing them directly to Jesus's actions during his public ministry.

What, then, are the roles of experience and of Scripture in our search for God? It is certainly accurate to say that both have a unique and authoritative role. God does remain with us and does reveal God's self through events. Scripture, correctly understood, is our greatest source for understanding God's self-revelation to God's people. For Christians to correctly discern God's will in their lives, it is essential that, in addition to listening to the teaching voice of the Church, they prayerfully reflect on their own experience and listen carefully to what God is teaching them through inspired biblical authors. To fail to do so would be to ignore the Catholic Church's teaching and a shared Christian belief: We are to be nourished and ruled by Scripture.

CONTINUING THE CONVERSATION

1. Do you think that you have some knowledge of God and God's will? If so, how did you come by this knowledge?
2. In hindsight, do you think you have learned more about God and God's will by reflecting on your own experience? Explain.
3. Are you a contextualist or a fundamentalist? Why?
4. Do you consider the Bible a reliable source for learning about God? Why?
5. Have you ever experienced the Bible as a living word? Explain.

Chapter Three

Can Catholic Church Teaching Change?

On Change

But if the Supreme Pontiffs in their official documents purposely pass judgment on a matter up to that time under dispute, it is obvious that that matter, according to the mind and will of the Pontiffs, cannot be any longer considered a question open to discussion among theologians.
—Pius XII in *Humani Generis*, 1950

It is the duty of theologians to keep themselves regularly informed of scientific advances in order to examine if such be necessary, whether or not there are reasons for taking them into account in their reflection or for introducing changes in their teaching.
—Pope John Paul II in an address in the Pontifical Academy of Science, reported in *L'Osservatore Romano*, November 4, 1992

On Ecumenism

We therefore declare, say, affirm, and announce that for every human creature to be submissive to the Roman Pontiff is absolutely necessary for salvation.
—Boniface VIII in *Unam Sanctam*, 1302, before the Reformation but later applied to the post-Reformation setting

The Spirit of Christ has not refrained from using them [i.e., separated brethren, whether considered as individuals or as communities and Churches] as means of salvation.
—Second Vatican Council, *Decree on Ecumenism*, 1964

On Textual Criticism Applied to Scripture

To aid them in this they call to their assistance that branch of criticism which they call *textual*, and labour to show that such a fact or such a phrase is not in its right place. . . . Hence anybody who embraces it and employs it [this criticism] . . . places himself in opposition to Catholic faith.
—Pius X in *Encyclical on the Doctrines of the Modernists, Pascendi Dominici Gregis*, 1907

In the present day indeed this art, which is called textual criticism and which is used with great and praiseworthy results in the editions of profane writings, is also quite rightly employed in the case of the Sacred Books.
—Pius XII in *Encyclical on Promoting Biblical Studies, Divino Afflante Spiritu*, 1943

51

Later chapters of this book will argue that the Catholic Church is being called to be open to change in some of its teachings and in some of its practices. As was acknowledged in the introduction, in regard to change in teachings, some faithful Catholics would vehemently disagree. They believe that once Rome has spoken, the discussion is over.

To lay a foundation for both the possibility of change and the necessity for change, chapter 1 noted that the teaching voice of the Catholic Church requires us to follow our well-formed consciences. Chapter 2 pointed out that the very existence of Scripture rests on the fact that people reflected on their own experiences in order to come to an understanding of God and what God would have them do to cooperate with God's will. Chapter 2 also pointed out that the Catholic Church has instructed us to be nourished and ruled by Scripture, to understand what the original authors were teaching, and to hear Scripture as a living word in the context of our own lives.

This chapter will illustrate that the Catholic Church has itself set the example that change is both possible and necessary by recently (in the twentieth century) changing its teachings on at least two very important issues: how to be in right relationship with other Christians and how to correctly interpret Scripture. These changes have occurred in the lifetime of many present-day adult Catholics. Those who have lived through these changes know from experience that the Catholic Church can change its teaching on a moral matter.

THE CATHOLIC CHURCH AND ECUMENISM

Before the Second Vatican Council (1962–1965), twentieth-century Catholics were taught that it would be a mortal sin to worship in a Christian church that was not a Catholic church. In *Examination of Conscience for Boys and Girls*, first published in 1927 and in its twenty-ninth printing in 1951, with the authority of both a *Nihil obstat* and an *Imprimatur*, children were instructed to ask themselves: "DID I WILLINGLY ATTEND NON-CATHOLIC SERVICES OR NON-CATHOLIC SUNDAY SCHOOL?" This question is asked in the context of the first commandment: "I am the Lord thy God; Thou shalt not have strange gods before Me." The question is in caps because, as the booklet explains, "Mortal sins are shown in large letters like these: MORTAL."[1]

A mortal sin, of course, is the most serious kind of sin. As *Baltimore Catechism No. 1* explains: "Mortal sin takes away the life of the soul. . . .

Mortal sin kills the supernatural life of a man as truly as any bullet kills the natural life of a man."[2]

This booklet for the examination of conscience reflects what Catholic youth learned and memorized from the catechisms used throughout the United States. For instance, when teaching the first commandment, *Baltimore Catechism No. 1* asks: "How does a Catholic sin against faith?" The answer is: "A Catholic sins against faith by not believing what God has revealed, and by taking part in a non-Catholic worship."[3] The catechism goes on to explain: "Catholics know that there is only one true religion, and that God wants us to worship Him according to that one true religion. To take part in a non-Catholic (Protestant, Jewish, etc.) worship is like saying that we do not believe that there is only one true religion."[4]

In the first part of the twentieth century, the idea that joining fellow Christians in their worship was a mortal sin was a teaching of long standing. In fact, Richard McBrien in his book *Catholicism* tells us that well before the Reformation, anyone not in right relationship with the pope had been condemned in Catholic teaching. Pope Boniface VIII in *Unam Sanctam* (1302) declared: "We therefore declare, say, affirm, and announce that for every human creature to be submissive to the Roman Pontiff is absolutely necessary for salvation."[5]

Despite the fact that this teaching had existed for centuries, it changed with the Second Vatican Council. In its *Decree on Ecumenism* the council acknowledged that "all who have been justified by faith in baptism are incorporated into Christ; they therefore have a right to be called Christians, and with good reason are accepted as brothers [and sisters] by the children of the Catholic Church."[6] The document also states unequivocally that "the Spirit of Christ has not refrained from using them [i.e., separated brethren, whether considered as individuals or as communities and Churches] as means of salvation."[7]

So as not to encourage further prejudice against fellow Christians, the decree encourages Catholics to make "every effort to avoid expressions, judgments, and actions which do not represent the condition of our separated brethren with truth and fairness and so make mutual relations with them more difficult."[8] The decree encourages Catholics to become involved in ecumenical activities such as dialogue and common prayer, activities that had previously been forbidden by Pius XI in *Encyclical on Religious Unity, Mortalium Animos* (1928). In addition, all, including Catholics, are reminded that we are "led to examine [our] own faithfulness to Christ's will for the

Church and, wherever necessary, undertake with vigor the task of renewal and reform"(par. 4)[9].

In changing this teaching, the Catholic Church was growing in its understanding and was responding to the Spirit of Christ calling Catholics to change. Such growth calls for a conversion of heart. It also necessitates an acknowledgment of past blindness and a repentance for having acted toward others with prejudice, even if in the name of trust of authority or obedience.

Many Catholics are unaware that they are now called to be ecumenical and to work for the visible unity of Christ's body, the Church. The visible sign of that unity is that Christians will all someday be united around one Eucharistic table. The path to unity is not one on which everyone else will have to undergo growth and change, but Catholics will not. Catholics, too, are called to undertake the task of renewal and reform. (We will take up this topic again in chapter 10.)

THE CATHOLIC CHURCH AND THE PROPER WAY TO INTERPRET SCRIPTURE

In chapter 2 we explained the Catholic Church's present teaching regarding how to correctly interpret Scripture. This contextualist approach to Scripture was first officially taught in Pius XII's *Encyclical on Promoting Biblical Studies*, *Divino Afflante Spiritu* (1943), often called the Magna Carta of Catholic biblical scholarship. In the years before 1943, the Catholic Church had condemned much of what is now accepted in regard to the textual criticism of biblical texts. Before the promulgation of *Divino Afflante Spiritu*, a person who embraced the ideas explained in chapter 2 would have been accused of being a Modernist, a school of thought condemned by Pius X.

What ideas did the Modernists support that Pius X condemned? The answer to this question can be found in Pius X's *Encyclical on the Doctrines of the Modernists, Pascendi Dominici Gregis* (1907).[10]

- The Modernists gave a role to experience in one's search for God that Pius X condemned.
- The Modernists argued that revelation developed over years and that dogma, too, develops. Pius X points out that Pius IX had already condemned this idea in his *Syllabus of Errors*, where he said it is an error to maintain that "Divine revelation is imperfect, and therefore subject to continual and indefinite progress, corresponding with the progress of human reason."[11]

- The Modernists claimed that our expressions of truth are inadequate to their objects. Therefore, these formulas, "to be living, should be, and should remain, adapted to the faith and to him who believes."[12] Pius X responds to this claim with the charge: "Blind that they are, and leaders of the blind, inflated with a boastful science, they have reached that pitch of folly where they pervert the eternal concept of truth and the true nature of the religious sentiment."[13] Later Pius X quotes the First Vatican Council, which said,

  > The doctrine of the faith which God has revealed has not been proposed to human intelligences to be perfected by them as if it were a philosophical system, but as a divine deposit entrusted to the Spouse of Christ to be that which our Holy Mother the Church has once declared, nor is this sense ever to be abandoned on plea or pretext of a more profound comprehension of the truth.[14]

- Most important for our present discussion, however, is the Modernist approach to Scripture, which Pius X condemned. Pius says:

  > The Modernists have no hesitation in affirming commonly that these books, and especially the Pentateuch and the first three Gospels, have been gradually formed by additions to a primitive brief narration—by interpolations of theological or allegorical interpretation, by transitions, by joining different passages together. This means, briefly, that in the Sacred Books we must admit a *vital evolution*, springing from and corresponding with evolution of faith. . . . To aid them in this they call to their assistance that branch of criticism which they call *textual*, and labour to show that such a fact or such a phrase is not in its right place." (par. 34)[15]

Pius X goes on to say that anyone who employs this kind of criticism "places himself in opposition to Catholic faith."[16]

Every priest who was ordained between 1910 and 1967 was required to take Pius X's Oath against Modernism. The oath was "to be sworn to by all clergy, pastors, confessors, preachers, religious superiors, and professors in philosophical-theological seminaries."[17] This oath begins, "I . . . firmly embrace and accept each and every definition that has been set forth and declared by the unerring teaching authority of the Church, especially those principal truths which are directly opposed to the errors of this day." It goes on to state:

- Therefore, I entirely reject the heretical misrepresentation that dogmas evolve and change from one meaning to another different from the one which the Church held previously.
- I also condemn every error according to which, in place of the divine deposit which has been given to the spouse of Christ to be carefully guarded by her, there is put a philosophical figment or product of a human conscience that has gradually been developed by human effort and will continue to develop indefinitely.
- Furthermore, with due reverence, I submit and adhere with my whole heart to the condemnations, declarations, and all the prescripts contained in the encyclical *Pascendi* and in the decree *Lamentabili*.[18] (These two documents are the *Encyclical on the Doctrines of the Modernists* [1907], which was previously quoted, and the *Syllabus Condemning the Errors of the Modernists* [1907]).

To demand that all priests take this Oath against Modernism was to dig in the Catholic Church's heels against change. It was also to place dedicated, holy, intelligent, and faithful priests in a very difficult situation. However, the Spirit blows where the Spirit will. This strong stand against growth, against change, did not prevail.

THE CATHOLIC CHURCH'S RESPONSE TO THE SPIRIT'S CALL

In today's Catholic Church there are still some who are adamantly against present-day Catholic biblical scholarship and who quote Pius X to affirm their position. They believe that Catholic Church teaching cannot change, even in the light of new knowledge or in response to new contexts. They believe that to admit that Catholic Church teaching can change calls everything into question: the Catholic Church's ability to affirm anything at all about God, every dogma and doctrine that the Catholic Church has taught, and the present authority of the Catholic Church to teach on any subject at all. To affirm that the Catholic Church can, has, and must continue to change simply yanks the spiritual rug out from under their feet.

In order to respond pastorally to the needs of these faith-filled people who love the Catholic Church, one must be able to illustrate that the very Spirit-filled Catholic Church in which they have placed so much trust is the Spirit-filled Catholic Church that is now calling its people to a new understanding.

Experience has forced the Catholic Church to grow and to change, and many Catholics are now embracing that experience as a call from the Spirit.

To have a new understanding of an issue does not mean that Catholics have to abandon the truths that they have been taught for years. It means that Catholics have to grow in their understanding in the light of new knowledge. The truth remains firm. It is the way of understanding and expressing that truth that changes in the light of new knowledge. An example of this process, one that grows out of Catholic biblical scholarship and a consideration of literary form, is the Catholic Church's teaching on original sin.

The *Baltimore Catechism No. 2*, which Catholics used before Vatican Council II, says the following:

THE CREATION AND THE FALL OF MAN

Man is a creature composed of body and soul, and made to the image and likeness of God. Man's likeness to God is chiefly in the soul. The soul is like God because it is a spirit having understanding and free will. The soul is destined to live forever.

The first man and woman were Adam and Eve. They were the first parents of the whole human race. The chief gift God bestowed on Adam and Eve was sanctifying grace. This made them children of God and gave them the right to heaven. God bestowed other gifts on Adam and Eve: happiness in the Garden of Paradise, a great knowledge, control of the passions by reason, and freedom from suffering and death.

God gave Adam and Eve the commandment not to eat of the fruit of a certain tree that grew in the Garden of Paradise. However, Adam and Eve did not obey this commandment. They ate of the forbidden fruit. On account of their sin, Adam and Eve lost sanctifying grace, the right to heaven, and their special gifts. They became subject to death, to suffering, and to a strong inclination to evil. They were driven from the Garden of Paradise.

Because of the sin of Adam we, his descendants, come into the world deprived of sanctifying grace. This sin in us is called original sin. We inherit Adam's punishment as we would have inherited his gifts had he been obedient to God. The chief punishments of Adam which we inherit through original sin are: death, suffering, ignorance, and a strong inclination to sin. [19]

This passage obviously relies on the story of the man and woman in the garden that appears in Genesis 2:4–3:24. The paragraph treats that story as though it is teaching not only theology, but biology and history. The *Baltimore Catechism* claims that Adam and Eve are biologically the first parents of the whole human race, and that there is a cause-and-effect relationship between Adam and Eve's disobedience and the suffering that human beings experience. It names the punishment that we inherit from Adam and Eve "original sin," a name that was drawn not from the story itself but from the writings of St. Augustine in the fourth century AD. In the light of present-day biblical scholarship, can all of these claims be supported?

As we have already said, in 1943, in the encyclical *Divino Afflante Spiritu*, the Catholic Church first taught the importance of considering context in order to determine the intent of inspired human authors. In this encyclical, Pius XII embraced the work of textual critics: "In the present day indeed this art, which is called textual criticism and which is used with great and praiseworthy results in the editions of profane writings, is also quite rightly employed in the case of the Sacred Books."[20]

In addition, the pope embraced the absolute importance of considering the variety of literary forms found in the Bible: Pius XII says that the Catholic commentator should determine "to what extent the manner of expression of the literary mode adopted by the sacred writer may lead to a correct and genuine interpretation; and let him be convinced that this part of his office cannot be neglected without serious detriment to Catholic exegesis."[21]

The pope encourages Catholics to pursue these studies even though the conclusions reached will raise questions, the solutions to which may not be immediately self-evident but will be reached over time: "New beginnings grow little by little and fruits are gathered only after many labors. . . . Hence, there are grounds for hope that those [i.e., disputed points] also will by constant effort be at last made clear, which now seem most complicated and difficult."[22]

With this encyclical Pius XII gave Catholic biblical scholars the freedom and encouragement they needed to bring new knowledge to bear on present teaching. He says, "This true liberty of the children of God, which adheres faithfully to the teaching of the Church and accepts and uses gratefully the contributions of profane science, this liberty, upheld and sustained in every way by the confidence of all, is the condition and source of all lasting fruit and of all solid progress in Catholic doctrine."[23]

When a person follows Pius XII's direction and applies the concept of literary form to the story of the man and woman in the garden, the conclusions reached challenge some of what is claimed in the *Baltimore Catechism*. The literary form of the story is obviously neither scientific writing nor historical writing. The inspired author makes this perfectly evident by using several well-known literary devices: symbolic language and personification.

Among the obvious symbols in the story are Adam and the two trees. In English, *Adam* sounds like a masculine, singular noun, but in Hebrew it is a neuter collective noun. *Adam* is each one of us and all of us. The trees in the story are also symbols, not actual trees. There is a tree of life. As long as one eats its fruits that person will not die. In addition, there is a tree of knowledge of good and evil. This tree represents the fact that a moral order exists in creation, a moral order that has been revealed to us.

The plot of the story involves a talking snake. We all know that snakes do not talk. The author expects us to know this and, therefore, to correctly understand that this story has been composed to teach an eternal truth. The author is not claiming that the events are historical.

What eternal truth is the author teaching? The author is teaching that sin always causes suffering because it destroys all of our relationships: our relationship with self (naked, but ashamed), with others ("She made me do it!"), with God (the man and woman hide from God), and with the earth (the man must work by the sweat of his brow; the woman will bear children in pain). The fact that there is a moral order and that sin, acting contrary to that moral order, inevitably leads to suffering is a truth that our society, indeed every person, needs to take to heart.

However, the story cannot support the claims made for it in the *Baltimore Catechism*. A symbolic story cannot be the basis for biological or historical claims: It cannot support the claim that we all descended from Adam and Eve or that Adam's sin is a historical fact and that we inherited his punishment.

Although it was Pius XII who gave Catholic biblical scholars the freedom to raise such issues, it was also Pius XII who took a step backward from his own directions once the questions were raised. In regard to the question of whether or not Adam and Eve are the biological parents of the whole human race, Pius in his encyclical *Humani Generis* (1950) says:

> When however, there is question of another conjectural opinion, namely polygenism, the children of the Church by no means enjoy such liberty. For the faithful cannot embrace that opinion which maintains that either after Adam there existed on this earth true men who did not take their origin through natural generation from him as from the first parent of all, or that Adam represents a certain number of first parents. Now it is in no way apparent how such an opinion can be reconciled with that which the sources of revealed truth and the documents of the teaching authority of the Church propose with regard to original sin, which proceeds from a sin actually committed by an individual

Adam and which, through generation, is passed on to all and is in everyone as his own.[24]

Pius XII wrote *Humani Generis* to argue against some of the theological ideas that were developing after World War II. However, over the succeeding years, many of these ideas became accepted. Catholic theologians no longer insist that the truth being taught through the phrase "original sin," which was coined by St. Augustine, is dependent on a historical Adam and Eve from whom we biologically inherited our tendency to do that which we know to be wrong. We know we have this tendency from experience. We believe that we have been redeemed from slavery to this tendency through Jesus Christ.

In fact, when Paul, in his letter to the Romans, teaches the universal salvific effect of Jesus's saving acts, he uses Adam as a type of Jesus who had the opposite effect: condemnation for all. Paul says, "Yet death exercised dominion from Adam to Moses, even over those whose sins were not like the transgression of Adam, who is a type of the one who was to come" (Rom 5:14). Paul's point is not to insist that Adam is a historical person whose sin was biologically inherited, but to teach that Jesus redeemed the whole human race. We continue to grow in our understanding of the sources of the disorders we experience.

The most recent catechism, the *Catechism of the Catholic Church* (1997), partially accommodates this new understanding and partially insists on the older understanding. It says, "The account of the fall in Genesis 3 uses figurative language, but affirms a primeval event, a deed that took place *at the beginning of the history of man*."[25]

To say that Adam's sin was "a deed that took place at the beginning of the history of man" is not to teach a theological truth but to make a historical claim. The Catholic Church learned from its reflection on the Galileo case that when theologians try to speak definitively on subjects outside of their areas of expertise they open themselves to error.

Pope John Paul II, in an address before the Pontifical Academy of Science printed in the November 4, 1992, issue of *L'Osservatore Romano*, spoke of the separation of roles that must exist between various areas of study. The pope affirms that people in every area of study, including theologians, must have "an informed awareness of the field and the limits of their own competencies."[26]

In explaining what the Church had learned from its condemnation of Galileo's teaching regarding the relationship of the planets to each other, the pope states: "Thus the new science, with its methods and the freedom of research which they implied, obliged theologians to examine their own criteria of scriptural interpretation. Most of them did not know how to do so."[27]

The pope then draws his first conclusion:

> The birth of a new way of approaching study of natural phenomena demands a clarification on the part of all disciplines of knowledge. It obliges them to define more clearly their own field, their approach, their methods, as well as the precise import of their conclusions. In other words, this new way requires each discipline to become more rigorously aware of its own nature.[28]

The pope then goes on to warn theologians and biblical scholars not to reject truths discovered by historians. He says:

> Another crisis, similar to the one we are speaking of, can be mentioned here. In the last century and at the beginning of our own, advances in the historical sciences made it possible to acquire a new understanding of the Bible and of the biblical world. The rationalist context in which these data were most often presented seemed to make them dangerous to the Christian faith. Certain people, in their concern to defend the faith, thought it necessary to reject firmly-based historical conclusions. That was a hasty and unhappy decision. . . . It is a duty of theologians to keep themselves regularly informed of scientific advances in order to examine if such be necessary, whether or not there are reasons for taking them into account in their reflection or for introducing changes in their teaching.[29]

The pope then names exactly the problem with making historical or biological claims based on the story of Adam and Eve. It is the same mistake that was made in the case of Galileo: "The majority of theologians did not recognize the formal distinction between Sacred Scripture and its interpretation, and this led them unduly to transpose into the realm of the doctrine of the faith a question which in fact pertained to scientific investigation."[30] Whether or not the whole human race is descended from one couple is just such a question. It is a question that, when answered, will be answered by scientists, not by theologians.

There can be no doubt that Catholics are now called to embrace truth no matter what area of study discovers that truth. As Catholics grow in their knowledge of the world in which we live they will have to reimage some of the truths that have been received through revelation. To do so is not to abandon Scripture or Tradition. However, as they reimage core truths, Catholics will have to act as contextualists in relation to both Scripture and Tradition in order to separate those core truths from descriptions that include presumptions of the time and from applications that are not equally applicable in a new setting.

As scholars continue to grapple with the issue of just what we mean by "original sin" and with many other issues, Catholics must discard neither the core truths of Catholic traditional teachings nor the new knowledge that has been gained from many diverse areas of study. The Spirit is at work in God's people and in the whole world, not just in the Catholic Church and in the Catholic hierarchy.

Were the Catholic Church not able to grow in the light of knowledge gained from every area of study, Catholics would not be able to have intellectual integrity. They would have either to compartmentalize their experience and knowledge in one area and their faith in another, or they would have to choose between their specific areas of knowledge and the teaching voice of a Church that refuses to grow and change. In such a conflict, either choice—to dismiss truths learned from experience and from our areas of expertise, or to dismiss the Catholic Church as a credible teaching voice—would be a tragedy.

Catholics believe that Christ is alive and in our midst. Catholics believe that Christ's Spirit is, among other places, present in Christ's body, the Church. Catholics should never be afraid to follow the promptings of that Spirit and to grow beyond the present understanding of who God is, who God is calling us to be, and what God is calling us to teach.

CONTINUING THE CONVERSATION

1. When you bring your experience to bear on the question "Can Catholic Church teaching change?" how do you reply? Why is this your response?
2. Does the fact that the Catholic Church's teaching on important topics has changed over the years add or subtract from the credibility of the Church's teaching voice for you personally? Why?
3. What is your area of expertise? Does the knowledge you have gained from your own experience and from your area of work challenge the Catholic Church to reexamine and perhaps redefine some of its teachings? Explain.

4. Have you tried to pass on your faith to others, either as a parent, a friend, or a teacher? Have those others brought up questions that you found challenging? What were those questions? Where did you go, or where might you go, to find thoughtful and credible responses?

5. Do you believe that truths learned in other fields that challenge the Catholic Church's previous thinking on a topic are a threat or a gift to the Catholic Church? Why?

Chapter Four

Contraception

Since, therefore, the conjugal act is destined primarily by nature for the begetting of children, those who in exercising it deliberately frustrate its natural power and purpose sin against nature and commit a deed which is shameful and intrinsically vicious.

—Pius XI, *Encyclical on Christian Marriage, Casti Connubii*, n. 54

Small wonder, therefore, if Holy Writ bears witness that the Divine Majesty regards with greatest detestation this horrible crime and at times has punished it with death. As St. Augustine notes, "Intercourse even with one's legitimate wife is unlawful and wicked where the conception of the offspring is prevented. Onan, the son of Juda, did this and the Lord killed him for it."

—Pius XI, *Encyclical on Christian Marriage, Casti Connubii*, n. 55

Married couples should regard it as their proper mission to transmit human life and to educate their children. . . . This involves . . . the formation of correct judgment through docile respect for God and common reflection and effort; it also involves a consideration of their own good and the good of their children already born or yet to come, an ability to read the signs of the times and of their own situation on the material and spiritual level, and, finally an estimation of the good of the family, of society, and of the Church. It is the married couple themselves who must in the last analysis arrive at these judgments before God.

—Vatican Council II, *Pastoral Constitution on the Church in the Modern World, Gaudium et Spes*, n. 50

In chapter 3 we noted that the Catholic Church, in the twentieth century, set the example that to be faithful to the call of the Spirit, as that call was revealed through experience and through new knowledge, the Catholic Church changed its teaching regarding how to be in right relationship with other Christians and how to interpret Scripture. When faithful Catholics look back on the twenty-first century, will they describe other changes that have occurred?

There are three teaching areas in which experience and new knowledge may be calling Catholics to new understanding in the twenty-first century: the Magisterium's teaching on the intrinsic evil of all methods of contraception other than the rhythm method; the teaching that women cannot be ordained in the Catholic Church; and the teaching that sexual activity between committed homosexuals is intrinsically disordered. Therefore, homosexual couples should be deprived of marrying their chosen partners in a civil ceremony.

To suggest change in the Catholic Church's teaching on the use of contraception within marriage is far from an original or bold suggestion. Even before the Second Vatican Council (1962–1965), a review of the Catholic Church's present teaching was in process. For many years a great deal of conversation had taken place in the Catholic Church about whether or not the teachings in the 1930 encyclical *Casti Connubii*, which forbade the use of artificial methods of birth control, should change.

Therefore, before we examine the Catholic Church's present teaching forbidding the use of contraceptives, we will first review the events that led up to that teaching as it is presented in Paul VI's *Humanae Vitae* (1968). We will also note what Scripture has to say on the topic.

Casti Connubii (*On Christian Marriage*; 1930) had taught that contraception was wrong. There were two bases for the teaching: Scripture and natural law. The Scriptural argument rested on a story in Genesis, the story of Onan (see Genesis 38:8–10). Pius XI says:

> Small wonder, therefore, if Holy Writ bears witness that the Divine Majesty regards with greatest detestation this horrible crime and at times has punished it with death. As St. Augustine notes, "Intercourse even with one's legitimate wife is unlawful and wicked where the conception of the offspring is prevented. Onan, the son of Juda, did this and the Lord killed him for it."[1]

Today, Catholic biblical scholars would not support this use of the Genesis text. Onan's sin was that he failed to fulfill his familial responsibility to provide his brother's widow with offspring. Genesis says:

> Then Judah said to Onan, "Go to your brother's wife and perform the duty of a brother-in-law to her; raise up offspring for your brother." But since Onan knew that the offspring would not be his, he spilled his semen on the ground whenever he went in to his brother's wife, so that he would not give offspring to his brother. (Gen 38:8–10)

It is certainly an abuse of Scripture to use this passage to give biblical authority to a teaching against the use of contraceptives.

Because the condemnation of birth control was considered to be supported by natural law, all people of good will should have been able to see the wisdom of the teaching. For that reason, the pope's hope was that birth control devices would be illegal. *Casti Connubii* says, "Governments can assist the Church greatly in the execution of its important office, if, in laying down their ordinances, they take account of what is prescribed by divine and ecclesiastical law, and if penalties are fixed for offenders."[2]

Of course, the truth of this teaching was not self-evident to all. In fact, the Anglican bishops, at their August 1930 Lambeth Conference, had voted to allow the use of contraceptives. *Casti Connubii* (December 1930) was, in part, a reaction to that decision.

Between 1930 and the beginning of Vatican Council II, several other important events occurred. In 1951 the rhythm method of birth control was accepted because this method did not interfere with the sexual act and was viewed as cooperating with nature rather than acting against the natural law. However, this decision turned out to be a major step toward change because it affirmed that having intercourse with the intent of not conceiving a child is acceptable.

In 1958 the pill was discovered. This discovery really rocked the boat because, some argued, using the pill did not interfere with the integrity of the sexual act. However, Pius XII condemned the use of the pill for the purpose of contraception.

By the time the Second Vatican Council began to meet, more and more questions were being raised about the credibility of the natural law argument as supporting the prohibition against contraception. As discussed in our introduction, whether one believes that a teaching based on natural law can change would depend on whether one considers natural law static or dynamic. If a person emphasizes physicalism, the biological realities as they are presently understood, and thinks human beings should conform to the fixed order of nature, that person would consider the teaching unchangeable. If a person emphasizes personalism, the role of reason as it applies new knowledge to a variety of social contexts, that person would be open to the possibility that a teaching could change in the light of new knowledge.

Some of this debate over the possibility of change was public—the debate among the bishops preparing to write the Vatican II document *Gaudium et Spes* (*Pastoral Constitution on the Church in the Modern World*)—and some of it was initially private: John XXIII had appointed a special commission to study the Church's teaching on contraception. Evidently, it was Pope John's intention to have the commission advise the council members, but that is not the way things worked out. Pope John died (June 1963) between session meetings. Paul VI inherited the commission and expanded its membership, but he used the commission to advise himself, not the council deliberations. In the end, he rejected the advice of this commission.

After careful study and several years of deliberation, the commission advised the pope that its members, by a solid majority, did not find either the Scriptural or natural law arguments against the use of contraception within marriage persuasive. They believed that the prohibitions in *Casti Connubii* should be changed.

Paul VI was confronted with the very question that we discussed in chapter 3: Can Church teaching change? Evidently, he was persuaded that it could not because he was concerned that such a change would undercut the teaching authority of the Magisterium (evidence for this conclusion is given later in this chapter). The dilemma Paul VI faced is stated clearly and succinctly in a question reported in Robert McClory's book *Turning Point: The Inside Story of the Papal Birth Control Commission.* A priest, when confronted with the idea of change, asked, "What then with the millions we have sent to hell, if these norms are not valid?"[3] The response from Patty Crowley, a member of the commission, was, "Do you really believe God has carried out all of your orders?"[4] In *Humanae Vitae* (1968), Paul VI reaffirmed the teaching against all methods of birth control other than the rhythm method.

After *Humanae Vitae* was promulgated, there were worldwide negative reactions. Even bishops' groups spoke up, reminding people that while they must listen carefully to what the Magisterium teaches, they still must follow their conscience. According to surveys, a vast majority of Catholics, in good conscience, decided not to obey. The pope's action, based on a desire to maintain the authority of the teaching voice of the Catholic Church, apparently had the opposite effect, at least on this one subject.

WHAT DOES SCRIPTURE HAVE TO SAY?

Scripture remains silent on the issue of birth control. We have seen that the passage from Genesis about Onan was misused to give biblical authority to the teaching in *Casti Connubii*. The mistake of using that passage to support the teaching was not repeated in *Humanae Vitae*.

One might assume that Scripture remains silent on the topic of contraception because this is a modern problem. Perhaps the ancients lacked knowledge on this subject and so it was not an issue. However, John T. Noonan, in his classic work *Contraception*, says, "The existence of contraceptive methods in the world from which Christians came is established."[5] Noonan says that, in regard to Roman literature, the "absence of reference . . . is perhaps best understood as due to a general calm acceptance of contraceptive practice."[6]

So, instead of talking about what Scripture has to say about a specific topic on which it remains silent, we will instead address the question: What moral stance do the Gospels teach us to have when trying to correctly discern how to live so as to please God? It is this question that *Humanae Vitae* has raised for many Catholic married couples who have had to make a conscience decision about whether or not to obey the Magisterium's teaching on contraception.

In the Gospels, Jesus consistently tries to get his listeners, who are prone to judge everyone, including themselves, on the basis of their obedience to the law, to use a different criterion. Jesus wants them to ask themselves: "Am I loving God and my neighbor?" When obeying a law had the unintended effect of preventing one from loving a neighbor, the love of neighbor trumped obeying the law.

For instance, Jesus tells the story of the prodigal son to Pharisees and scribes to help them realize that, although they obey the law, they fail at the all-important commandment: love of neighbor. The Pharisees and scribes are criticizing Jesus because he spends too much time with sinners (see Luke 15:2). They do not realize that Jesus is spending time with sinners when he is spending time with them. To help the Pharisees and scribes gain some insight about themselves, Jesus tells them a parable about a man who has two sons (see Luke 15:11–32). On hearing this story, the Pharisees and scribes would never identify with the younger son. He is an obvious sinner. However, they would identify with the older son, who is obedient, self-righteous, and judgmental, just like the Pharisees and scribes. As the father lovingly corrects his older son, Jesus is lovingly correcting his critics. They, too, are sinners because they fail to love other sinners.

These law-abiding, self-righteous characters were constantly critical of Jesus for disobeying the law. Jesus was an active, faithful Jew. He regularly taught in the Jewish synagogues. He knew the law and the prophets inside and out. He celebrated Passover with his fellow Jews. What he did not do was allow what he believed to be human law, presented as God's law, to stand in the way of his loving his neighbor.

Jesus makes this distinction between God's law and human law, presented as God's law, very clearly in his condemnations of some of the Pharisees and scribes. They ask Jesus:

> "Why do your disciples break the tradition of the elders? For they do not wash their hands before they eat." He answered them, "And why do you break the commandment of God for the sake of our tradition? For God said, 'Honor your father and your mother,' and, 'Whoever speaks evil of father or mother must surely die.' But you say that whoever tells father or mother, 'Whatever support you might have had from me is given to God,' then that person need not honor the father. So, for the sake of your tradition, you make void the word of God. You hypocrites! Isaiah prophesied rightly about you when he said: 'This people honors me with their lips / but their hearts are far from me; / in vain do they worship me / teaching human precepts as doctrines.'" (Matt 15:1–9)

The invitation of the Gospel is to become a disciple of Jesus Christ, to have Jesus Christ become our model of moral decision making. Jesus's focus was not only, or primarily, on the law, although he certainly knew the law and, for the most part, obeyed it. Jesus's focus was on his relationship with God, who he knew loved him, and whom he loved above all others and all else. In addition, Jesus's focus was on announcing and effecting the coming of the kingdom of God. This should be Christians' focus, too, as disciples of Jesus Christ. Jesus knew and taught that love of God and of neighbor fulfills the law and the prophets and brings about the coming of the kingdom. The focus of all Christians, including Catholics, as would-be disciples of Jesus Christ, should be on becoming loving people.

So, the question the Gospels would have us ask in regard to the use of contraceptives is the same question the Gospels would have us ask in regard to every other moral dilemma: What is the loving thing to do?

PRESENT CATHOLIC CHURCH TEACHING

As explained earlier, during the Second Vatican Council the Catholic Church's teaching forbidding all types of contraception except the rhythm method was under study. This is evident in the Second Vatican Council document *Gaudium et Spes*, issued in December 1965. This document addresses the topic of married love, saying:

> Married couples should regard it as their proper mission to transmit human life and to educate their children. . . . This involves . . . the formation of correct judgment through docile respect for God and common reflection and effort; it also involves a consideration of their own good and the good of their children already born or yet to come, an ability to read the signs of the times and of their own situation on the material and spiritual level, and, finally an estimation of the good of the family, of society, and of the Church. It is the married couple themselves who must in the last analysis arrive at these judgments before God.[7]

The document goes on to say:

> In questions of birth regulation the sons of the Church, faithful to these principles, are forbidden to use methods disapproved of by the teaching authority of the Church in its interpretation of the divine law.[8]

A footnote then directs the reader to a number of documents, including *Casti Connubii*. The footnote then adds:

> By order of the Holy Father, certain questions requiring further and more careful investigation have been given over to a commission for the study of population, the family, and births, in order that the Holy Father may pass judgment when its task is completed. With the teaching of the magisterium standing as it is, the Council has no intention of proposing concrete solutions at this moment.[9]

From 1965 until July 1968, the world waited with bated breath to hear if there would be a change in the teaching. News of what was happening in the commission leaked, and the world knew, as explained earlier, that the commission had recommended change. However, when Paul VI passed judgment on the advice of the commission, he decided to turn it down and reaffirmed the earlier teaching, although with a somewhat different justification.

HUMANAE VITAE

Paul begins *Humanae Vitae* (1968) by acknowledging that times have changed: He refers to the growth in the world population, to the increased expenses involved in raising and educating a family, to a new understanding of the dignity of women, to the appreciation of the value of love in marriage, and to man's "domination . . . of the forces of nature" through new discoveries.[10]

Paul also acknowledges that new questions are being asked, such as: "Could it not be admitted . . . that procreative finality applies to the totality of married life rather than to each single act? Should not . . . the transmission of life . . . be regulated by [the couple's] intelligence and will rather than through the specific rhythm of their own bodies?"[11]

The encyclical then turns to what was evidently the major question in Paul VI's mind: the authority of the Magisterium to teach on moral matters. Paul says:

> Let no Catholic be heard to assert that the interpretation of the natural moral law is outside the competence of the Church's Magisterium. It is in fact indisputable, as our Predecessors have many times declared, that Jesus Christ, when he communicated his divine power to Peter and the other apostles and sent them to teach all nations his commandments, constituted them as the authentic guardians and interpreters of the whole moral law, not only that is, of the law of the gospel but also of the natural law, the reason being that the natural law declares the will of God, and its faithful observance is necessary for men's eternal salvation.[12]

The pope then goes on to thank the commission for its work, but to reject its advice because there was not complete unanimity on the commission and because it advised a change in Church teaching.

Humanae Vitae says that sexual activity between husband and wife is honorable and good; it strengthens the love between the spouses. At the same time, "it is absolutely required that in any use whatever of marriage there must be no impairment of its natural capacity to procreate human life."[13] The document reiterates that there is "an inseparable connection, established by

God, which man on his own initiative may not break between the unitive significance and the procreative significance" of the marriage act. [14]

The document goes on to forbid "any action, which either before, or at the moment of, or after sexual intercourse, is specifically intended to prevent procreation—whether as an end or as a means." [15] Because these actions are intrinsically wrong, they cannot be justified by a good intent: "It is never lawful, even for the gravest reasons, to do evil that good may come of it." [16]

As *Humanae Vitae* continues, the thrust of the message is not to persuade others that its teaching is true by presenting cogent reasons that support its conclusions, but to implore everyone to accept the teaching authority of the Magisterium. For instance, in its Pastoral Directive to Priests, the document says: "In the performance of your ministry you must be the first to give an example of this sincere obedience, inward as well as outward, which is due to the Magisterium of the Church. For, as you know, the Pastors of the Church enjoy a special gift of the Holy Spirit in teaching the truth. And this, rather than the arguments they put forward, is why you are bound to such obedience." [17]

Subsequent Church documents, such as *Familiaris Consortio* and *Veritatis Splendor*, have continued to affirm the Magisterium's teaching against the use of any method of birth control other than the rhythm method.

QUESTIONS AND CONCERNS

Humanae Vitae left the whole world with many questions and concerns. Not only were married couples presented with a painful dilemma, but so were bishops and priests in their teaching and pastoral roles. National groups of bishops, while they, of course, did not recommend disobedience, emphasized the preeminent role that conscience must play in moral decisions. For instance, Richard McBrien, in his book *Catholicism*, reports the reaction of the Dutch bishops. The Dutch bishops said that although Catholics must show "respect to the authority and pronouncements of the pope," there are "many factors which determine one's personal conscience regarding marriage rules, for example, mutual love, the relations in a family, and social circumstances." [18]

In addition, the document appears to suggest that the Catholic Church's teaching on this subject could never change, even in the light of new knowledge. In giving his reasons for rejecting the advice of the commission, the pope says that his decision was necessary because "certain approaches and criteria for a solution to this question had emerged which were at variance with the moral doctrines on marriage constantly taught by the Magisterium of the Church."[19]

One of the first questions addressed in this book is whether Church teaching can grow, can change. We have demonstrated that Church teaching has changed on some very important topics, such as our understanding of how to interpret the Bible and our posture toward other Christians. Since we know that Catholic Church teaching has changed on other topics, the question becomes: Can Catholic Church teaching change on the morality of the use of contraceptive methods, other than the rhythm method, within the context of marriage?

One of the reasons that members of the commission advised change is that they were convinced that the Catholic Church's teaching on this subject had already evolved over centuries. John T. Noonan, the author of *Contraception*, had appeared before the commission and had demonstrated that Catholic Church teaching evolves. Noonan was an expert on this subject in relation to both usury and contraception.

McBrien summarizes the changes that Noonan described to the commission:

> The early Fathers of the Church held that the use of sex in marriage was justified *only* for procreation. Later it was admitted that a sterile woman might marry and enjoy full conjugal relations. Eventually intercourse during the so-called safe period was approved. The next step would be to admit that the procreative value of the conjugal act is not bound up with every individual act of intercourse.[20]

Evidently the pope thought it would be a scandal to the laity to have the Magisterium change a teaching that it had not only taught but enforced. Gary Wills in his *Papal Sin* explains that "Pius [XI] gave priests a mandate to patrol individual consciences that was unparalleled in past instruction on contraception."[21] Wills then quotes Pius XI's *Casti Connubii*:

> "We admonish, therefore, priests who hear confessions, and others who have the care of souls, in virtue of Our supreme authority and in Our solicitude for the salvation of souls, not to allow the faithful entrusted to them to err regarding this most grave law of God, much more that they keep themselves immune from such false opinions, in no way conniving in them. If any confessor or pastor of souls, which may God forbid, lead the faithful entrusted to him into these errors or should at least confirm them by approval or by guilty silence,

let him be mindful of the fact that he must render a strict account to God, the Supreme Judge, of the betrayal of his sacred trust, and let him take to himself the words of Christ: 'They are blind and leaders of the blind, and if the blind lead the blind, both fall into the pit.'"[22]

It must have been a priest who diligently obeyed this instruction who, when hearing of the suggestion of change, responded, "What then with the millions we have sent to hell, if these norms were not valid?"

This brings us to two other questions which *Humanae Vitae* raises, neither of which have anything directly to do with birth control. However, answers to these questions will affect the decision couples make when deciding how to act, given the Magisterium's present teaching on birth control. The first question has to do with the Magisterium's teaching role, the second with each person's individual conscience.

- Does the Magisterium, because of its teaching role, have more access to truth than do other baptized people?
- Can the teaching voice of the Magisterium relieve an individual baptized person from taking responsibility for his or her own moral decisions?

The first question is raised because of what Paul VI says as he defends the teaching role of the Magisterium. As we noted earlier, Paul VI says:

It is in fact indisputable, as Our Predecessors have many times declared, that Jesus Christ, when he communicated his divine power to Peter and to the other apostles and sent them to teach all nations his commandments, constituted them as the authentic guardians and interpreters of the whole moral law, not only, that is, of the law of the gospel but also of the natural law, the reason being that the natural law declares the will of God, and its faithful observance is necessary for men's salvation.[23]

Paul VI doesn't exactly say, but he seems to imply, that if he and previous popes disagree with the advice of others, such as the expert commission, the Magisterium must be right and the experts wrong because Jesus communicated his divine power and the instruction to teach all nations to Peter and the apostles, not to the community as a whole. Is that what Paul means? Scripture cannot support that claim.

The footnote that accompanies the passage refers us to Matthew 28:18–19. Jesus says to the eleven, "All authority in heaven and on earth has been given to me. Go therefore and make disciples of all nations, baptizing them in the name of the Father and of the Son and of the Holy Spirit." However, as we discussed in chapter 1, this is not the only passage in the Gospels that deals with Jesus's giving authority to others.

Another passage is the one in which Jesus says to Peter: "And I tell you, you are Peter, and on this rock I will build my church, and the gates of Hades will not prevail against it. I will give you the keys of the kingdom of heaven, and whatever you bind on earth will be bound in heaven, and whatever you loose on earth will be loosed in heaven" (Matt 16:18–20). This passage certainly affirms Peter, and by extension, the Petrine role. However, Peter is not the only one given authority.

Just two chapters later in Matthew, when Jesus is speaking not just to Peter and the other apostles but to unspecified disciples, Jesus gives many other instructions, including: "Truly I tell you, whatever you bind on earth will be bound in heaven, and whatever you loose on earth will be loosed in heaven. Again, truly I tell you, if two of you agree on earth about anything you ask, it will be done for you by my Father in heaven. For where two or three are gathered in my name, I am there among them" (Matt 18:18–20).

Other scriptural passages about power being given appear in Acts. For instance, at Pentecost, the Spirit does not descend just on Peter and the apostles. We are told that "they were all gathered in one place" (Acts 2:1). When we look back to see who "all" includes we read not only the names of the apostles, but also "certain women, including Mary the mother of Jesus, as well as his brothers" (Acts 1:13–14). There are about 120 people in all. Luke tells us that "a tongue [of fire] rested on *each* of them. *All* of them were filled with the Holy Spirit" (Acts 2:3b–4a).

Later, when God wants Peter, for the good of the Church, to grow in knowledge, he not only inspires Peter's dream, but he sends Peter to the house of Cornelius. There Peter learns that the Gentiles are having an experience of the presence of the Spirit that Peter finds very enlightening. It forces Peter to grow beyond his earlier understanding that he was to go only to the Israelites. Peter then reports his experience to the Church at Jerusalem (Acts 10–11:18). Peter, despite his preeminence, has to learn from the experience of others and has to be open to new understandings and new teachings.

The gifts of wisdom and understanding are given not only to the Magisterium. If the Magisterium is called to fulfill its teaching role on a subject with which it has absolutely no personal experience other than observation, such as married love, the Magisterium must, by necessity, listen to the witness of faithful Catholics who are married and who are seeking to know and do God's will.

Humanae Vitae also raises the question: Can a teaching Church relieve an individual of his or her responsibility to make moral decisions? The document seems to ask both married couples and priests to trust that what the Magisterium is saying is true, to accept it, and to act on it, even if, in the depth of their being, they simply cannot agree.

Many bishops around the world were evidently concerned with this issue, too, evidenced by the fact that they responded to the document by reaffirming the Catholic Church's teaching on the priority of conscience.

Certainly, if a woman is blessed with a regular cycle and the rhythm method is not too great a burden for either the wife or the husband, the rhythm method is a good method of family planning: It does demand discipline and self-control, but those are good qualities to develop. The rhythm method keeps people aware that what might become routine is really a marvelous gift from God and is not to be taken for granted. That, also, is a benefit.

However, there are many circumstances that could be understood to make using the rhythm method irresponsible: What if another pregnancy would endanger the life of the wife and mother? What if the husband or wife develops a disability, and the healthy spouse cannot support the family the couple already has, much less a bigger family? What if a spouse's job entails a great deal of travel and he or she isn't home during the infertile times? What if the amount of abstinence required leads to temptations to infidelity for either the husband or the wife? What if one of the children is a special needs child and absolutely requires a great deal of parental time, attention, and resources? The *what ifs* could go on and on and on.

In any of these circumstances, would any form of birth control other than total abstinence or the rhythm method be allowed by the Magisterium? At present, the answer is no, because separating the unitive and procreative goals of marriage is understood to be intrinsically wrong. One cannot choose an evil means to achieve a good end, no matter what the circumstances or how great the good of the final end.

The flaw in this argument for many is that they can't find the intrinsic evil that the Magisterium believes is present. In order to consider the morality of an act, one must consider such things as the situation of the person acting, the act itself, the person's motive, and the consequences.

In the past, when procreation was considered the only or the primary purpose of intercourse, one could not defend a married couple having intercourse and shutting off the possibility of conceiving. But that is no longer the case. The mutual expression of love between husband and wife is also a purpose, and even *Humanae Vitae* does not make it a secondary purpose.

In the past, when the intent to prevent conception was considered wrong, one could not defend a married couple's having intercourse and shutting off the possibility of conceiving. However, when the rhythm method was accepted, the intent to prevent conception was also accepted.

So, in the development of the Catholic Church's thinking, both intercourse without the possibility of conception and intercourse when conception is possible but not desired have become accepted. We also now know, thanks to science, that there is a natural rhythm when conception is possible and when it is not. We also know, thanks to science, how to control fertile and infertile times. Why do we not consider this knowledge a kind of truth, a gift from God, and feel free to use it?

If a mother of three very young children is told that a fourth pregnancy would endanger her life, and that mother takes a pill (not an act that is intrinsically evil, or one would not be able to do it no matter what the intent) with the intent of not conceiving (not an intrinsically evil intent, or it would not be allowed with the rhythm method) in order to preserve her life so that she can fulfill her responsibilities to her husband and children (a worthy outcome), why should she not make that choice?

The Catholic Church teaches the priority of conscience. The Magisterium cannot relieve any one of us from the responsibility of doing what we believe to be God's will, whether we are a wife, a husband, a bishop, or a priest. Surely, listening to the Magisterium's teaching is part of the process of conscience formation. But listening to that teaching, according to the Magisterium itself, cannot take the place of forming one's conscience and acting on it.

Surveys report widespread disagreement with and disobedience to the teachings in *Humanae Vitae* among Catholics, undoubtedly because the encyclical insists on conclusions that it does not persuasively defend. Ironically, it appears that in order not to scandalize Catholics by changing a teaching, the pope unwittingly reinforced another important teaching of the Catholic Church: the Catholic's obligation to follow a well-formed conscience. It is obvious from the reaction to *Humanae Vitae* that the vast majority of Catholics are not scandalized by change. They are open to new knowledge, to growth, and to change.

CONTINUING THE CONVERSATION

1. What beliefs do you have, based on your own experience, on the topic of birth control? Why do you hold these beliefs?
2. Using Jesus as your model, what do you believe should be the moral stance out of which Christians make their moral decisions?
3. Have you ever had to distinguish between what you believe to be God's law and what you believe to be human law represented as God's law? Explain.
4. Do you believe that the Magisterium, because of its teaching function, has greater access to the truth than do all others? Explain.
5. Do you believe that the teaching voice of the Magisterium can relieve you of your responsibility to make moral decisions? Why or why not?

Chapter Five

Ordination and Women's Role in the Church

Again, the same holds good between man and the other animals: tame animals are superior in their nature to wild animals, yet for all the former it is advantageous to be ruled by man, since this gives them security. Also, as between the sexes, the male is by nature superior and the female inferior, the male ruler and the female subject.

—Aristotle in *Politica*, 1254 b-12

Each faith community should be free to celebrate all of the sacraments as frequently as the Spirit moves led by a sacramental minister who is part of the community. We see a strong need for open dialogue about these issues which have been suppressed by the hierarchy of the church.

—Regional report published in a *Cross Roads* supplement, December 28, 1997, iv

In accord with the prescriptions of law, those who have received sacred orders are capable of the power of governance, which exists in the Church by divine institution and is also called the power of jurisdiction.

—Canon 129 in *The Code of Canon Law*

The Church, in fidelity to the example of the Lord, does not consider herself authorized to admit women to priestly ordination.

—*Inter Insigniores*, n. 1

One of the reasons that many young people of the twenty-first century do not find the teaching voice of the Catholic Church credible is the Magisterium's present position against the ordination of women. The Magisterium adamantly denies that this refusal to ordain women has anything to do with prejudice, instead attributing it to fidelity to Jesus Christ, who did not choose a woman to be one of the twelve (to be discussed later).

However, some prejudices are so deeply embedded in one's culture that they are not recognized as prejudice; they are accepted as God's own order. In this chapter we will give evidence that prejudice against women has deep roots in Western civilization, we will look carefully at what Scripture has to say on women's role in the Church, and we will look at what the Catholic Church presently teaches. Finally, we will try to discern how the prejudice against women, which has been part and parcel of the thinking of Western civilization, has also affected the Magisterium of the Catholic Church and, therefore, has limited the ways in which women can serve the Catholic Church, no matter their God-given gifts or the needs of the Eucharistic community.

THE NATURE OF WOMEN: INFERIOR AND A MISTAKE

It comes as a shock to young people of the twenty-first century who are growing up in Western civilization to learn what great thinkers of the past have thought about women. For instance, Aristotle (384 BC–322 BC) thought that women were defective by nature. They were merely the field in which the male planted his seed. At that time, people believed that the semen contained the whole person. Women could not produce semen and so were defective. In his *Generation of Animals*, Aristotle says that "a woman is as it were an infertile male."[1] She is female by virtue of something she lacks.

Aristotle thought that men had superior intelligence and, therefore, should rule over women. In *Politica* Aristotle says: "Again, the same holds good between man and the other animals: tame animals are superior in their nature to wild animals, yet for all the former it is advantageous to be ruled by man, since this gives them security. Also, as between the sexes, the male is by nature superior and the female inferior, the male ruler and the female subject."[2]

Augustine (354–430) and Thomas Aquinas (1225–1274), foundational thinkers in Catholic theology, would not have had the reaction of a person who lives in today's Western civilization when presented with such ideas:

one of total astonishment. Their thinking was in accord with Aristotle's. Thomas, in his *Summa Theologica*, quotes Augustine's *Animal Conception* when he says:

> As regards the individual nature, woman is defective and misbegotten, for the active force in the male seed tends to the production of a perfect likeness in the masculine sex; while the production of woman comes from defect in the active force or from some material indisposition, or even from some external influence; such as that of a south wind, which is moist, as the Philosopher observes. (De Gener. Animal. Iv. 2)[3]

As we will see when we discuss what Scripture has to say on this topic, Jesus seems to have been unaffected by ideas such as Aristotle's. However, when Christianity moved out into the Gentile world, the Hellenized world, women's roles in the Church became severely restricted compared to what they had originally been.

WHAT DOES SCRIPTURE HAVE TO SAY?

About Ordination to Priesthood

If our question is, "What does Scripture have to say about ordination to Christian priesthood?" the answer is: nothing. Ordination, in the way the word is used in the Catholic Church, did not develop until the third century AD. Many Catholics presume that Jesus ordained his apostles at the Last Supper on the evening before he died. This idea has been reinforced by the fact that Catholics celebrate the priesthood in a liturgical setting on Holy Thursday. However, in the historical context of Jesus's public ministry, Jesus, who was Jewish, was not a priest himself, and Jesus did not ordain anyone.

It isn't that priesthood was unheard of in Jesus's time. In fact, it had a long history. The role of the priest, to mediate between God and God's people, was established soon after the Israelites settled in Canaan. Once David united the twelve tribes and moved the political and cultic center of the kingdom to Jerusalem, and once the temple was built in Jerusalem, the priests had an even more important role as they offered sacrifice in the Jerusalem temple. After the Babylonian exile, because the Israelites no longer had a king, the priests who served in the rebuilt temple became the leaders of the Jewish people. John the Baptist's father, Zachariah, was a Jewish priest. However, Jesus was not a Jewish priest who served in the temple, offering sacrifice. No person contemporary with Jesus would have called him a priest.

Priesthood is spoken about in the New Testament. In 1 Peter the author tells the people: "But you are a chosen race, a royal priesthood, a holy nation, God's own people, in order that you may proclaim the mighty acts of him who called you out of darkness into his marvelous light" (1 Peter 2:9). According to this passage, all in the Christian community are priests. However, this is what later began to be called "the priesthood of the laity."

But nowhere in the New Testament is there any mention of there being a particular person, or a particular office of people, who presided at Eucharist. Rather, it was the whole community who presided at Eucharist. In the earliest days of Christianity, Christians gathered to break bread together in each other's homes. The individual who was the host or hostess at the gathering, who presided, was most probably the man or woman in whose home the gathering took place.

The New Testament, by analogy, also describes Jesus as a priest. The author of Hebrews compares the old covenant to the new covenant, and the role of Jesus to the role of the Jewish high priests. Hebrews says:

> Now the main point in what we are saying is this: we have such a high priest, one who is seated at the right hand of the throne of the Majesty in the heavens, a minister in the sanctuary and the true tent that the Lord, and not any mortal, has set up. . . . But Jesus has now obtained a more excellent ministry, and to that degree he is the mediator of a better covenant, which has been enacted through better promises. (Heb 8:1–2, 6)

The author of Hebrews goes on to teach that Jesus, as high priest, offered the perfect sacrifice, himself, so that his sacrifice need never be repeated. "But when Christ came as a high priest . . . he entered once for all into the Holy Place, not with the blood of goats and calves, but with his own blood, thus obtaining eternal redemption" (Heb 9:11–12). The author is not claiming that historically Jesus was a priest who offered sacrifice in the temple. Rather, he is using an analogy to compare Jesus's perfect sacrifice of himself to the sacrifices offered in the temple.

The Book of Revelation also refers to priests, but these references, like the one in 1 Peter, are referring to all who have been redeemed, not to a particular order of ordained men. In his greeting to the seven churches, John says: "To him who loves us and freed us from our sins by his blood, and made us to be a kingdom, priests serving his God and Father, to him be glory and dominion forever and ever: Amen" (Rev 1:5b–6). When describing why only the lamb is worthy to open the sealed scroll, John pictures those in the heavenly court singing, "For you were slaughtered and by your blood you ransomed for God saints from every tribe and language and people and nation; you have made them to be a kingdom and priests serving our God, and they will reign on earth" (Rev 5:9).

Later, in describing the redeemed in heaven, John says: "Blessed and holy are those who share in the first resurrection. Over these the second death has no power, but they will be priests of God and of Christ, and they will reign with him a thousand years" (Rev 20:6). None of these passages is referring to an ordained priesthood as Catholics understand priesthood today. Rather, the word *priests* is referring to the whole Christian community.

As Ray Noll explains in his book *Sacraments: A New Understanding for a New Generation*, priestly and sacrificial terminology began to be applied to the role of Christian church leaders by the apostolic fathers in the second century and reached its full flower in the third century under the influence of St. Cyprian, the bishop of Carthage (d. 258). Noll quotes Edward Schillebeeckx's *The Church with a Human Face: A New and Expanded Theology of Ministry*, who says:

> "Cyprian (and already Tertullian before him) had a clear predilection for the Old Testament priestly sacrificial terminology, to which he compared the Christian Eucharist. In this way the sacerdotalizing of the vocabulary of the Church's ministry in fact developed gradually, though this was first in an allegorical sense. Furthermore, Cyprian is also the first who says of the *sacerdos,* i.e., at that time the bishop who presides over the community and therefore at the Eucharist, that he does this *vice Christi*, in Jesus' place. By contrast, Augustine continues to refuse to call bishops and presbyters 'priests' in the real sense, in the sense of being mediators between Christ and the community."[4]

So, although the New Testament authors are familiar with the concept of priesthood, they say not a word about there being any ordained Christian priests who had a specific sacral, cultic role in the first hundred-plus years of Christianity. We have no evidence to support the idea that Jesus ordained anyone. Neither Jesus himself, the twelve, nor the apostles were priests in either a Jewish or Christian context.

About Women's Role in the Early Church

If, however, instead of asking what Scripture has to say about ordination to priesthood, we ask what Scripture has to say about leadership in the early Church, we have a good deal more to offer.

There seems to be no question that Jesus did not exclude women from important roles in his ministry. Luke does the best job of reporting women's roles. He tells us that women accompanied and supported Jesus throughout his ministry:

> Soon afterwards [Jesus] went on through cities and villages, proclaiming and bringing the good news of the kingdom of God. The twelve were with him, as well as some women who had been cured of evil spirits and infirmities: Mary, called Magdalene, from whom seven demons had gone out, and Joanna, the wife of Herod's steward Chuza, and Susanna, and many others, who provided for them out of their resources. (Luke 8:1–3)

The women are present at the crucifixion: "But all his acquaintances, including the women who had followed him from Galilee, stood at a distance, watching these things" (Luke 23:49). It was the women who first told the apostles the good news of Jesus's resurrection: "Then they remembered his words, and returning from the tomb, they told all this to the eleven and to all the rest. Now it was Mary Magdalene, Joanna, Mary the mother of James, and the other women with them who told this to the apostles. But these words seemed to them an idle tale, and they did not believe them" (Luke 24:8–11).

The eleven are not alone when Jesus appears to them and commissions them; they are with other disciples, including women. Luke tells us that the two disciples on the road to Emmaus (many think Cleophas and his wife [see Luke 25:18; John 19:25]), returned to Jerusalem and "found the eleven and their companions gathered together" (Luke 24:33). As Luke's story continues in Acts, Luke tells us that their companions include women; all are told to wait for the coming of the Spirit. When the Spirit comes, Luke describes the "all" who were "gathered in one place" (Acts 1:14–15; 2:1). The group consists of about 120 persons, including "certain women, including Mary the mother of Jesus" (Acts 1:14–15). We see, then, that not just the eleven, but women, were commissioned. Not just the twelve (Judas's successor was chosen before Pentecost), but women, received the Holy Spirit.

Another important point to remember when we speak of apostles is that the expression "the twelve" is not synonymous with the term "the apostles." Paul considered himself an apostle, as is obvious from the way he begins many of his letters. For instance, as Paul begins Romans he says, "Paul, a servant of Jesus Christ called to be an apostle, set apart for the gospel of God" (Rom 1:1). Yet Paul was not one of the twelve. Nor did he attribute his ministry to the twelve, but to Christ himself. Paul tells the Galatians: "For I want you to know, brothers and sisters, that the gospel that was proclaimed by me is not of human origin; for I did not receive it from a human source, nor was I taught it, but I received it through a revelation of Jesus Christ" (Gal 1:11–12).

In fact, not all the people who are called apostles in the New Testament are men. When Paul sends greetings in his letter to the Romans, among those he greets are "Andronicus and Junia, my relatives who were in prison with me; they are prominent among the apostles, and they were in Christ before I was" (Rom 16:7). "Junia" is, of course, a female name. Paul also refers to a woman as "deacon." In Romans Paul says, "I commend to you our sister Phoebe, a deacon of the church at Cenchreae" (Rom 16:1 NRSV; the New American Bible translates the Greek word *diakonos* as "minister" rather than "deacon" in this passage).

Ministry in the early Church was initially not hierarchical. Everyone was called to one kind of ministry or another. What ministry each person fulfilled depended on the gifts that each received for the good of the community.

> Now there are varieties of gifts, but the same Spirit; and there are varieties of services, but the same Lord; and there are varieties of activities, but in the same God who activates all of them in everyone. To each is given the manifestation of the Spirit for the common good. To one is given through the Spirit the utterance of wisdom, and to another the utterance of knowledge according to the same Spirit, to another faith by the same Spirit, to another gifts of healing by the one Spirit, to another the working of miracles, to another prophecy, to another the discernment of spirits, to another various kinds of tongues, to another the interpretation of tongues. All these are activated by one and the same Spirit, who allots to each one individually just as the Spirit chooses. (1 Cor 12:4–11)

Whether the person who received the Spirit was a man or a woman was irrelevant, as Paul tells the Galatians: "For in Christ Jesus you are all children of God through faith. As many of you as were baptized into Christ have clothed yourselves with Christ. There is no longer Jew or Greek, there is no longer slave or free, there is no longer male and female; for all of you are one in Christ Jesus" (Gal 3:26–27).

As time went on, certain formal ministries started to develop: teachers, prophets, those who administered the community goods. Some of the words used to describe these roles are *episkopos*, which is translated "overseer" or "bishop"; *presbyteroi*, which is translated "presbyter" or "elder"; and *diakonoi*, which is translated "minister" or "deacon" (see 1 Timothy and Titus). The Church, over time, developed the threefold ministry of bishop, presbyter (elder; priest), and deacon.

Even after Paul's generation, women served the Church in the role of deacon. In 1 Timothy, a letter attributed to Paul but written in the late first or early second century, instructions are given about the personal characteristics needed for a person to serve as a deacon. These instructions describe both men and women:

> Deacons likewise must be serious, not double-tongued, not indulging in much wine, not greedy for money; they must hold fast to the mystery of the faith with a clear conscience. And let them first be tested; then, if they prove themselves blameless, let them serve as deacons. Women likewise must be serious, not slanderers, but temperate, faithful in all things. Let deacons be married only once, and let them manage their children and their household well, for those who serve well as deacons gain a good standing for themselves and great boldness in the faith that is in Christ Jesus. (1 Tim 3:8–13)

The ministries described in 1 Timothy developed in response to the community's life and the community's needs. While as early as Paul's time, there was a laying on of hands, a kind of commissioning and sending forth, a formal recognition of role, there was not what we call "ordination." The ministerial roles did not involve privilege or spiritual power to which others had no access, but service and authority exercised for the ordering of community life. Jesus had made it abundantly clear that anyone who ministers in his name must act, not as a king or a prince, as one above others, but as a servant (Mark 9:35; Matt 20:26; 23:8–12).

Women's Role Diminishes

Although, as we have seen, Paul calls women both "apostle" (Rom 16:7) and "deacon" (Rom 16:1), we also see in Paul's first letter to the Corinthians evidence that, as time went on, roles that women had fulfilled in the early Church were giving offense to some and so they were pulled back. Such roles for women were even more countercultural then than they are now. In first-century Christendom, wives and slaves were still property. In Gentile lands, to give women any kind of leadership role was to challenge Roman society and perhaps to invite persecution.

For instance, in First Corinthians Paul gives instructions on how a woman is to dress when she prays or prophesies in a worship setting: "Any woman who prays or prophesies with her head unveiled disgraces her head" (1 Cor 11:5a). Here, it is assumed that women will be speaking in Church.

However, later in the letter we read: "Women should be silent in the churches. For they are not permitted to speak, but should be subordinate, as the law also says. If there is anything they desire to know, let them ask their husbands at home. For it is shameful for a woman to speak in church" (1 Cor 14:34–35). Scripture scholars deduce that the first passage describes conditions in Corinth when Paul wrote his letter. The second passage was inserted later when the cultural setting had changed and the local community was attempting to avoid inciting trouble.

A similar clamping down on women's roles is evident in 1 Timothy (late first century or early second century): "Let women learn in silence with full submission. I permit no woman to teach or to have authority over a man; she is to keep silent" (1 Tim 2:11–12).

Are these and similar passages misused to support limiting women's roles today? In some settings they are. However, Catholic biblical scholars do not support such a fundamentalist interpretation. If they did they would also have to support slavery, as Ephesians and Colossians direct not only women to obey their husbands, but slaves to obey their masters (see the household codes in Ephesians 5:21–6:9 and Colossians 3:18–25). Once the Catholic Church embraced a contextualist approach to Scripture (1943), those teaching in the name of the Catholic Church could explain why the Church cannot use Scripture to support the institution of slavery. The Catholic Church also learned not to use these same passages to support the subjugation of women. The Catholic Church allows women to speak as they proclaim the Word (but not the Gospel) at mass, to be extraordinary ministers of the Eucharist (that is, not to consecrate the bread and wine, but to distribute Eucharist after the consecration), and to teach. However, the Catholic Church does not yet allow women to be ordained, whether as deacons, priests, or bishops.

At the same time, we can't but note that as recently as 1930, the subjugation of women was part of the thinking of the Catholic Church. This was, of course, thirteen years before the publication of *Divino Afflante Spiritu* (1943), the Magna Carta of Catholic biblical scholarship. In his *Encyclical on Christian Marriage, Casti Connubii* (1930), Pius XI says:

> Domestic society being confirmed, therefore, by this bond of love, there
> should flourish in it the "order of love," as St. Augustine calls it. This order
> includes both the primacy of the husband with regard to the wife and children,
> the ready subjection of the wife and her willing obedience, which the Apostle
> commends in these words: "Let women be subject to their husbands as to the
> Lord, because the husband is the head of the wife, and Christ is the head of the
> Church." (Eph 5:22–23)[5]

Now that Catholics are biblical contextualists (see chapter 2), Catholics acknowledge that the author of the household code in Ephesians is applying an
eternal truth—that we must model God's love for every single person—to a
particular social setting, the Greco-Roman social order in which women were
property. The author is teaching the Ephesians to love each other; he is not
teaching that the Greco-Roman social order is God's social order.

PRESENT CATHOLIC CHURCH TEACHING

The Second Vatican Council document *Gaudium et Spes* teaches against the
discrimination of women:

> But forms of social or cultural discrimination in basic personal rights on the
> grounds of sex, race, color, social conditions, language or religion, must be
> curbed and eradicated as incompatible with God's design. It is regrettable that
> these basic personal rights are not yet being respected everywhere, as is the
> case with women who are denied the chance freely to choose a husband, or a
> state of life, or to have access to the same educational and cultural benefits as
> are available to men.[6]

Obviously, the Magisterium does not think that excluding women from ordination, precisely because they are women, is an example of discrimination.

The document that most fully explains the Magisterium's present position
on this topic is titled *Inter Insigniores*, or the *Declaration on the Question of
Admission of Women to the Ministerial Priesthood*. It was issued by the
Sacred Congregation for the Doctrine of the Faith in 1976.

Basically, there are three reasons presented for the exclusion of women
from priestly ordination. These reasons are:

- Jesus did not choose a woman, even his own mother, to be one of the
  twelve, so the Catholic Church lacks the power to ordain women as
  priests.

- A priest's role at Eucharist requires that he be able to image Jesus Christ, who was male, so only a male can succeed in doing this.
- The Church is Christ's bride, and Christ is the bridegroom. Therefore, the priest, who represents Christ, must be male.

Before responding to these reasons in the "Questions and Concerns" section, let us first note the arguments that the document offers to support each of these reasons.

In the document's introduction, it states with great clarity the teaching that women cannot be priests: "The Church, in fidelity to the example of the Lord, does not consider herself authorized to admit women to priestly ordination."[7] In section 1, the document says: "The Catholic Church has never felt that priestly or episcopal ordination can be validly conferred on women. . . . The Church intends to remain faithful to the type of ordained ministry willed by the Lord Jesus Christ and carefully maintained by the Apostle"[8] (more about this later).

When we get to the second reason, the idea that women can't image Christ at Eucharist, the document warns us that, in order to understand what follows, we have to think analogically rather than logically: "It is not a question here of bringing forward a demonstrative argument, but of clarifying this teaching by the analogy of faith."[9] The point is that the authors want to demonstrate something by analogy and by an appeal to our faith, not try to persuade us by presenting a logical argument.

The document then goes on to explain that the priest, at mass, is not acting in his own name, but in the name of Christ. He is "taking the role of Christ, to the point of being his very image, when he pronounces the words of consecration. . . . There would not be this 'natural resemblance' which must exist between Christ and his minister if the role of Christ were not taken by a man: in such a case it would be difficult to see in the minister the image of Christ."[10]

In regard to the third point, that because Christ is the Church's bridegroom the priest must be male, the document says:

> Christ is the Bridegroom; the Church his Bride, whom he loves because he has gained her by his blood and made her glorious, holy and without blemish, and henceforth he is inseparable from her. . . . It is through this Scriptural language, all interwoven with symbols, and which expresses and affects man and woman in their profound identity, that there is revealed to us the mystery of God and Christ, a mystery which of itself is unfathomable.

> That is why we can never ignore the fact that Christ is a man. And there-
> fore . . . it must be admitted that in actions which demand the character of
> ordination and in which Christ himself, the author of the covenant, the Bride-
> groom, the Head of the Church, is represented, exercising his ministry of
> salvation . . . his role . . . must be taken by a man.[11]

The document then goes on to insist that this teaching cannot be changed
because it is the fruit of revelation—it is Christ's will:

> It is opportune to recall that problems of sacramental theology, especially
> when they concern the ministerial priesthood, as is the case here, cannot be
> solved except in the light of Revelation. The human sciences, however valu-
> able their contribution in their own domain, cannot suffice here, for they
> cannot grasp the realities of faith: the properly supernatural content of these
> realities is beyond their competence.[12]

These teachings were reaffirmed in John Paul II's *Apostolic Letter on Reserving Priestly Ordination to Men Alone, Ordinatio Sacerdotalis* (1994).
John Paul says:

> Wherefore, in order that all doubt may be removed regarding a matter of great
> importance, a matter which pertains to the Church's divine constitution itself,
> in virtue of my ministry of confirming the brethren (cf. Lk 22:32) I declare that
> the Church has no authority whatsoever to confer priestly ordination on wom-
> en and that this judgment is to be definitively held by all the Church's faith-
> ful.[13]

QUESTIONS AND CONCERNS

Before asking questions and expressing concerns regarding the teaching in
Inter Insigniores, we should first address the question of infallibility in relationship to this teaching. Why do many dedicated, loyal Catholics consider
the question of women's ordination still open for discussion? John Wright
addresses this question in an article in *Theological Studies*. First, Wright
gives the background for addressing the question:

> On October 28, 1995, the Vatican Congregation for the Doctrine of the Faith
> (CDF) responded to a dubium: "Whether the teaching that the Church has no
> authority whatsoever to confer priestly ordination on women, which is present-
> ed in the Apostolic Letter *Ordinatio Sacerdotalis* to be held definitively, is to
> be understood as belonging to the deposit of faith." The congregation an-

swered: In the affirmative. This teaching requires definitive assent, since, founded on the written Word of God, and from the beginning constantly preserved and applied in the Tradition of the Church, it has been set forth infallibly by the ordinary and universal Magisterium (cf. Second Vatican Council,*Dogmatic Constitution on the Church, Lumen Gentium* 25, 2).

... The Congregation here neither claimed to be infallible itself nor did it attach infallibility directly to Pope John Paul II's Apostolic Letter of May 1994. Rather it appealed to the constant universal teaching of the Church's magisterium as teaching this infallibly. It did not offer at this time any evidence to show that this is indeed the case. [14]

The reason many Catholics do not regard the teaching against women's ordination to be taught infallibly is that the conditions for infallibility have not been met. The Congregation is not claiming that the pope has taught this infallibly. The Congregation itself is not infallible. The claim for infallibility rests on the "constant universal teaching of the Church's magisterium." Therefore, the next step is to examine the evidence for this claim. Is the evidence persuasive?

After examining the evidence himself, Wright concludes:

What does emerge from much of the patristic evidence cited by the CDF is the conviction that women by nature, temperament, and social status are inferior to men. For this reason they cannot be ordained priests. Even the practice and intention of Jesus are set within the context of this inferiority. But the CDF does not admit or argue from the inferiority. Why not? The Fathers are clearly teaching it. However, the Second Vatican Council reversed nearly two thousand years of popular teaching when it proclaimed the equality of all human beings and deplored the kinds of discrimination still found in society, particularly in the case of women. . . . Thus the CDF recognizes, as all intelligent persons recognize today, that the ancient Fathers were voicing a prejudice they shared with their contemporary society.

If the Fathers are wrong on the inferiority of women, why may they not be wrong on the inability of women to be ordained priests, since this inferiority is the basic reason for their stance on ordination?

It seems to me that if the examples cited by the CDF as the testimony of the Fathers are at all representative of what tradition has to offer, we must acknowledge that their testimony offers meager support for the claim that the tradition of not ordaining women was motivated primarily by the Church's intention to remain faithful to the will of Christ. [15]

The problem with the teaching in *Inter Insigniores* is that many people cannot find any logical connection between the statement that Jesus did not choose a woman to be one of the twelve and the statement that the Church cannot choose women to be priests. The document seems to assume that the twelve, the apostles, and ordained priests are all the same. "The twelve" and "the apostles" are not synonyms, and none of them were ordained priests.

If the Catholic Church believes that it cannot do anything not taught by word or example by Jesus Christ during his public ministry, it wouldn't have ordained priests at all. Where did the Catholic Church get the authority to begin to ordain anyone, even males? The Catholic Church can't claim that Jesus set that example because there is absolutely no evidence of that. The practice of ordination developed many years after Jesus's public ministry and resurrection, Catholics believe, under the influence of the Holy Spirit.

The reason it is compatible with Catholic teaching to believe that the Catholic Church can grow and change is that Catholics believe that the Spirit of the risen Christ is still with the Church, in the people's midst, guiding and inspiring them. That was true not just in the first two hundred years of Church history. It is equally true now. If the Catholic Church was empowered to ordain men in the late second to early third century, something Jesus himself did not do, could the Catholic Church not be equally empowered to ordain women if the Church believes that the Spirit is leading it to do so?

In response to the second reason given in the document, we must ask, "Can a woman image Christ as well as a man?" If we were to accept the argument that a woman cannot, we would have to be thinking very literally and concretely, not analogically. If we were to think that literally, wouldn't we also be undercutting some of our most basic beliefs?

For instance, based on Paul's analogy, Paul's comparison of the Church to a physical body in which different people have received different gifts but all the gifts are necessary for the good of the whole, the Catholic Church teaches that baptism incorporates people into the body of Christ. Baptism incorporates both males and females into the body of Christ. That would not make sense if a person reverts to literal thinking: Wouldn't a person have to conclude that because Christ was male, a female cannot be incorporated into his body? Should females, then, be baptized?

In addition, Christians are to be Christ for each other. That idea is inspiring and motivating if Christians think about it analogically and with faith. The idea is destroyed if one thinks literally and says that because Christ was male, only males can be other Christs.

Are not all Christians called to see Christ in, and be Christ for, the poor, the lame, prisoners, and so on? Are Christians to see Christ in the poor, the lame, and prisoners only if they are male? Of course not. Just as every person is made in the image of God, male and female, so can every person be an image of the risen Christ, the Word who became flesh and dwells among us. Both women and men are called to image Christ in all that they do. Far from masking Christ, having female celebrants might well help others see Christ where they may not have been able to see Christ before.

Finally, *Inter Insigniores* invites readers to ask, "If the Church is the bride and Christ the bridegroom, doesn't the person who presides at Eucharist and represents Christ have to be male?" This argument takes many Catholics by surprise because Catholics have been taught that the whole Church is cele-brating the mass; the priest is representing not just Christ, but the whole Church. Presumably, it is because any member of the community could represent the community at Eucharist that the whole topic of who presided never even came up in the New Testament.

Inter Insigniores itself responds to this observation:

> However, it will perhaps be further objected that the priest, especially when he presides at the liturgical and sacramental functions, equally represents the Church; he acts in her name with "the intention of doing what she does." In this sense, the theologians of the Middle Ages said that the minister also acts in persona Ecclesiae, that is to say, in the name of the whole Church and in order to represent her. And in fact, leaving aside the question of the participa-tion of the faithful in a liturgical action, it is indeed in the name of the whole Church that the action is celebrated by the priest: he prays in the name of all, and in the Mass he offers the sacrifice of the whole Church. [16]

Then why cannot a woman represent Christ at liturgy? The document ex-plains: "It is true that the priest represents the Church, which is the Body of Christ. But if he does so, it is precisely because he first represents Christ himself, who is the Head and the Shepherd of the Church." [17] This answer takes us back to question two: Can a male better represent Christ than a female? In the eyes of many faithful Christians, men and women are equally able to represent Christ.

This brings us to the meaning of a symbol. Whether or not a symbol is successful in conveying meaning depends entirely on the eyes of the behold-er. The meaning is not innate to the symbol itself but to the person's ability to attach meaning to that symbol. Is there any chance that the negative view of women that is a sorry part of the history of Western civilization has resulted in those who have been affected by this view, the Magisterium included, being unable to see Christ clearly in women?

Again, the authors of *Inter Insigniores* have realized that the question of the effect of past prejudices in regard to present teaching might arise. The document says: "It is true that in the writings of the Fathers, one will find the undeniable influence of prejudices unfavorable to woman, but nevertheless, it should be noted that these prejudices had hardly any influences on their pastoral activity and still less on their spiritual direction."[18]

But did these prejudices influence the Magisterium? We know they did at least until 1930, as demonstrated in the passage quoted earlier from *Casti Connubii*. Are these prejudices still exerting themselves in our present practice? The Magisterium says no. As we have said, the document insists that in teaching that women cannot be priests "the Church intends to remain faithful to the type of ordained ministry willed by the Lord Jesus Christ and carefully maintained by the Apostles."[19]

It is this claim that many find most puzzling: the claim that the Catholic Church cannot change this teaching because it has been "willed by Jesus Christ and carefully maintained by the Apostles." With this assertion the Magisterium is not falling back into the Catholic Church's old bad habit of proof texting, taking an out-of-context passage to prove that the Catholic Church is right about something that developed later. Instead, the Magisterium is making the claim without offering any scriptural evidence at all that the claim is true. How could the Magisterium offer such evidence, since Scripture remains silent on the whole question of Christians' ordaining anyone to be priests?

As the ordained priesthood developed, is it accurate to say that women were not among the ordained? Some argue from archaeological evidence that women were among the ordained. Nevertheless, the practice of ordaining women as well as men did not become the norm. Why? Historians suggest that as Christians appropriated the idea of priesthood from their Jewish ancestors, they also appropriated some of the Israelites' ideas about ritual purity, about what is clean and unclean. Bodily fluids, such as semen and menstrual flow, were understood to make one ritually unclean. Women could not be priests because they menstruate. Married men could still be priests if they abstained from intercourse before the Sunday celebration. However, when the Church started to celebrate mass every day, the demand for celibacy increased. Only a celibate male could remain ritually clean for the daily celebration.

THE EFFECT: DISCRIMINATION

Is the fact that the Magisterium of the Catholic Church does not call women to ordination, either to priesthood or to the diaconate, an example of discrimination against women? Many think that the answer is self-evident: yes. In addition, even if discrimination is not the intent, discrimination is turning out to be the effect.

The question of ordination is no longer limited to the topic of women priests or bishops. Now that the Catholic Church has reinstituted the diaconate, the question of whether or not women can be ordained as deacons is also on the table. Since deacons do not preside at Eucharist, the argument in *Inter Insigniores* that women cannot image Christ at the consecration is irrelevant. There is certainly no scriptural block to women becoming deacons. We know that there were women deacons in the early Church. As we have already noted, in Romans, Paul sends greeting to "Phoebe, a deacon of the church at Cenchreae" (Rom 16:1). In 1 Timothy the personal characteristics needed to be a deacon are described in reference to both men and women (1 Tim 3:8–13).

The reinstitution of a deaconate that excludes women has limited women's opportunities to serve the Church in many ways. The events described below are the story of one diocese, but similar stories could be told by dioceses throughout the United States. This story illustrates how the addition of another all-male ordained ministerial role, the deaconate, has had the effect of depriving women of opportunities to serve the Catholic Church in ways in which they have previously served. These elements of the story are common to many locations and emblematic of a systemic pattern that results in discrimination against women:

- A shortage of priests
- The desire to keep worshipping communities intact
- Women duly appointed by their bishops to fulfill a variety of administrative and teaching functions in a parish
- A reasoned and respectful questioning about present practice based on prayerful discernment, including reflection on experience
- A negative reaction by some to women in duly delegated leadership roles, to a Spirit-filled discernment process that involves the whole faith community, and to the truth speaking that results when people are invited to speak

- A reassertion of authority on the part of newly appointed bishops, choosing ordained (men) over nonordained (women) to fulfill not only priestly duties but administrative duties as well

One Diocese's Story

A mission diocese that includes much of Appalachia had a shortage of priests. Many priests had responsibility for two or even three parishes and/or missions. The bishop's priority was to keep faith communities intact and to make sure that they had access to the sacraments. In order to meet the pastoral needs of parishes, the bishop appointed a woman religious to administer a program called New Faces of Ministry.

The purpose of New Faces of Ministry was to ensure that parishes and missions had effective leadership for the future. A process was designed that ensured that all who would be affected by the decisions made would have a voice in those decisions.

As the process was under way, the diocesan newspaper included a supplement that informed everyone about what was proposed regarding future staffing patterns and invited everyone's response before final decisions were made. A first draft of the regional and parish plans was included.

In an accompanying letter the bishop explained that staffing plans would include the placement of qualified lay and vowed religious people, as well as priests, in a variety of parish leadership positions. The bishop then invited everyone to attend regional meetings so that everyone's voice would be heard before decisions were reached.

The supplement in the diocesan newspaper included a section called "Issues and Concerns" from each of the regions of the diocese. Some of these "Issues and Concerns" sections respectfully disagreed with present Catholic Church practice regarding ordination. Here is an example:

> There is a need for education to prepare people for the future. In general, we believe that the Holy Spirit is not calling Mountain East Catholics to the above compromises, but to new possibilities in ministry and sacrament. We believe there needs to be increased lay leadership and a commitment to a broader understanding of ordination. Ordination is, fundamentally, the faith community calling forth its leaders . . . and should be open to all with appropriate training and deep spirituality, including married men and women. Each faith community should be free to celebrate all of the sacraments as frequently as the Spirit moves, led by a sacramental minister who is part of the community.

We see a strong need for open dialogue about these issues which have been suppressed by the hierarchy of the church. [20]

The bishop's accompanying letter made it clear that the supplement was not the plan. It was one step in a conversation that would lead to a plan. Nor were the "Issues and Concerns" sections part of the plan. They were part of the conversation. They reported, without censoring the material, what the people had said.

An organized group in the diocese who had a different view of the Catholic Church than did the bishop was outraged. The January 22, 1998, issue of *The Wanderer* covered the story. *The Wanderer* article began:

> One of the first indications of how American bishops will respond to the Holy See's instruction of last November sharply limiting the roles laity can play in parish life and at Mass comes from [a] small rural Diocese. . . .
>
> The Holy See's *Instruction on Certain Questions Regarding the Collaboration of the Nonordained Faithful in the Sacred Ministry of Priests*, signed by eight curial heads and approved by the Pope, will have no effect. . . .
>
> Late last month (Dec. 28th), the diocese published *New Faces of Ministry*, the first draft of a "staffing plan" designed to accelerate the development of priestless parishes run by nuns, deacon-couples, or small faith communities. . . .
>
> Among the unique features of . . . [the] plan, however, are the explicit rejection of the Holy See's instruction, and, with the bishop's consent, the call for the ordaining of women and married men to the priesthood. . . .
>
> The plan, according to one priest who has worked in the diocese for decades, "is to make the church in the area Protestant. Everything is organized in that direction.
>
> "Why else," he wonders, "would the bishop retire priests at a time when he needs them most? Why else would he appoint nuns to run these newly vacant parishes? Why else would he spend all his time talking about developing 'small faith communities'?
>
> "Nobody—neither the priests nor the people—has ever asked for this 'plan.'" [21]

With the New Faces of Ministry supplement, both the woman religious who oversaw the discerning process and the bishop became targets of a group organized to thwart the implementation of the plan. Later, this woman religious would be one of five lay people, four of them women, to be dismissed when a new bishop restructured the diocese (see chapter 9). After the new bishop came, much of New Faces of Ministry was dismantled.

After the five lay people were abruptly dismissed, an angry argument raged throughout the diocese. People demanded answers to their questions: Why were all these people dismissed? What could possibly be the reason? The debate was not only local but national, because similar events were taking place in other dioceses. New bishops, after being present for one year, were "restructuring," and lay employees, most of whom were women, were being dismissed.

However, some in the diocese were feeling triumphant. Their hard work to stop women from doing all the things that they had been doing was beginning to bear fruit. Their understanding was that women were forbidden to do things, not only in the priestly area, but also in the areas of prophet (teaching) and king (administration).

PRIEST, PROPHET, AND KING

Catholics are familiar with the idea that at present in the Roman Catholic Church only men can be ordained as priests, and only ordained priests can preside at Eucharist, give absolution in the sacrament of Reconciliation, and administer the sacrament of Anointing. True, in one way, we are all priests, but in the Catholic tradition ordained priests have a special priesthood that only they can exercise. In addition, some Catholics claim that ordination gives the ordained particular power, not just in their priestly role, but in their roles as prophet (teaching) and king (administration). This understanding rests partially on their interpretation of canon 129. This canon says:

> In accord with the prescriptions of law, those who have received sacred orders are capable of the power of governance, which exists in the Church by divine institution and is also called the power of jurisdiction.
>
> Lay members of the Christian faithful can cooperate in the exercise of this power in accord with the norm of law. [22]

The commentary on the canon goes on to say:

> Only those who have been ordained are capable of possessing the power of governance in the Church—which may be received in a variety of ways. This reflects canon 118 of the 1917 Code. The canon, however, extends to lay persons a role of cooperation in the exercise of the power of governance for individual causes provided it has been granted by the Holy See. . . .

> The distinction between possessing the power of governance and merely
> sharing in its exercise is new, and it is not at all clear what it means to
> cooperate in the exercise of a power that a person cannot hold. [23]

The *usurpation* of the responsibilities of the ordained in their prophetic
(teaching) and kingly (administrative) roles was seen by some in the diocese
as taking place in the New Faces of Ministry Program. For instance, in
parishes and missions that had a nonordained pastoral director and an ordained sacramental minister it appeared to some that the priest was accountable to the lay person, although officially he was not. Also, nonordained
people were giving homilies or reflections. Some felt that this was simply
wrong and had to be stopped.

It appears that the bishop who oversaw the New Faces of Ministry process and his successor, the bishop who oversaw the restructuring and the
dismissal of the five lay employees, had different interpretations of this canon. The first bishop wanted to empower every baptized person, male or
female, to offer his or her gifts in service to the Catholic Church, whether
that person was ordained or not. So, he interpreted the canon as liberally as
possible and, through delegation, empowered women as much as he could.

Many thought that the bishop who oversaw the restructuring was instructed by congregations in Rome to do just that, to *clean up* after women
had been empowered beyond the comfort level of the Vatican. If so, he was
acting in obedience and loyalty to the heirarchy. It appeared that the ecclesiology out of which the first bishop acted was based primarily on Scripture and
embraced women's roles in the Catholic Church. On the other hand, the
ecclesiology out of which the second bishop acted gave more emphasis to
canonical and hierarchical views of the Catholic Church and limited to a
much greater extent the ways in which women could offer their gifts in
service to the Catholic Church.

Of course, the work that had been done by the five diocesan leaders who
were let go still needed to be done. However, none of the dismissed lay
persons was initially replaced by a nonordained person. Their responsibilities
were delegated to second-career deacons whose backgrounds were in bank-
ing and in the military. They were good men and good at their jobs. However, the question remains: Why were the deacons more qualified than the lay
people? The answer seems to be that they were ordained. Ordination makes
all the difference, and, of course, only men can be ordained.

Such experiences lead many to ask, "If God has given women the desire,
the intelligence, the knowledge, and the pastoral skills to serve the Catholic

Church in ministerial roles, and if the Catholic Church needs their services, why can't the Catholic Church call women to serve the Church in ordained roles?" Unless that question is answered in a persuasive manner or the Catholic Church becomes open to change, the Catholic Church will continue to be accused of having an unrecognized and so unacknowledged prejudice toward women, and it will continue to lose a credible teaching voice for many people of the twenty-first century.

CONTINUING THE CONVERSATION

1. What personal experience do you have to bring to bear on the topics of ordination and women's role in the Catholic Church? What conclusions have you drawn based on these experiences?
2. Were you under the impression that Jesus ordained the twelve? If so, why? If not, why not?
3. Do you believe women should be allowed to become priests and/or deacons? Why or why not?
4. If the pope, in an apostolic letter, says that a teaching is definitive, do you feel free to continue to discuss that teaching? Why or why not?
5. Do you think that men and women can each image Christ? Why or why not?

Chapter Six

Homosexuality

Basing itself on Sacred Scripture, which presents homosexual acts as acts of grave depravity, tradition has always declared that "homosexual acts are intrinsically disordered." They are contrary to the natural law. They close the sexual act to the gift of life. They do not proceed from a genuine affective and sexual complementarity. Under no circumstances can they be approved.
—*Catechism of the Catholic Church*, par. 2357

They [i.e., people whose sexual orientation is homosexual] do not choose their homosexual condition; for most of them it is a trial. They must be accepted with respect, compassion, and sensitivity. Every sign of unjust discrimination in their regard should be avoided.
—*Catechism of the Catholic Church*, par. 2358

Here then is the norm for human activity—to harmonize with the authentic interests of the human race, in accordance with God's will and design, and to enable men as individuals and as members of society to pursue and fulfill their total vocation.
—*Pastoral Constitution on the Church
in the Modern World*, n. 35

Sexual orientation is a relatively new concept. In fact, although same sex behavior has always existed, the idea of a homosexual identity or a homosexual person is only about 100 years old.
—from a policy statement of the American
Psychiatric Association

The potential risks of "reparative therapy" are great, including depression, anxiety and self-destructive behavior, since therapist alignment with societal prejudices against homosexuality may reinforce self-hatred already experienced by the patient.
—from a position statement of the American
Psychiatric Association

In chapter 3 we gave evidence to support the claim that the Catholic Church's teaching on very important issues changed in the twentieth century. One of those areas was the prejudicial way in which Catholics were instructed to treat our fellow Christians. Catholics had been taught that it would be a mortal sin to worship with them. In hindsight, many Catholics regret that we acted with prejudice, thereby failing to love other beloved children of God, other members of the body of Christ.

In chapter 5 we gave evidence that prejudice against women has been part of Western civilization at least since the time of Aristotle. Church saints and foundational thinkers, such as Augustine and Thomas Aquinas, shared in this prejudice. So did the Magisterium until at least 1930. We asked the question: Is the Catholic Church still participating in this prejudicial behavior in the twenty-first century by refusing to allow women to receive orders?

In this chapter we will once again examine a present teaching of the Catholic Church: the teaching that sexual acts between people whose sexual orientation is toward those of their own sex are intrinsically disordered and that marriage for such people is always wrong because it is against the natural law. We will ask if this teaching, too, reflects a prejudice that has existed for centuries, a prejudice that can no longer be taught because we now interpret Scripture as contextualists and because, thanks to science, we now think that homosexuality is something that one discovers about oneself, not something that one chooses.

To discuss the present teaching of the Catholic Church regarding homosexuality and homosexual actions within a loving, exclusive, committed, and lifelong relationship, we will first look at what Scripture has to say. We will then listen carefully to the present teaching of the Catholic Church. We will then discuss the questions that remain.

WHAT DOES SCRIPTURE SAY?

Historically, the Catholic Church has based its teaching about the immorality of all homosexual acts on Scripture, especially on the story of Sodom and Gomorrah, after which sodomy is named. Can Catholic biblical scholars affirm that the biblical texts support our teaching? We will look at the texts one at a time and see.

The story of Sodom and Gomorrah appears in Genesis 19:1–11:

The two angels came to Sodom in the evening, and Lot was sitting in the gateway of Sodom. When Lot saw them, he rose to meet them, and bowed down with his face to the ground. He said, "Please, my lords, turn aside to your servant's house and spend the night, and wash your feet; then you can rise early and go on your way." They said, "No; we will spend the night in the square." But he urged them strongly; so they turned aside to him and entered his house; and he made them a feast, and baked unleavened bread, and they ate. But before they lay down, the men of the city, the men of Sodom, both young and old, all the people to the last man, surrounded the house; and they called to Lot, "Where are the men who came to you tonight? Bring them out to us, so that we may know them." Lot went out of the door to the men, shut the door after him, and said, "I beg you, my brothers, do not act so wickedly. Look, I have two daughters who have not known a man; let me bring them out to you, and do to them as you please; only do nothing to these men, for they have come under the shelter of my roof." But they replied, "Stand back!" And they said, "This fellow came here as an alien, and he would play the judge! Now, we will deal worse with you than with them." Then they pressed hard against the man Lot, and came near the door to break it down. But the men inside reached out their hands and brought Lot into the house with them, and shut the door. And they struck with blindness the men who were at the door of the house, both small and great, so that they were unable to find the door. (Gen 19:1–11)

This passage is part of a legend about the destruction of Sodom and Gomorrah. God is about to destroy these cities because of their prior sinfulness, and he sends two angels, who appear to be men, to save Lot and his family. The men of Sodom threaten to sexually violate the angels. In the story, the sinfulness of Sodom is illustrated by the people's desire ("all of the people to the last man") to gang-rape Lot's guests. Because Lot does not want his guests mistreated he offers to send out his virgin daughters instead!

What conclusions can we draw from this story? What is the author teaching? The story uses the people's desire to gang-rape Lot's guests as an example of sinfulness. Sin is punished.

Since the daughters are offered in the guests' place, the story certainly cannot be used as an "example story" that teaches the truth about the morality of sexual acts. Lot seems to regard the people's demand as a sin against hospitality rather than a sexual sin. Certainly the story does not address the question we are asking: Are sexual acts between homosexuals in the context of a lifelong committed relationship sinful? To use this story to answer that question is to abuse Scripture.

Two passages in Leviticus appear, when read out of context, to forbid a man to lie down with another man. The passages are part of the holiness code (Lev 17:1–26:46), the list of laws that instructed the Israelites about how to be holy as God is holy. As always, to correctly understand what the passages are teaching, we must read them in context.

The holiness code begins with regulations regarding the sanctuary and sacrifice. Within this context the code goes on to warn the Israelites against any behaviors that were practiced by their pagan neighbors as part of their fertility rites in worship of false gods. Leviticus says:

> You shall not approach a woman to uncover her nakedness while she is in her menstrual uncleanness. You shall not have sexual relations with your kinsman's wife, and defile yourself with her. You shall not give any of your offspring to sacrifice them to Molech, and so profane the name of your God: I am the Lord. You shall not lie with a male as with a woman; it is an abomination. You shall not have sexual relationships with any animal and defile yourself with it, nor shall any woman give herself to an animal to have sexual relations with it; it is perversion. Do not defile yourselves in any of these ways, for by all these practices the nations I am casting out before you have defiled themselves. (Lev 18:19–24)

> If a man lies with a male as with a woman, both of them have committed an abomination; they shall be put to death; their blood is upon them. (Lev 20:13)

In this passage we see that one of the ritual practices of the pagans was child sacrifice. The Israelites, in contrast to their pagan neighbors, are not to offer any of their children as human sacrifices to Molech. Nor are they to involve themselves in fertility rites, such as having sexual intercourse with prostitutes, male or female. Such practices were believed by the pagans to affect the fertility of the land. To involve oneself in any of these common practices was to fail to worship Yahweh, to fail to be holy as God is holy. To introduce cultic fertility rites into the worship of Yahweh was an abomination.

The ritual purity demanded of the Israelites in the holiness code also extended to their dietary laws. Leviticus says:

> You shall therefore make a distinction between the clean animal and the unclean, and between the unclean bird and the clean; you shall not bring abomination on yourselves by animal or by bird or by anything with which the ground teems, which I have set apart for you to hold unclean. (Lev 20:25)

We cannot take passages from the Israelites' holiness code, passages that forbid men to lie with male prostitutes as part of pagan fertility rites, and claim that the words are forbidding people whose sexual orientation is homosexual to have sexual relationships in the context of committed, lifelong relationships. If we interpreted Scripture in this way we would obey the Israelites' dietary laws, too. We would also be insisting on the death penalty for anyone who involves himself or herself in such behavior.

The Gospels do not say anything relevant to our topic. It is certainly true that whenever marriage is discussed the presumption is that marriage will be between a man and a woman. Jesus, when asked whether or not a man can divorce his wife, quotes Genesis to teach that marriage is intended to be permanent: "But from the beginning of creation, 'God made them male and female.' 'For this reason a man shall leave his father and mother and be joined to his wife, and the two shall become one flesh.' So they are no longer two, but one flesh. Therefore what God has joined together, let no one separate" (Mark 10:6–9).

In this passage Jesus is teaching the Pharisees that they should not divorce their wives for trivial reasons, as was their practice. Jesus's words do not cast light on our question about homosexual acts in the context of a committed relationship because that is not the question the Pharisees have asked him. In fact, the Pharisees could never have asked our question because the idea of a homosexual orientation and the very word *homosexual* did not enter our thinking or our discourse until the late nineteenth century.

Paul, however, does, at first glance, appear to say something specific about homosexual activity in his first letter to the Corinthians and in his letter to the Romans. In 1 Corinthians Paul says: "Do you not know that wrong doers will not inherit the kingdom of God? Do not be deceived! Fornicators, idolaters, adulterers, male prostitutes, sodomites, thieves, the greedy, drunkards, revilers, robbers—none of these will inherit the kingdom of God!" (1 Cor 6:9–10).

Here Paul lists a number of sinful behaviors including male prostitutes and sodomites. In the New American Bible translation, which is used in the Catholic Lectionary in the United States, these words appear as "boy prostitutes" and "practicing homosexuals." Since our word *homosexual*, as well as the concept behind it (a person whose sexual orientation is toward his or her own sex), was unknown when 1 Corinthians was written, we must ask what Paul intended to say when he used the Greek word αρσενοκοιται (arseno [male] koitai [bed]).

A boy prostitute was a boy who was kept for the purpose of prostitution. The word αρσενοκοιται, translated "sodomite" or "practicing homosexual," is thought to refer to adult males who have sexual relationships with boy prostitutes. This was not an uncommon practice in the Gentile culture. So, Scripture scholars surmise that in this passage Paul is teaching against males using boy prostitutes.

This same Greek word, αρσενοκοιται, appears in 1 Timothy. Among the sinners that the author names are "fornicators, sodomites, and slave traders" (1 Tim 1:10a). Once more, Scripture scholars think that the word translated "sodomites" refers to men who used boy prostitutes.

In Romans Paul says:

> For this reason God gave them up to degrading passions. Their women ex-changed natural intercourse for unnatural, and in the same way also the men, giving up natural intercourse with women, were consumed with passion for one another. Men committed shameless acts with men and received in their own persons the due penalty for their error. (Rom 1:26–27)

Paul is teaching the Romans that both Jews and Gentiles have sinned and need to be redeemed. Both Jews and Gentiles have failed to put their faith in God, as evidenced by their various sins. Among the sins that the Gentiles have committed, in addition to being "gossips, slanderers, God-haters, inso-lent, haughty, boastful, inventors of evil, rebellious toward parents, foolish, faithless, heartless, and ruthless" (Rom 1:29b–31), are that they have ex-changed "natural intercourse for unnatural" and have been "consumed with passion" for members of their own sex.

Notice that the behavior that Paul describes as sinful is behavior that is freely chosen: the women and men have "exchanged," "given up" natural intercourse for unnatural intercourse. Paul is, of course, assuming that heterosexual people are choosing to act in homosexual ways.

In addition, the behavior Paul describes is not rooted in love, but in lust; the Gentile sinners are "consumed with passion for one another." Paul is teaching that sexual activity between people of the same sex that is freely chosen and that is rooted in lust is sinful. Of course, sexual activity between heterosexual people that is freely chosen and rooted in lust, not love, is also sinful.

What are we to conclude from examining these passages? There is a great degree of consensus among Catholic biblical scholars on the following con-clusions:

- Certainly the Bible teaches against any sexual activity that is rooted in violence, power, idolatry, or lust, whether heterosexual or homosexual.
- Paul assumes, rather than teaches, that sex between two people of the same gender is unnatural, much as biblical authors assume, rather than teach, that the earth is flat. No biblical author ever heard of, or considered, the idea of homosexual orientation.
- The Bible discusses same-gender sex only in the contexts of violence, fertility rites, freely chosen unnatural acts rooted in lust, and male prostitution with boys.
- The Bible remains silent on whether or not sexual activity between two homosexual people who love each other and are committed to each other could be natural and not sinful. That question is never raised nor addressed.

PRESENT CATHOLIC CHURCH TEACHING REGARDING HOMOSEXUALITY

The *Catechism of the Catholic Church* summarizes the Catholic Church's present teaching regarding homosexuals and homosexual activity:

> Homosexuality refers to relations between men or between women who experience an exclusive or predominant sexual attraction toward persons of the same sex. It has taken a great variety of forms through the centuries and in different cultures. Its psychological genesis remains largely unexplained. Basing itself on Sacred Scripture, which presents homosexual acts as acts of grave depravity, tradition has always declared that "homosexual acts are intrinsically disordered." They are contrary to the natural law. They close the sexual act to the gift of life. They do not proceed from a genuine affective and sexual complementarity. Under no circumstances can they be approved.
>
> The number of men and women who have deep-seated homosexual tendencies is not negligible. They do not choose their homosexual condition; for most of them it is a trial. They must be accepted with respect, compassion, and sensitivity. Every sign of unjust discrimination in their regard should be avoided. These persons are called to fulfill God's will in their lives and, if they are Christian, to unite to the sacrifice of the Lord's Cross the difficulties they may encounter from their condition.
>
> Homosexual persons are called to chastity. By the virtues of self-mastery that teach them inner freedom, at times by the support of disinterested friendship, by prayer and sacramental grace, they can and should gradually and resolutely approach Christian perfection. [1]

This teaching corrects a common misperception about homosexuality: People whose sexual orientation is homosexual have not chosen that orientation any more than heterosexuals have chosen their sexual orientation.

The Catholic Church's present teaching is defended by calling on Scripture to support the teaching: "Basing itself on Sacred Scripture, which presents homosexual acts as acts of grave depravity, tradition has always declared that 'homosexual acts are intrinsically disordered.'"[2] However, this "tradition" that has "always" condemned homosexual acts preceded, for the most part, the change in the Church's posture regarding how to interpret Scripture in context, how to determine what the inspired authors intended to say rather than using out-of-context passages to give authoritative answers to questions that the inspired authors were not addressing. As we have demonstrated, Scripture does not address the questions we are asking today.

In addition, our present teaching does not take into account the role of the human sciences. The Catechism acknowledges that pertinent scientific information is, as yet, unknown: "Its [homosexuality's] psychological genesis remains largely unexplained."[3] In stating our lack of knowledge in this regard, the Catechism limits the source of homosexuality to psychological rather than to physical origins. That, too, is more than we presently know. Is homosexuality the result of nature or nurture? As long as we do not know the answer, even that question is simplistic. Homosexuality may be a product of one or the other or both, or either of these and additional components. So far, we don't know why some people, without choosing, are homosexual.

The Catechism then states that homosexual activity is "contrary to the natural law."[4] As we have already discussed in our introduction and in chapter 4, not everyone agrees on whether or not a teaching based on natural law can change. If one emphasizes the role of reason and new knowledge in our understanding of natural law, then one sees the possibility of change because human beings gain new knowledge over time. This is not to deny that an objective moral order, established by God the creator, does exist.

One way of explaining that a moral order is part and parcel of the created order is to refer to the story of the man and woman in the garden. In that story, God tells the man and the woman that there is a "tree of knowledge of good and evil," from which they must not eat. That tree symbolizes the belief that there is a moral order built into creation. Right and wrong are not just a matter of human consensus, but have their source in God. Human beings cannot flourish if we choose to do what is wrong. The day we eat the fruit of the tree of knowledge of good and evil we die, spiritually.

In the Genesis story, an anthropomorphic God explains the moral order. In the concept of the natural law, the order can be known, not through revelation, but through observation and reason. That is why truths that are known through natural law are not specific to one religion, but can be known by the whole human race. The Catholic Church teaches that natural law exists, and that it can be known.

Paul refers to a person's ability to perceive a moral order innate to nature in his letter to the Romans. Paul tells the Romans that even those who have not yet heard the Gospel are responsible for their sinful behavior. Paul says: "For what can be known about God is plain to them, because God has shown it to them. Ever since the creation of the world his eternal power and divine nature, invisible though they are, have been understood and seen through the things he has made" (Rom 1:19–20).

If homosexual acts are contrary to natural law, then it follows that homosexual acts are always sinful, no matter what the circumstances. However, the Catholic Church's teaching that those acts are against the natural law rests on a previous lack of knowledge about exactly what causes a person to be homosexual. Now that we know that a homosexual orientation is not chosen and that a certain percentage of people across centuries and across cultures are homosexual, the Catholic Church is called to reconsider its past teaching and ask: Is homosexuality a *condition* to be cured, or is a homosexual person exactly who God wants a homosexual person to be? No one can answer that question definitively until science tells us more about the origins of homosexuality than we now know.

INCORPORATING SCIENTIFIC KNOWLEDGE WITH CATHOLIC CHURCH TEACHING

If, in respect to the knowledge that science offers, we turn to the American Psychiatric Association for information, we learn several things that should become part of our conversation. In their policy statement regarding homosexuality the American Psychiatric Association says: "Sexual orientation is a relatively new concept. In fact, although same sex behavior has always existed, the idea of a homosexual identity or a homosexual person is only about 100 years old."[5] This statement confirms what we said earlier about the context in which we must interpret biblical statements. No biblical author considered the possibility that some people, without choosing, discover that their sexual orientation is toward members of their own sex.

The American Psychiatric Association also has something to say about the effect that nonacceptance of a homosexual orientation has for the homosexual person. Some people, unable to accept a homosexual orientation as normal, attempt reparative therapy. That is, through therapy they try to turn a homosexual person into a heterosexual person. The American Psychiatric Association says:

> The potential risks of "reparative therapy" are great, including depression, anxiety and self-destructive behavior, since the therapist's alignment with societal prejudices against homosexuality may reinforce self-hatred already experienced by the patient. Many patients who have undergone "reparative therapy" relate that they were inaccurately told that homosexuals are lonely, unhappy individuals who never achieve acceptance or satisfaction. The possibility that the person might achieve happiness and satisfying interpersonal relationships as a gay man or lesbian is not presented, nor are alternative approaches to dealing with the effects of societal stigmatization discussed. [6]

The Catholic Church, like reparative therapy, starts with the belief that the homosexual person has a *condition*. The Catholic Church teaches that such a person must remain celibate in order to be in right relationship with God and with God's people. The Catholic Church, too, does not present the possibility that a homosexual orientation is within the order of nature and that homosexual people are capable of loving, life-giving, committed marriage that witnesses God's love to the two partners and to the world.

The dilemma caused by trying to act in a loving way and refusing to consider the possibility that a homosexual orientation could be within the natural order became evident in a 1997 document written by the United States Conference of Catholic Bishops addressing questions regarding homosexuality titled *Always Our Children: A Pastoral Message to Parents of Homosexual Children and Suggestions for Pastoral Ministers*. In this document the Catholic bishops do their best to counsel and comfort parents of homosexual children. However, since the Church teaches that a homosexual orientation is a disorder and that any sexual relationship between homosexual people, even one within the context of a lifelong loving commitment, is sinful, the document has to advise parents within those parameters. Therefore, some of the advice is, "Do not blame yourselves for a homosexual orientation in your child." "Seek help for yourself, perhaps in the form of counseling or spiritual direction, as you strive for understanding, acceptance, and inner peace."[7]

The whole tone of the advice is to comfort the parents while, at the same time, affirming that if their children act in accord with their sexual orientation, those actions are disordered. How much more comforting it would be to consider the possibility that a homosexual person's actions are not disordered, that within the natural order there is a continuum of sexual attractions, and that a homosexual person's actions are no more disordered than a heterosexual person's actions. Either could act in sexual ways that would be unloving and harmful, and either could act in sexual ways that would be loving and life-giving.

The Catholic Church teaches that any sexual activity between homosexual persons is disordered because it closes the sexual act to the gift of life. However, the Catholic Church does allow marriage between heterosexual persons when nature itself has closed the sexual act to the gift of life in the sense of conceiving a child. A woman who is postmenopausal or who has had a hysterectomy is still free to marry. Such a sexual relationship is not open to conceiving new life, but it is open to the expression of mutual love, which is life-giving in itself. Remember, the Catholic Church does recognize two equally important purposes of marriage. The expression of love between the spouses is one of those purposes.

The bishops' document *Always Our Children* also advises parents always to express love for their children. However, this expression of love "does not have to include approving of all related attitudes and behavioral choices. In fact, [parents] may need to challenge certain aspects of a lifestyle that [they] find objectionable."[8] In other words, a loving parent would not accept uncritically the sexual orientation of a homosexual child. Rather, whenever the child acted in a way that expressed that homosexuality, the parent should feel free to comment. That would be the loving thing to do. Might such comments from a parent have the same effect as reparative therapy? Might they contribute to homosexual people's inability to accept themselves as the people God made them to be?

DISCRIMINATION AGAINST HOMOSEXUAL PEOPLE

The Catechism teaches us that we must never discriminate against homosexual people: "They must be accepted with respect, compassion, and sensitivity. Every sign of unjust discrimination in their regard should be avoided."[9] A question presently being raised in the United States is whether or not denying homosexual couples the opportunity to have a civil marriage is, by necessity, a form of discrimination. Many are convinced that it is.

The present Catholic Church teaching argues strongly that it is not. In 1997 the Secretariat for Doctrine and Pastoral Practices and the Secretariat for Family, Laity, Women, and Youth of the National Conference of Catholic Bishops put out a resource paper titled *Same-Sex Unions and Marriage: A Legal, Social, and Theological Analysis.* In an introductory letter the authors explain that the resource paper was put out to offer bishops "some guidance concerning the claim by some in our society that persons of the same sex have a right to marriage."

This document states:

> [The Church has] a pastoral responsibility to ensure that a vigorous defense of marriage does not at the same time stir up hatred against homosexual persons. The Church must show how it is possible simultaneously to oppose same-sex marriage and to stand against prejudice and unjust discrimination toward homosexual people; to stand for the traditional meaning of marriage and to support the basic human rights of homosexual persons, including their rights to respect, friendship and justice. [10]

The document notes that surveys show that "a majority of people oppose same sex 'marriage' simply because they think it isn't a 'good idea.' The challenge, therefore, is to provide sound reasons that will reinforce right instinct."[11] Certainly, the challenge *is* to provide sound reasons for the Catholic Church's present teaching. However, one must also ask if the "right instinct" cited in the study is right instinct or a well-taught, deeply imbedded prejudice.

The authors of this document believe that it is possible in the United States to deny homosexual couples a civil marriage and, at the same time, refrain from discriminating against them. Many would disagree. They point out that the 1996 Defense of Marriage Act, which defines marriage as being the legal union of a man and a woman, makes it possible for the federal government to deny legally married, same-sex couples hundreds of federal protections and benefits that are given to heterosexual couples. Some examples are Social Security survivor benefits, the ability to file joint tax returns, and the ability to take family medical leave to take care of each other.

QUESTIONS AND CONCERNS

Obviously, the questions revolving around the issue of homosexuality are extremely complex.

- Is a homosexual orientation against the natural law, or not? Can that question be answered definitively before we know why some people's sexual orientation is homosexual? When the question is answered, won't it be answered by scientists rather than by theologians? Since more knowledge is necessary before the question can be answered definitively, shouldn't the Catholic Church acknowledge this and refrain from teaching or thinking that the sexual acts of homosexual people are intrinsically disordered until it knows more?

- Does Scripture address the morality of homosexual actions by homosexual people within a loving, lifelong committed relationship? We have seen that it does not. If it does not, can the Magisterium continue to use Scripture to argue its case?

- Is homosexual marriage a threat to traditional, heterosexual marriage and to the stability of society? If so, why is it a threat? A committed homosexual relationship can be just as stable as a committed heterosexual relationship. So, where is the threat?

- In Catholic circles, the celibacy required of priests has been described as a gift, a special grace. Is it realistic to think that all homosexual people are offered the gift of celibacy? Is there no way in God's creative order for them to express their sexuality in a mutually life-giving way?

- Is it possible, in the United States, to deny homosexual couples the right to legally marry and not, at the same time, discriminate against them? If so, how is this possible?

- Is a homosexual marriage always sinful? If it is, then it will not, by necessity, promote the flourishing of the two people involved. Is this the experience of committed homosexual couples? Does their union add to their ability to be fully human and fully alive, or does it detract from that goal? Should the Catholic Church take their lived experience into account?

- If homosexual couples, in good conscience, get married, what is their relationship to the Catholic Church? Can they continue to worship as Catholics? Can they receive communion? Are others in the congregation entitled to judge their action?

To change the present teaching of the Catholic Church would certainly lead to a number of unanswered questions. However, in the light of solid Catholic biblical scholarship, and in the light of new scientific discoveries, many twenty-first-century Catholics think that the Magisterium has to at least be open to growing in its present understanding. The Magisterium should not state definitively what no one yet knows: that the sexual acts of a homosexual person are disordered. In doing so the Magisterium may be teaching an unrecognized prejudice, not the natural law. In addition, we should all be very, very careful that we do not inadvertently discriminate against homosexual people.

According to the Second Vatican Council's *Pastoral Constitution on the Church in the Modern World*, the norm for human activity is "to harmonize with the authentic interests of the human race, in accordance with God's will and design, and to enable men as individuals and as members of society to pursue and fulfill their total vocation."[12] Given this norm, perhaps we should view the marriage of homosexual people in a different light. Perhaps the two people involved *are* pursuing their total vocation and *are* growing in love.

CONTINUING THE CONVERSATION

1. What personal experience can you bring to bear on the topic of homosexuality? What truths do you firmly believe, based on this experience?

2. Do you think Scripture addresses the question "Are sexual acts between homosexuals committed to each other in a lifelong relationship moral or immoral?" Explain.

3. Do you think morality has its source in God or in human beings' customs and consensus? Do you believe that human beings' understanding of natural law can change with new scientific knowledge, or must it remain static?

4. Do you think marriages between homosexuals are a threat to heterosexual marriages and to the fabric of society?

5. Do you think states that forbid marriage to homosexual couples necessarily discriminate against homosexual people? Why or why not?

Chapter Seven

Abortion: Church, State, Conscience, and Effective Witness

Life once conceived must be protected with the utmost care; abortion and infanticide are abominable crimes.

> —*Pastoral Constitution on the Church in the Modern World, Gaudium et Spes*, 51

Man is a creature composed of body and soul, and made to the image and likeness of God. Man's likeness is chiefly in the soul. The soul is like God because it is a spirit having understanding and free will. The soul is destined to live forever.

> —the *Baltimore Catechism* definition of a human person

But someone will ask, "How are the dead raised? With what kind of body do they come?"

> —1 Corinthians 15:35

[Man must not] be prevented from acting according to his conscience, especially in religious matters.

> —*Catechism of the Catholic Church*, par. 1782

Modern man listens more willingly to witnesses than to teachers, and if he does listen to teachers, it is because they are witnesses.

> —Paul VI in *Evangelization in the Modern World, Evangelii Nuntiandi*, par. 41

In the last three chapters we argued that the Magisterium of the Catholic Church should be open to the possibility of change in regard to its teaching on three topics: contraception, women's ordination, and homosexuality. In this chapter and in future chapters we will discuss the possibility of change, not in regard to Catholic Church teaching, but in regard to Catholic Church actions. We will ask whether or not the present practice of the Catholic Church is the best way to give witness to its teachings. The first topic to be addressed is the topic of abortion.

In recent years some Catholics, including some bishops, have focused solely on the life issue of abortion, claiming its absolute and preeminent importance over all other life issues. In addition, some Catholic Church leaders have attempted to speak with authority not just on the morality of abortion but on its legality, as though there were no distinction between the two. Finally, some bishops have insisted that Catholics must agree with them on the singular importance of this issue and express that agreement in the voting booth. Some bishops have even gone so far as to suggest that Catholics who do not vote as instructed should be deprived of Eucharist.

Before we discuss the wisdom and effectiveness of these actions, let us first look carefully at what Scripture has to say on the topic and what the Catholic Church has taught and is presently teaching on the topic. In that context we will be better prepared to examine whether the Catholic Church's present strategies are successful or counterproductive to both teaching and witnessing to the Catholic Church's belief in the dignity of each person.

WHAT DOES SCRIPTURE HAVE TO SAY?

At its very core, the Catholic Church's teaching against abortion rests on the understanding that every human being is created in the image and likeness of God. This conclusion is drawn from the very first story in the Bible, the story of creation. On the sixth day God says: "'Let us make humankind in our image, according to our likeness. . . .' So God created humankind in his image, in the image of God he created them; male and female he created them. . . . God saw everything that he had made, and indeed, it was very good" (Gen 1:26a, 27, 31a).

This understanding of each person's dignity is the foundation of all of the Catholic Church's teachings on life issues, including not only abortion but euthanasia, health care, the death penalty, just wages, and so on. The Catholic Church understands every single person to be a beloved child of God. In addition, Catholics are taught that the way they treat others is the way they are treating Christ (see Matt 25:31–46). Catholics do not refrain from killing only *innocent* people. They understand life on earth as a gift that God gives and only God can take away. To choose abortion is to disobey the commandment "You shall not murder" (Ex 20:13).

However, if we ask the specific question at the core of the abortion debate we ask, "When does a person become a person?" Obviously, if a person becomes a person at the moment an egg and sperm meet, then preventing that fertilized egg from being implanted in a womb is killing a person. That is the present teaching of the Catholic Church. Can we claim that Scripture has revealed this truth to us?

We cannot. No biblical author addresses the question "When does a person become a person?" True, we do have passages in which the authors presume that a person is a person in the womb. For instance, in Psalm 51, when the psalmist is admitting that he is a sinner and asks for pardon, he says, "Indeed, I was born guilty, a sinner when my mother conceived me" (Ps 51:5).

In Psalm 139, when the psalmist is exclaiming over God's intimate knowledge of him, he says:

> For it was you who formed my inward parts;
> you knit me together in my mother's womb.
> I praise you, for I am fearfully and wonderfully made.
> Wonderful are your works;
> that I know very well.
> My frame was not hidden from you,
> when I was being made in secret,
> intricately woven in the depths of the earth.
> Your eyes beheld my unformed substance.
> In your book were written
> all the days that were formed for me,
> when none of them as yet existed. (Ps 139:13–16)

Job, when he remonstrates with God, never questions that God made him. Job says:

> Your hands fashioned and made me;
> and now you turn and destroy me.
> Remember, that you fashioned me like clay;
> and will you turn me to dust again? . . .
> You clothed me with skin and flesh,
> and knit me together with bones and sinews.

> You have granted me life and steadfast love,
> and your care has preserved my spirit. (Job 10: 8–9, 11–12)

All in all, Scripture presumes that every living person has been made by God and belongs to God. As the author of Psalm 100 tells us, we are to "know that the Lord is God / It is he that made us, and we are his; / we are his people, and the sheep of his pasture" (Ps 100:3). Scripture does not tell us when a person becomes a person.

PRESENT CATHOLIC CHURCH TEACHING

As we have said, the present teaching of the Catholic Church is that, from the moment the egg and sperm meet, the spiritual soul of each person is created by God. Therefore, any destruction of a fertilized egg, whether in or outside the womb, is tantamount to killing a child of God.

The Congregation for the Doctrine of the Faith, in its "Instruction on Respect for Human Life in Its Origin and on the Dignity of Procreation: Replies to Certain Questions of the Day," states that the Magisterium "constantly reaffirms the moral condemnation of any kind of procured abortion. This teaching has not been changed and is unchangeable."[1]

This document reiterates that "from the moment of conception, the life of every human being is to be respected in an absolute way because man is the only creature on earth that God has 'wished for himself' and the spiritual soul of each man is 'immediately created' by God."[2] Based on this core principle, a fertilized egg must be treated with the dignity with which one would treat any other person: "No objective, even though noble in itself, such as a foreseeable advantage to science, to other human beings or to society, can in any way justify experimentation on living human embryos or foetuses, whether viable or not, either inside or outside the mother's womb."[3]

The document also reiterates the Church's teaching against any kind of conception that separates the unitive and procreative purposes of marriage: "The Church's teaching on marriage and human procreation affirms the 'inseparable connection, willed by God and unable to be broken by man on his own initiative, between the two meanings of the conjugal act: the unitive meaning and the procreative meaning.'"[4] Obviously, any fertilization of eggs outside the woman's body would violate this teaching.

The document also comments that "[no] biologist or doctor can reasonably claim, by virtue of his scientific competence, to be able to decide on people's origin and destiny."[5] It is certainly true that certain truths regarding a human person lie outside the bounds of scientific study.

However, it is also true that the Church has a history of finding it very difficult to separate what are conclusions that can legitimately be drawn by theologians, and what are truths that, when known, will be discovered by scientists. For instance, it was science, after the discovery of the microscope, that corrected the Catholic Church's mistaken presumption that the tiny human, worthy of our utmost respect, resided in the semen alone. Given that belief, masturbation was seen as a kind of mass murder. Scientific knowledge will, with regularity, make it necessary for the Catholic Church to reimage the truths that are being taught regarding people's origin and destiny.

WHEN DOES A PERSON BECOME A PERSON?

While it is true that the Catholic Church has always taught that it is wrong to kill a person in the womb, it is not true that Church leaders have always agreed on what constitutes a person. Historically, the question was posed as "When does *ensoulment* take place?" Human beings were defined as being made up of body and soul. Most Christians are familiar with these categories of thought. In fact, many Catholics memorized the definition of a human being using just these categories. The *Baltimore Catechism*, in its format of question and answer, asked, "What is man?" and answered: "Man is a creature composed of body and soul, and made to the image and likeness of God." The *likeness to God* is chiefly in the soul because the soul is "a spirit having understanding and free will, and is destined to live forever."[6]

Although from the beginning of Christendom many, many teachers taught just what the Catholic Church teaches now, not all did. St. Augustine (354–430) did not think that a human soul could live in an unformed body. Therefore, an abortion that preceded animation, while seriously wrong, was not murder.

Later, St. Thomas Aquinas (thirteenth century) agreed with Augustine on this question, as did Pope Gregory XIV (late sixteenth century). Not until the seventeenth and eighteenth centuries did the Catholic Church's present teaching on this topic gain widespread acceptance. It was Pius IX (1792–1878) whose teaching did not make any distinction between an animated fetus and a fetus that was not yet animated: "Pius IX officially eliminated the Catholic distinction between an animated and a non-animated fetus and required excommunication for abortion at any stage of pregnancy."[7] He taught that a fetus has a soul from the time of conception. To have an abortion at any stage of a pregnancy is to kill a human being.

"Body" and "soul" are not the only categories of thought that the Christian tradition has used when probing the origin and destiny of human beings. Paul, in his first letter to the Corinthians, does not speak of body and soul, but of "fleshly body" and "spiritual body." While on earth, a person has a fleshly body. However, flesh and blood do not inherit eternal life. After death a person has a spiritual body. The same person is present in each body.

Paul explains all this in the fifteenth chapter of his first letter to the Corinthians. Paul says:

> But someone will ask, "How are the dead raised? With what kind of body do they come?" . . . There are both heavenly bodies and earthly bodies, but the glory of the heavenly is one thing, and that of the earthly is another. . . . What I am saying, brothers and sisters, is this: flesh and blood cannot inherit the kingdom of God, nor does the perishable inherit the imperishable. Listen, I will tell you a mystery! We will not all die, but we will all be changed, in a moment, in the twinkling of an eye, at the last trumpet. . . . For this perishable body must put on imperishability, and this mortal body must put on immortality. When this perishable body puts on imperishability, and this mortal body puts on immortality, then the saying that is written will be fulfilled: Death has been swallowed up in victory. (1 Cor 15:35, 40–41, 50–52a, 53–54)

When Paul speaks of the "last trumpet" he is referring to a definitive event, the coming of the Son of Man in glory, an event that Paul expected to occur during his own lifetime. That is why he says, "We will not all die." What Paul is teaching in this passage is that the Corinthians will rise from the dead just as Christ has risen from the dead.

Then Paul attempts to discuss what is a mystery: What kind of body will the Corinthians have when they rise as Christ has risen? In speaking of the body, Paul refuses to equate it with flesh. Paul uses the word *body* as it was used in Hebrew and Greek thought, not to name a thing but to describe a function. The body has two functions: it allows a person to be a distinct individual, and it makes it possible for a person to be in relationship with other distinct individuals. We use the word *body* in a similar way when we say "somebody."

To say that we use a word to describe a function, not a thing, becomes more understandable when we compare it to our use of the word *angel. Angel* means "messenger." So, when we say that we believe in angels, we are saying that we believe God sends messengers. We are not claiming that we know what an angel actually is.

Paul did not know, nor do we, just what a spiritual body will be like. That is, Christians do not know how they will still be unique, relational individuals, once they leave earth. But Christians do believe in life after death. They do believe that people will still be alive as unique individuals and still be able to be in relationship with other unique individuals for all eternity.

With this understanding of "body" in mind, our question about a fetus can be reworded, reimaged, from "When does a fetus have a soul?" to "When does a fetus become a person destined for eternal life?" Might becoming a person be the end result of a creative process rather than the result of a single creative act that takes place when an egg and sperm meet? That is the question that was being debated in earlier centuries with the words *ensoulment* and *animated fetus*.

The question of when a person becomes a person has arisen again in the twentieth and twenty-first centuries. Science has taught us things we did not previously know about what happens naturally. For instance, many eggs that are fertilized through sexual intercourse never get implanted in the womb. Implantation is, obviously, a necessary part of conception. In fact, we often use the word *conception* to refer to implantation rather than to the union of egg and sperm. We say that a woman has conceived a child. In the natural order, are billions of unborn people being killed by this lack of implantation, or have these "people" never existed in the first place?

In addition, a fertilized egg can divide and eventually become more than one person. Also, two fertilized eggs can merge and eventually become one person. Does the Catholic Church want to claim that one soul, present from the moment that an egg and sperm meet, divides and becomes two souls? On the other hand, does the Catholic Church want to claim that two souls present from the moment that two eggs and two sperms meet merge and become one soul? The Catholic Church makes no such claim, but the questions are raised by the insistence by the Magisterium that a person exists from the moment an egg and sperm meet, even if that fertilized egg is not yet implanted in a woman's womb.

The question of when a person first exists is not an unimportant or esoteric question. The answer affects people's understanding of the morality of in vitro fertilization, the morning-after pill, and stem cell research. A Catholic position might be that, given our present state of knowledge, no one can answer the question with certitude. Given this lack of knowledge, we must assume that a person does exist. Otherwise we might inadvertently be killing our own children. At the same time, the Catholic Church undercuts the credibility of its teaching if it states with certitude that which is beyond anyone's knowledge. The Magisterium should not claim to know more than it does know.

ABORTION AND THE STATE

So far we have examined what both Scripture and the Church teach us in response to the question "When does a person become a person destined for eternal life?" Based on the Catholic teaching that a person is a person from the moment of conception, we can draw the conclusion that to choose to have an abortion is always objectively morally wrong because it involves, or could involve, killing another human being. Let us now change the topic from the morality of abortion to the legality of abortion. There are a number of questions to be addressed:

- Since abortion is always objectively immoral, does that mean that it should also necessarily be illegal in the United States?
- Is it reasonable to conclude that any Catholic who disagrees with the idea that abortion should be illegal (as distinct from being immoral) is being unfaithful to the Catholic Church?
- Is it reasonable to conclude that if a Catholic votes for a candidate who does not want abortion to become illegal, but who agrees with Catholics on many other life issues, the Catholic, by casting that vote, has sinned and should not present himself or herself for communion?

These are questions that are very much in the public eye. In addition, Catholic bishops do not agree with each other on the correct answers. Many Catholics of the twenty-first century think that the answer to each of these questions is no.

Is it possible for a Catholic to disagree that abortion should be made a crime and, in concluding this, still be faithful to Catholic teachings and Catholic values? A Catholic, seeking to know and do God's will, might ask the following questions and come to the following conclusions:

- Does the very fact that an action is always immoral mean that it should also always be illegal? Catholics certainly don't hold that standard for other immoral actions. For instance, adultery is always immoral. However, adultery is no longer illegal in every state, nor are Catholics encouraged, in defense of marriage, to try to make adultery illegal. The question of morality and the question of legality are two separate questions.

- Is the Catholic conviction that a person is a person from the moment of conception an obvious conclusion that all reasonable and well-meaning people would accept as true? Catholics know from talking with their fellow citizens that it is not. Many people's thinking is more in line with Augustine and Thomas Aquinas. They disapprove of late-term abortions because they agree that such an abortion is killing a person. However, they do not have this same conviction about unimplanted fertilized eggs or about the earliest days of a pregnancy.

- Should freedom of conscience be denied to people who are not Catholic and who disagree with the Catholic Church's teaching on when a human person's life begins? Consider the case of a person who is not Catholic and is pregnant as the result of rape. Consider the case of a person whose life is endangered because of her pregnancy. Should that person be allowed to choose what she believes to be the right path, or should this choice be made for her? Certainly an argument could be made that if Catholics do not want laws passed that violate Catholics' freedom of conscience, Catholics should be equally sensitive to the fact that others should have that same right.

- In social settings in which citizens do not agree on the morality of abortion, who should make the decision as to whether or not an abortion is possible: the individual or the state? If we say that the state has the right to make the decision we could be opening the door to a situation that Catholics would find intolerable. If it is the state's right to decide matters of reproduction, the state could decide to limit the number of children a couple can have; instead of saying that abortion is illegal, the state could say that having a fifth child is illegal. This is not an absurd idea. In China a couple that has more than one child is severely penalized.

THE CATHOLIC TEACHING ON CONSCIENCE

As part of the Church's political posture on the question of abortion, the Church insists that the law must respect freedom of conscience. No Catholic doctor should have to participate in an abortion against his or her conscience.

In addition, the Catholic Church teaches the priority of a well-formed conscience. Catholics are not only allowed to follow a well-formed conscience, Catholics are required to do so. The *Catechism of the Catholic Church* states this truth with great clarity:

> Conscience is a judgment of reason whereby the human person recognizes the moral quality of a concrete act that he is going to perform, is in the process of performing, or has already completed. In all he says and does, man is obliged to follow faithfully what he knows to be just and right. It is by the judgment of his conscience that man perceives and recognizes the prescriptions of the divine law.[8]

Man has the right to act in conscience and in freedom so as personally to make moral decisions. "He must not be forced to act contrary to his conscience. Nor must he be prevented from acting according to his conscience, especially in religious matters."[9]

Given this teaching, let us consider the situation of a faithful Catholic, elected to public office, who has a well-formed conscience and who disagrees with the local bishop's political agenda. The bishop wants to make what both the bishop and the elected official believe to be an immoral action, having or participating in an abortion, an illegal action in the United States. Does not the Catholic Church's teaching regarding the necessity of following one's conscience teach that the Catholic elected official must act in accordance with his or her conscience, even if that means disobeying the local bishop? In addition, should not any voter who finds himself or herself in this situation also follow his or her conscience?

The United States Conference of Catholic Bishops' statement *Catholics in Political Life* seems to disagree with these conclusions. The statement, in trying to persuade legislators to vote to make what they believe to be immoral also illegal, argues:

> Catholics who bring their moral convictions into public life do not threaten democracy or pluralism but enrich them and the nation. The separation of church and state does not require division between belief and the public action, between moral principles and political choices, but protects the right of believers and religious groups to practice their faith and act on their values in public life.[10]

A legislator who agrees that he must protect the rights of those with whom he disagrees to act on *their* values might vote against criminalizing abortion for that very reason.

Because the bishops could not agree on how to respond to Catholic legislators who honestly do not agree with them on this issue, the bishops decided that each bishop should decide on the best action in his diocese: "Bishops can legitimately make different judgments on the most prudent course of pastoral action."[11]

True, each bishop must follow his conscience and exercise his office as he judges best. However, exactly the same thing can be said about each legislator. When a bishop reacts to the fact that Catholic public officials do not recognize his authority in dictating how they should carry out the duties of their offices, or when he reacts to the fact that Catholics don't vote as he thinks they should vote by suggesting, or insisting, that the disobedient people should be deprived of Eucharist, how is one to respond? Again, one could argue that to be a faithful Catholic one must follow his or her own conscience.

The idea of denying Eucharist as a way of disciplining a legislator who feels duty bound to use his or her own best judgment, rather than the bishop's best judgment, on a legislative matter, seems to many Catholics to be harmful rather than helpful in furthering the Catholic agenda.

HOW ARE CATHOLICS TO BE EFFECTIVE WITNESSES IN OUR SOCIETY?

Given the fact that Catholics believe that they are to be witnesses of their beliefs to the world, how should Catholics act in the present circumstances here in the United States in order to educate and persuade others to the truth of their insights and thus to accomplish their goal of abolishing abortion?

In recent years the Catholic Church's major tactic seems to have been to try to make abortion illegal, to criminalize abortion. So far, the Catholic Church has not had success in moving toward that goal. However, there are many other ways in which the Catholic Church could pursue the goal of abolishing abortion, ways that might be a great deal more successful.

First, the Catholic Church could do a better job of teaching what Catholics believe. If more Catholics were loving and persuasive teachers on this topic, fewer people might choose to have abortions. The Catholic Church could also do many more things to alleviate those problems that are the causes of a person's choosing abortion, be it shame, lack of family support, poverty, lack of health care, and the like. Catholics could help people see that abortion is their worst choice, not their best choice among bad choices.

In addition, it is very, very important that Catholic leaders—bishops, priests, or lay people—refrain from using bullying tactics to impose their will on others. To do so is to undercut the credibility of the teaching voice of the Catholic Church. The effect is that people want to dismiss the teaching that is being imposed upon them rather than listen to it and carefully consider its merits.

Catholics must also scrupulously avoid misrepresenting the facts by calling contraceptive methods abortifacients (something that causes an abortion rather than prevents conception). True, the present teaching of the Catholic Church is that to use either contraceptives or abortifacients is seriously wrong. However, there is a difference between the two, and people have both a right and a need to know the difference when they are making these important decisions.

Science is more and more able to inform us about how a contraceptive device is functioning. If the contraceptive is preventing ovulation or slowing down the progress of a sperm so that the egg and sperm do not meet, it is simply dishonest to lump these devices with others that prevent implantation or dislodge an already implanted fertilized egg. Catholics do not further their cause by obscuring the difference between a contraceptive and an abortifacient.

Also, in the course of discussing contentious issues about which both sides feel passionately, Catholics must avoid mischaracterizing the positions of those with whom they disagree by referring to them with inaccurate labels. For instance, people who are pro-choice are not necessarily pro-abortion. Even if people do not agree that abortion is immoral, or that it should be illegal, they do not necessarily think that abortion is a wonderful thing. They may think it is the least bad of the bad options they perceive.

Catholics also do harm when those who believe that abortion is immoral try to distinguish themselves from all of their opponents by calling themselves pro-life. People who go to heroic efforts and great expense to conceive a child through in vitro fertilization and people who believe it is all right to use fertilized eggs for stem cell research in hopes of discovering medical breakthroughs are also pro-life.

Even the label pro-choice is misleading. A person might agree that no woman has a moral right to choose to deprive her own child of life. However, that person might still believe that in the United States, where there is a choice to be made, that choice should be made by the individual, not by the state.

In addition, the Catholic Church should not state with certainty that which is a matter of belief and cannot be proven. If Catholics claim that they know fertilized eggs stored in a laboratory freezer have souls, and the person with whom they are speaking disagrees with them, that person will ask how Catholics know this. The answer "Because that is the teaching of the Catholic Church" will not persuade a person who is not a Catholic and who does not have a particular respect for the teaching voice of the Catholic Church. Catholics must have sound reasons to support conclusions when trying to persuade others that these conclusions are true.

It is both more honest and more persuasive to say that, until we have definitive evidence to the contrary, it seems the wiser choice to treat fertilized eggs with the respect given a human person. Otherwise we might inadvertently be killing a person. That statement can certainly be defended.

Finally, Catholics would do well to remember what Paul VI, in his encyclical *Evangelization in the Modern World*, had to say about effective witness: "The men of our day are more impressed by witness than by teachers, and if they listen to these it is because they also bear witness."[12]

If Catholics are going to teach others about the dignity of human life, Catholics must be witnesses of that teaching by the dignity and love with which they treat those with whom they disagree. It is both wrong and counterproductive to ridicule, misrepresent, or dismiss those with whom one disagrees. Catholics cannot ride roughshod over other people's consciences. After all, as mentioned above, Catholics believe that those with whom they disagree are also God's beloved children, and that the way Catholics treat them is the way they are treating Christ himself.

CONTINUING THE CONVERSATION

1. Based on what you have been taught and on your own experience, what are your present beliefs about the morality of abortion? Why do you hold these beliefs? What are your beliefs about the legality of abortion? Why do you hold these beliefs?

2. What does the word *conceived* mean to you? Do you think a fertilized egg outside a womb is a child? Why do you think this? Why is the answer to this question important?

3. What do you think a person is obliged to do if the state passes a law that violates his or her conscience? Do you think the criminalization of abortion could violate anyone's conscience? Why or why not?

4. As you read how the abortion debate is unfolding, do you think that some tactics and some behaviors do more harm than good? Explain.

5. What do you think would be the most effective ways to give public witness to the Catholic goal to abolish abortion? Why do you think these actions would be most effective?

Chapter Eight

Marriage and Annulments

"What God has joined together, let no one separate."

—Jesus's answer to the Pharisees' question,
"Is it lawful for a man to divorce his wife?"
as it appears in Mark 10:9

The matrimonial covenant, by which a man and a woman establish between themselves a partnership of the whole of life, is by its nature ordered toward the good of the spouses and the procreation and education of offspring; this covenant between baptized persons has been raised by Christ the Lord to the dignity of a sacrament.

—*Catechism of the Catholic Church*, par. 1601

A sacrament is an outward sign instituted by Christ to give grace.

—the *Baltimore Catechism* definition of a sacrament
that I learned as a child

A sacrament is an act of worship through which we come into intimate relationship with the risen Christ.

—the definition of a sacrament that I learned when
teaching a catechist certification course on basic
Catholic teachings in the 1970s

In such a case the brother or sister is not bound. It is to peace that God has called you.

—Paul to the Corinthians, making an exception
to the teaching against divorce (1 Cor 7:15b)

In this chapter we will discuss the Catholic Church's present response to the tragic situation in which a person's marriage has ended in divorce and that person wants to remarry in the Catholic Church. As was true with the Church's stance on abortion, the problem is not with the Catholic Church's basic teaching: a sacramental marriage is a covenant relationship, a witness on earth to God's covenant relationship with God's people. As such, marriage is understood to be an unbreakable bond. The problem is with the way the Catholic Church is presently living out that core teaching through the canonical annulment process.

To give context to our discussion we will first see what Scripture has to say on the permanency of marriage. We will then examine carefully what the Roman Catholic Church has taught and presently teaches on the subject. Next we will look at the annulment process as it presently exists. Finally we will note the questions and concerns that our discussion has raised.

WHAT DOES SCRIPTURE HAVE TO SAY?

Throughout Scripture, marriage is a presumed, cross-cultural reality. In the very first story of creation, the author describes God as creating human beings on the sixth day: "So God created humankind in his image, in the image of God he created them; male and female he created them. God blessed them, and God said to them, 'Be fruitful and multiply, and fill the earth. . . .' God saw everything that he had made, and indeed, it was very good" (Gen 1:27–28a; 31a).

In the second story in the Bible, the story of the man and woman in the garden, a very sophisticated view of marriage is expressed. After God finally succeeds in finding a suitable partner for the man, the man says, "This at last is bone of my bones and flesh of my flesh. . . ." The narrator then adds, "Therefore a man leaves his father and his mother and clings to his wife and they become one flesh" (Gen 2:23–24).

In addition, the Old Testament presents marriage as more than a necessary cultural reality in order for the race to propagate, and more than a relationship of intimate unity between a husband and wife (although not always with just one wife). Marriage is also seen, in some mysterious way, as a revelation of God's love for God's people. For example, the book of Hosea rests on this insight. Hosea is a husband, married to an unfaithful wife. Hosea understands his situation to be a living metaphor for the relationship between God and unfaithful Israel.

Hosea constantly uses the metaphor of husband and wife to picture God's love for and forgiveness of God's people. He pictures God assuring Israel: "I will take you for my wife forever; I will take you for my wife in righteousness and in justice, in steadfast love, and in mercy. I will take you for my wife in faithfulness; and you shall know the Lord" (Hos 2:19–20).

The Gospel according to Mark, which is believed to be the earliest of the four Gospels (AD 65), addresses the questions of marriage, divorce, and remarriage. In Mark the Pharisees ask Jesus,

> "Is it lawful for a man to divorce his wife?" [Jesus] answered them, "What did Moses command you?" They said, "Moses allowed a man to write a certificate of dismissal and to divorce her." But Jesus said to them, "Because of your hardness of heart he wrote this commandment for you. But from the beginning of creation, 'God made them male and female.' 'For this reason a man shall leave his father and mother and be joined to his wife, and the two shall become one flesh.' So they are no longer two, but one flesh. Therefore what God has joined together, let no one separate." Then in the house the disciples asked him again about this matter. He said to them "Whoever divorces his wife and marries another commits adultery against her; and if she divorces her husband and marries another, she commits adultery." (Mark 10:2–12)

If this were the only passage we have that addresses the topic of marriage, divorce, and remarriage, the subject would be less complicated than it is. From this passage it seems that Jesus, as he quotes from the story of creation (Gen 1:27b) and the story of the man and woman in the garden (Gen 2:24), expressly forbids both divorce and remarriage. However, this is not the only passage we have.

The Gospel according to Matthew is thought to be the second oldest of our four Gospels (AD 80). In addition, Scripture scholars believe that Mark's Gospel was a source for Matthew's Gospel. This is very useful information because it means that if there is a difference between Mark and Matthew's account of the same scene, Matthew has edited it purposefully. In Matthew we read:

> Some Pharisees came to him, and to test him they asked, "Is it lawful for a man to divorce his wife for any cause?" He answered, "Have you not read that the one who made them at the beginning made them male and female, and said, 'For this reason a man shall leave his father and mother and be joined to his wife, and the two shall become one flesh?' Therefore what God has joined together, let no one separate." They said to him, "Why then did Moses com-

mand us to give a certificate of dismissal and to divorce her?" He said to them, "It was because you were so hard-hearted that Moses allowed you to divorce your wives, but from the beginning it was not so. And I say to you, whoever divorces his wife, except for unchastity, and marries another commits adultery." (Matt 19:3–9)

When we compare Mark's and Matthew's passages we notice some changes. Matthew adds to the Pharisees' question, "Is it lawful for a man to divorce his wife?" the phrase, "for any reason." Many people, when they read this phrase, finish it in their minds with "no matter how serious." Catholics are prone to add this phrase because Catholics have been taught that a sacramental marriage cannot be undone, no matter what the circumstances. A sacramental marriage is unbreakable because it is a living metaphor for God's covenant love for God's people. Just as God's covenant with God's people is unbreakable, so is the covenant between a husband and wife.

However, those who lived at the time of Matthew's Gospel would have finished the sentence in their minds with: "no matter how trivial?" In the Israelite culture the man was allowed to dismiss his wife for any number of trivial reasons. However, the wife could not dismiss her husband. She belonged to the husband as long as he wanted her.

Matthew tells us that the Pharisees asked the question not to learn, but to *test* Jesus. They are experts when it comes to the law, and they are hoping that Jesus will contradict the law, thus putting himself at odds with his fellow Israelites. Jesus tells the Pharisees that, in this instance, the law is not strict enough. A man should not be able to put away his wife for trivial reasons.

In addition, Matthew adds an exception to Jesus's blanket statement against divorce. He pictures Jesus saying, "except for *unchastity*" (New Revised Standard Version). This word differs in various English translations of the passage. The *New American Bible*, the translation used in the Lectionary in the United States, says, "unless the marriage is *unlawful*." The *Good News Bible* translation uses the word *unfaithfulness*. The *Jerusalem Bible* says *fornication*.

The Greek word being translated is *pornia*, the root word for our word *pornography*. Scripture scholars are not sure exactly what exception Matthew is introducing, but there is no question that an exception has been added. One possibility is that Matthew is referring to marriages among Gentiles that violated Jewish laws of consanguinity, such as a marriage between a brother and a sister (see Acts 15:19–20).

Matthew is not the only inspired author who feels free to add an exception to what, in Mark, appears to be the blanket forbidding of divorce and remarriage. In Paul's first letter to the Corinthians (AD 54), he says:

> To the married I give this command—not I but the Lord—that the wife should not separate from her husband (but if she does separate, let her remain unmarried or else be reconciled to her husband), and that the husband should not divorce his wife. To the rest I say—I and not the Lord—that if any believer has a wife who is an unbeliever, and she consents to live with him, he should not divorce her. And if any woman has a husband who is an unbeliever, and he consents to live with her, she should not divorce him. For the unbelieving husband is made holy through his wife, and the unbelieving wife is made holy through her husband. Otherwise, your children would be unclean, but as it is, they are holy. But if the unbelieving partner separates, let it be so; In such a case the brother or sister is not bound. It is to peace that God has called you. (1 Cor 7:10–15)

Paul is discussing a situation where two nonbelievers have married, and one of the two becomes a believer. Is that person free to divorce his or her spouse and marry a believer? Paul says no. The believer must stay with the nonbeliever. The believing spouse may be the path through which the nonbeliever will come to believe. But what if the nonbeliever refuses to stay with the believer? Then the believer is not bound. To this day, Paul's exception stands, and is called the Pauline Privilege.

At the same time that Scripture acknowledges that exceptions to Jesus's teaching against divorce exist, it also teaches the holiness of marriage. Marriage was seen as a way to live "in the Lord" (see 1 Cor 7:39), a vocation through which the partners mysteriously experience God's love and become witnesses of that love to the community.

This idea is most clearly expressed in the letter to the Ephesians:

> Husbands, love your wives, just as Christ loved the church and gave himself up for her, in order to make her holy by cleansing her with the washing of water by the word, so as to present the church to himself in splendor, without a spot or wrinkle or anything of the kind—yes, so that she may be holy and without blemish. In the same way, husbands should love their wives as they do their own bodies. He who loves his wife loves himself. For no one ever hates his own body, but he nourishes and tenderly cares for it, just as Christ does the church, because we are members of his body. "For this reason a man will leave his father and mother and be joined to his wife, and the two will become one

flesh." This is a great mystery, and I am applying it to Christ and the church. (Eph 5:25–32)

In this passage the covenantal aspect of a marriage in the Lord is explicitly stated. Husbands are to love their wives as Christ loves the church. A marriage in which this vision becomes a reality is one in which not only the husband and wife mysteriously witness to each other the faithful and self-sacrificing love of Christ for his people, but they witness God's covenant love to the whole community. Such a marriage is indeed a vocation, a response by both husband and wife to God's call to grow in holiness.

WHAT IS PRESENT CATHOLIC CHURCH TEACHING?

The Catholic Church teaches that marriage is a sacrament. However, no Catholic could have made this claim in the first millennium of Church history. The word *sacrament* is not one that the biblical authors used. Augustine did speak of sacrament, but more in the context of mystery than in the context of something definable by law. The first official declaration of marriage as a sacrament happened at the Council of Verona in 1184.

The way the Catholic Church has taught what it means when it calls marriage a sacrament changed in the twentieth century. Many Catholics were taught that a sacrament is an outward sign instituted by Christ to give grace. Catholics were also taught that Jesus personally instituted marriage as a sacrament during his public ministry at the wedding at Cana.

The *Catechism of the Catholic Church* acknowledges that this was taught but moves away from such a concrete explanation when it says: "The Church attaches great importance to Jesus' presence at the wedding at Cana. She sees in it the confirmation of the goodness of marriage and the proclamation that thenceforth marriage will be an efficacious sign of Christ's presence."[1] Given what the Catholic Church now teaches about biblical interpretation, Catholics would have a very hard time defending this particular way of teaching that marriage is a sacrament.

A later definition of sacrament that I learned as a young adult teacher is that a sacrament is an act of worship through which we come into intimate relationship with the risen Christ. In this definition, a sacrament is understood not as a thing, but as a mysterious way of being involved in an ongoing relationship with the risen Christ.

For the first thousand years of Church history, although marriage between baptized Christians was understood as a path to grow in holiness, the wedding itself was not celebrated in the Church. Because of baptism, a person's whole life was understood as being lived in a sacramental context, as a life lived in the Lord. After their wedding, a civil and familial celebration, the couple would continue to worship with the gathered community and receive Eucharist, thus sealing their union as one body with each other by their reception of the body of Christ.

The first compilation of canon law appeared in the twelfth century. As people's understandings became more centered in law and less centered in sacramental mystery, people began to define marriage more in terms of a contract than in terms of a covenant. The response to the question "What constitutes a valid marriage?" focused on two specific aspects of marriage: consent and consummation.

The Church began to take over the celebration of marriage gradually. Originally the Church ceremony, once it was begun, was held at the entrance to the church. Only later was it moved into the church proper. It was the Council of Trent, in the sixteenth century, that insisted on the Catholic Church's right to define and regulate just what constituted a sacramental marriage. This Council was the first to teach that for a marriage to be valid and sacramental it had to be conducted in the presence of a priest and two witnesses.

The documents of the Second Vatican Council continued the growth process in the Catholic Church's understanding of the sacrament of marriage. The Council, in its documents *Lumen Gentium* and *Gaudium et Spes*, retrieved some of the early biblical insights that had lost prominence over the years and took into account knowledge gained from the human sciences. As was true with the two definitions of sacrament mentioned earlier, the Council put less emphasis on an understanding of the sacrament of marriage as a *thing* (an outward sign) that centered on matters legal and contractual, and gave renewed prominence to an emphasis on *relationship* (an act of worship through which we come into an intimate relationship with the risen Christ), the personal dimension of marriage.

This growth in understanding is reflected in the introduction to the *Rite of Marriage*, which teaches the following:

- A sacramental marriage is not simply a contract, but a covenant. As such, it is a source of grace to the couple and a witness to the community:

"Married Christians, in virtue of the sacrament of matrimony, signify and share in the mystery of that unity and fruitful love which exists between Christ and his Church. . . . Marriage arises in the covenant of marriage, or irrevocable consent, which each partner freely bestows on and accepts from the other."[2]

- The love of the two people is essential to the very existence of a sacramental marriage. God is the source of that love: "Christian couples, therefore, nourish and develop their marriage by undivided affection, which wells up from the fountain of divine love, while, in a merging of human and divine love, they remain faithful in body and in mind, in good times as in bad."[3]

- Marriage has a twofold purpose, no longer ranked as one more important than the other. These two purposes are the mutual love of husband and wife and the growth of God's family through the birth, loving, and educating of children: "Therefore, married Christians, while not considering the other purposes of marriage of less account, should be steadfast and ready to cooperate with the love of their Creator and Savior, who through them will constantly enrich and enlarge his own family."[4]

- Faith is also necessary. Marriage, like all sacraments, involves an act of worship by people of faith: "Priests should first of all strengthen and nourish the faith of those about to be married, for the sacrament of matrimony presupposes and demands faith."[5]

We see, then, that based on both Scripture and Tradition, the Catholic Church teaches the covenant nature of the sacrament of marriage and therefore the indissolubility of a valid, sacramental marriage. At the same time, the Church recognizes that not every marriage that initially appears to be a valid, sacramental marriage is in fact a valid, sacramental marriage. So, the dilemma is how to balance these two truths.

For a number of centuries the Catholic Church's response to the need to balance these two truths, which are in obvious tension with each other, has been primarily juridical rather than pastoral. However, the process is moving in the pastoral direction. We will first explain the annulment process as it now stands before we ask ourselves if this process is the most effective response to broken marriages that the Catholic Church can have and still remain true to its teaching about the sacramental nature of marriage between baptized people.

THE ANNULMENT PROCESS

Many people think of the annulment process as a "Catholic divorce." This is not really an accurate characterization of the process. Why? Because a divorce is a civil matter. It dissolves a legal marriage *contract* (a legally binding agreement between two people that can, with the consent of the two people, no longer be binding). An annulment is a Church matter.

Many American Catholics did not clearly understand that, at a Catholic Church marriage, two distinct things are taking place, until Grace Kelly got married. Since she was a well-known Hollywood star, her marriage to Prince Rainier of Monaco was covered in the U.S. news. She and the prince had two different ceremonies: one civil (a contract) and one religious (a covenant). When a person is married in a Catholic Church in the United States, the ordained person who witnesses the ceremony is representing both the Church and the state.

The Church, at its beginning and now, understands what is now called a sacramental marriage not in terms of contract, but in terms of covenant. A covenant cannot be dissolved any more than God can stop loving us. Therefore, a civil divorce has no effect on the binding nature of a sacramental marriage. A person who is sacramentally married, but civilly divorced, is not free to remarry in the Catholic Church. It is the annulment process that addresses whether or not a marriage is a sacramental marriage, a covenant relationship that cannot be dissolved.

An annulment states that the conditions for a sacramental marriage, a marriage covenant, to have taken place were not present at the time of the marriage. An annulment has no effect civilly. It does not affect the legitimacy of children, and it does not address the distribution of property, as does a civil divorce. The only purpose of an annulment is to decide whether or not the marriage that took place is a sacramental marriage or not.

There are three questions the annulment process asks to determine whether or not a valid, sacramental marriage exists:

1. Was there a lack of canonical form? Remember, the Council of Trent taught that a valid and sacramental marriage must take place before a priest and two witnesses. Today this requirement would mean that a valid and sacramental marriage must take place before a properly delegated person, usually but not always a priest or a deacon, and two

additional witnesses. Also, the ceremony must be true to the Catholic Church's rite for the sacrament of marriage.[6]

2. Was there an impediment to the marriage? An impediment to marriage could be any number of things: Was the person who married under age? Were the bride and groom close blood relatives? Was either the bride or the groom already married to someone else? If so, a valid, sacramental marriage did not take place.[7]

3. Was there a defect of consent? Most annulments rest on a defect of consent. If there is a serious defect in the consent that each person gives, then the marriage is not a sacrament—that is, a covenant marriage. We have the expression "ready, willing, and able." For each person to give full consent, each must be ready, willing, and able. Obviously, if a pregnancy is involved and the couple marries for that reason alone, a defect of consent exists. In any marriage where a clear understanding of the sacramental nature of the marriage is lacking, or the ability to carry out the responsibilities of marriage is lacking, a defect of consent is present.[8]

A person who is abusive, who is unable to stop his or her abusive treatment toward others, is unable to enter a sacramental marriage because that person is unable to be a witness of God's love to his or her spouse and children. This defect of consent may not be evident on the day of the marriage, but it becomes very evident in the lived experience of that marriage. In such a case, to quote Paul, but in a different context, the abused person is not bound. It is to peace that God calls God's beloved children (see 1 Cor 7:10–15).

THE INTERNAL FORUM

In addition to the annulment process, and only after the annulment process has failed for one reason or another, the Catholic Church has what is called the "internal forum" to respond to failed marriages.

The internal forum is a pastoral rather than a juridical response to a failed marriage. The priest, in private meetings with the person involved, helps that person reach an informed decision, based on that person's experience, knowledge, and conscience, as to the person's status and relationship with the Catholic Church.

The internal forum would allow a person for whom the annulment process is impossible, through no fault of his or her own, and who has chosen to remarry in good conscience (although not in a ceremony officially witnessed by the Catholic Church), to return to the sacraments of Reconciliation and Eucharist. The person would obviously not be confessing the second marriage, as this marriage has been carried out in good conscience. However, he or she must endeavor to return to the sacraments in a manner that does not cause scandal to others.[9]

QUESTIONS REGARDING THE CATHOLIC CHURCH'S RESPONSE TO FAILED MARRIAGES

Based on experience, Scripture, and Church teaching, many people are asking if the annulment process is the best way for the Church to respond to the tragedy of a failed marriage. Many have pointed out that the Eastern Church, whose sacraments the Catholic Church recognizes, has adopted a pastoral, rather than a juridical response, so it is obvious that a juridical response is not the only response possible.

Certainly the Catholic Church is giving society as a whole a gift in emphasizing the importance of a sacramental marriage as a witness to the spouses, the children, and, indeed, the whole community, of God's covenant love for God's people. Some marriages are able to live up to this ideal. But what are we to do if marriages have the opposite effect, if there is such a lack of love that the spouses and children begin to doubt the very existence of a loving God who loves them particularly and individually? Should we simply say "Tough it out"?

There is another truth, core to the Gospel, to which the present annulment process fails to give witness. As things stand now, the only reason for an annulment is that something was lacking at the time that the vows were exchanged. There is no possibility of an annulment if something has gone drastically wrong after that date. There is no possibility to acknowledge failure, to be forgiven for that failure, and to move forward with one's life. The truth to which the Catholic Church's present annulment process does not give witness is that God loves and forgives those who sin, who fail, for one reason or another, to be a constant witness through their actions to God's never-ending love. Christ came both to reveal that God is love and to call sinners to repentance and forgiveness. Every single one of us is a forgiven sinner as well as a constantly loved child of God. Why does the Catholic Church's response to failed marriages neglect to give witness to God's constant offer of forgiveness?

Another problem exists in the present juridical response to failed marriages: As things stand in the annulment process, the final decision regarding whether or not a marriage has been a valid, sacramental marriage is being made by the canon lawyers, not by the married people themselves. Why has the hierarchy usurped this decision from the ministers of the sacrament (if the marriage was a sacrament)—the husband and wife?

The Catholic Church teaches that at a sacramental marriage the bride and groom are the ministers of the sacrament. The institutional Church witnesses that sacrament. Only the bride and groom can truly discern whether full consent existed. Why does the institutional Church not once again act as a witness to their decision rather than making the decision for them?

If a pastoral response, such as the one used in the Eastern Church, or as the one used in the private forum, replaced the annulment process as the first response to failed marriages, the Catholic Church could respond to four deficiencies in the present practice:

- The Catholic Church could give witness not only to God's covenant love but to God's constant call to repentance and forgiveness.
- The Catholic Church could return the final decision to the couple, the ministers of the sacrament of marriage and the ones who have the greatest ability to know from experience the truth of the situation in which they find themselves.
- The Catholic Church could alleviate, to some extent, the question of scandal: Jesus came to call sinners. A person's broken marriage would, like every other area of failure, be considered primarily a private rather than a public matter, even though the public has a great stake in that person's choices.

    Those who take scandal at the return of a person who has failed in one way or another are just like the older brother in Jesus's parable of the prodigal son (see Luke 15:11–32), and just like the Pharisees to whom Jesus told this parable. They fail to recognize their own sin—their own lack of ability to love and to forgive.
- The Catholic Church could greatly lessen the amount of time necessary to complete the process. For the process to take years and years is an unnecessary burden on those seeking the annulment.

As a person who has been called to the sacrament of marriage, I do not want, for one second, to diminish the Catholic Church's counter-cultural teaching on marriage as a vocation that calls the spouses to holiness and that witnesses God's covenant love to the world. At the same time, it seems very wrong to dismiss people's lived experience and to insist that their marriage is sacramental when they know, from that lived experience, that their marriage is anything but a witness of God's love in their lives.

We are definitely taught that what "God has joined together no one should separate" (Mark 10:9). However, an unloving marriage is not an example of what "God has joined together." It is an example of what fallible human beings have joined together. Such a marriage is an obstacle, rather than a help, in living out one's call to holiness.

The Catholic Church is, after all, a pilgrim people, a pilgrim Church. Catholics should carefully consider whether or not the Catholic Church is succeeding in its goal of being a faithful witness of God's love for God's people by its present juridical response to failed marriages.

CONTINUING THE CONVERSATION

1. What personal experience do you have with marriage, sacramental or otherwise? What do you firmly believe, based on your own experience?
2. Do you have any personal experience with the annulment process? Do you believe that this juridical response to failed marriages is a faithful witness or a hindrance to the Catholic Church's teaching regarding the covenantal nature of a sacramental marriage?
3. Have you ever heard of the internal forum? What does this pastoral process offer that the annulment process fails to offer? What does the annulment process offer that the internal forum fails to offer?
4. Do you think that the Catholic Church's present annulment process respects the dignity of the two people involved? Does it respect the fact that the partners themselves are the ministers of the sacrament of marriage? Explain.
5. If you were to design the Catholic Church's response to failed marriages, what truths would you try to uphold? Where did you learn these truths? Based on these truths, what would the process you design involve?

Chapter Nine

Teaching Social Justice and Treating Employees Justly

The Church has the God-given mission and the unique capacity to call people to live with integrity, compassion, responsibility, and concern for others. Our seminaries, colleges, schools, and catechetical programs are called to share not just abstract principles but a moral framework for everyday action. The Church's social teaching offers a guide for choices as parents, workers, consumers, and citizens.

—United States Conference of Catholic Bishops, *Sharing Catholic Social Teaching: Challenges and Directions*, 1998

[The] confidential Release and Severance Agreement are confidential, and [the] Employee may not disclose the existence, terms or provisions of this Agreement without the written consent of the Diocese.

—Severance agreement offered to dismissed diocesan employees

The Church cannot redeem the world from the deadening effects of sin and injustice unless it is working to remove sin and injustice in its own life and institutions. All of us must help the Church to practice in its own life what it preaches to others about economic justice and cooperation.

—United States Catholic Bishops, *Economic Justice for All*, par. 24

Catholics can all be very proud of the Catholic Church's teachings on social justice. However, for many people, the credibility of that teaching has been undercut by the fact that the Catholic Church has not always practiced what it preaches. As events have unfolded in dioceses around the country, many Catholics have concluded that the lack of just treatment of Catholic Church employees is a systemic problem in the Catholic Church, one that needs to be named and addressed. Why? Because, as a church, Catholics do not want to be guilty of mistreating others, nor do Catholics want the teaching voice of the Catholic Church to lose its credibility on the important topic of social justice.

In this chapter we will first examine the biblical roots for the Catholic Church's teachings on social justice and then briefly explain the seven major themes of those teachings. We will then, as an example, discuss how those teachings regarding the just treatment of employees were systemically implemented in one diocese and subsequently not followed in the same diocese. We will then discuss what problems and concerns remain.

WHAT DOES SCRIPTURE HAVE TO SAY?

The Catholic Church's teachings in regard to social justice, and more particularly on the just treatment of employees, are the fruit of the Church's applying Scriptural truths to society and to the workplace. The most basic concept is the Catholic Church's understanding of the dignity of each person. Based on the very first story in the Bible, the story of the creation of the world, the Catholic Church understands every human being to have been created in the image of a loving God. Therefore, every person deserves to be treated with great dignity. No human being can ever be regarded as a functionary to carry out an agenda without the employer giving thought to the welfare of that person.

That workers should be treated justly and given a fair wage in a timely manner is an idea that recurs over and over in the Old Testament. In a way, the very rhythm of society revolved around this idea, in that six days were to be devoted to work and the seventh day to the Sabbath rest. Workers were to have one day of every seven free from work to devote to worship of God and personal renewal.

The importance of treating workers justly was part of the Israelites' holiness code (Lev 17:1–26:46). The code begins: "The Lord spoke to Moses, saying: Speak to all the congregation of the people of Israel and say to them:

You shall be holy, for I the Lord your God am holy" (Lev 19:1–2). The code goes on to say, "You shall not defraud your neighbor; you shall not steal; and you shall not keep for yourself the wages of a laborer until morning" (Lev 19:13).

The duty, in justice, to pay workers a fair wage in a timely manner is elaborated upon in Deuteronomy: "You shall not withhold the wages of poor and needy laborers, whether other Israelites or aliens who reside in your land in one of your towns. You shall pay them their wages daily before sunset, because they are poor and their livelihood depends on them; otherwise they might cry to the Lord against you, and you would incur guilt" (Deut 24:14–15). Of course the Israelites knew that God would hear the cry of the poor. As Psalm 34 says: "This poor soul cried, and was heard by the Lord / and was saved from every trouble" (Ps 34:6).

Perhaps the most striking calls for the just treatment of workers can be found in Amos. Amos is outraged because the people of the Northern Kingdom are getting richer and richer while grinding down the poor. Amos berates the people, saying:

> Seek the Lord and live,
> or he will break out against the house of Joseph like fire,
> and it will devour Bethel, with no one to quench it.
> Ah, you that turn justice to wormwood,
> and bring righteousness to the ground! (Amos 5:6–7)

Amos exhorts the people to change their evil ways:

> Seek good and not evil,
> that you may live;
> and so the Lord, the God of hosts, will be with you,
> just as you have said.
> Hate evil and love good,
> and establish justice in the gate;
> it may be that the Lord, the God of hosts,
> will be gracious to the remnant of Joseph. (Amos 5:14–15)

Amos makes it clear that religious observances are meaningless if the people are not treating each other justly:

> I hate, I despise your festivals
> and take no delight in your solemn assemblies.
> Even though you offer me your burnt offerings and grain offerings,
> I will not accept them;
> and the offerings of well-being of your fatted animals

I will not look upon.
Take away from me the noise of your songs;
I will not listen to the melody of your harps.
But let justice roll down like waters,
And righteousness like an ever-flowing stream. (Amos 5:21–24)

Jesus followed in the footsteps of his religious tradition as he taught people that in order to cooperate in the coming of the kingdom of God they must act justly. Like Amos, Jesus railed against religious leaders who paid attention to the minutiae of the law but did not treat others with justice: "Woe to you, scribes and Pharisees, hypocrites! For you tithe mint, dill, and cumin, and have neglected the weightier matters of the law; justice and mercy and faith. It is these you ought to have practiced without neglecting the others" (Matt 23:23).

Justice is rooted in Jesus's overall commandment to love God and neighbor: "'You shall love the Lord your God with all your heart, and with all your soul, and with all your mind.' . . . 'You shall love your neighbor as yourself.' On these two commandments hang all the law and the prophets" (Matt 22:37, 39b). On these commandments also hang all of the Catholic Church's teachings on social justice.

Jesus's command to act lovingly in every relationship was incorporated into household codes. The author of Colossians exhorts the people to act lovingly in every relationship, including those in which one person has authority over another, because they are all beloved by God.

As God's chosen ones, holy and beloved, clothe yourselves with compassion, kindness, humility, meekness, and patience. Bear with one another and, if anyone has a complaint against another, forgive each other; just as the Lord has forgiven you, so you also must forgive. Above all, clothe yourselves with love, which binds everything together in perfect harmony. And let the peace of Christ rule in your hearts, to which indeed you were called in the one body. And be thankful. Let the word of Christ dwell in you richly; teach and admonish one another in all wisdom; and with gratitude in your hearts sing psalms, hymns, and spiritual songs to God. And whatever you do, in word or deed, do everything in the name of the Lord Jesus, giving thanks to God the Father through him. . . . Masters, treat your slaves justly and fairly, for you know that you also have a Master in heaven. (Col 3:12–17, 4:1)

Both the Old and New Testaments are adamant in admonishing those who have authority over others that they also are accountable to authority; they are accountable to God. No amount of obedience to laws or ritual practices pleases God if those who obey and offer sacrifice fail to act justly toward those over whom they have authority.

CATHOLIC SOCIAL TEACHING: WORDS AND ACTIONS

The Catholic Church has an admirable history of being in the forefront of teachings on social justice. From Pope Leo XIII's groundbreaking encyclical *Rerum Novarum* (*On the Condition of Workers*, 1891), through John XXIII's *Mater et Magistra* (*Christianity and Social Progress*, 1961) and *Pacem in Terris* (*Peace on Earth*, 1963), to the 1986 pastoral letter of the United States bishops, *Economic Justice for All* (to name but a few), the Catholic Church has been a world leader in promoting justice for all.

The bishops of the United States have made a concerted effort to integrate Catholic social justice teachings into all levels of education. In 1998 the bishops put out a statement titled *Sharing Catholic Social Teaching: Challenges and Directions*. In this statement the bishops review and explain the major themes of Catholic social teaching. They begin by stating the urgency of their task:

> The Church's social teaching is a rich treasure of wisdom about building a just society and living lives of holiness amidst the challenges of modern society. It offers moral principles and coherent values that are badly needed in our time. In this time of widespread violence and diminished respect for human life and dignity in our country and around the world, the Gospel of life and the biblical call to justice need to be proclaimed and shared with new clarity, urgency, and energy.[1]

The bishops then proceed to name and briefly explain the major themes of Catholic social justice teachings.

The first theme, of course, is the *life and dignity of the human person*. Here the bishops explain that "the dignity of the human person is the foundation of a moral vision for society." The bishops declare: "We believe that every person is precious, that people are more important than things, and that the measure of every institution is whether it threatens or enhances the life and dignity of the human person."

The second major theme is the *call to family, community, and participation*. Here the bishops reiterate that the Catholic "tradition proclaims that the person is not only sacred but also social. How we organize our society—in economics and politics, in law and policy—directly affects human dignity and the capacity of individuals to grow in community." The bishops then go on to affirm that "the family is the central social institution that must be supported and strengthened, not undermined."

The third major theme is *rights and responsibilities*. Emphasizing the importance of both rights and responsibilities, the bishops say: "The Catholic tradition teaches that human dignity can be protected and a healthy community can be achieved only if human rights are protected and responsibilities are met." Individuals have duties and responsibilities "to one another, to our families, and to the larger society." A focus on both personal and social responsibilities is necessary.

The fourth major theme is the *option for the poor and vulnerable*. The bishops remind us that the story of the Last Judgment (Matt 25:31–46) "instructs us to put the needs of the poor and vulnerable first." A basic moral test that we should bring to bear on all decisions is to consider how this particular decision will affect the most vulnerable in our society.

The fifth major theme in Catholic social teaching is the *dignity of work and the rights of workers*. Since, in this chapter, we will be discussing how the Catholic Church treats its own workers we will pay particular attention to this theme. The bishops state their belief that the "economy must serve people, not the other way around." The bottom line cannot take precedence over the rights of workers. Among the rights that the bishops name are "the right to productive work, to decent and fair wages, to organize and join unions, to private property, and to economic initiative."

The sixth major theme is *solidarity*. The bishops quote John Paul II to explain what they mean by solidarity. It is "a firm and persevering determination to commit oneself to the common good; that is to say to the good of all and of each individual, because we are all really responsible for all." We *are* our brother and sister's keepers, and we must not be indifferent to the suffering of others.

The seventh and final theme of Catholic social teaching is *care for God's creation*. The bishops remind us that the "environmental challenge has fundamental moral and ethical dimensions that cannot be ignored. . . . The Catholic tradition insists that we show our respect for the Creator by our stewardship of creation."

The bishops acknowledge that they have not been able to cover all the complexity of Catholic social teaching. They also acknowledge that "there will be legitimate differences and debate over how these challenging moral principles are applied in concrete situations." Nevertheless, every Catholic is called upon to "know and apply these principles in family, economic, and community life."

The bishops then go on to describe the educational challenge with which the Catholic Church is presented. They state:

> The Church has the God-given mission and the unique capacity to call people to live with integrity, compassion, responsibility, and concern for others. Our seminaries, colleges, schools, and catechetical programs are called to share not just abstract principles but a moral framework for everyday action. The Church's social teaching offers a guide for choices as parents, workers, consumers, and citizens.

The Church's social teaching also offers a guide for choices for the bishops themselves as they implement, or fail to implement, Catholic social justice teachings in their own dioceses.

Many bishops have taken very seriously the Catholic Church's responsibility to practice what it preaches when it comes to the just treatment of employees. Others have not. To do so is not an easy task. For many years, women religious, who had taken a vow of poverty, staffed Catholic schools and did not receive just salaries. As the number of women religious went down and lay people took over their responsibilities, parish and diocesan budgets were severely challenged. Many lay employees were paid salaries far lower than were their counterparts in the public schools. In fact, many fully qualified teachers were treated more like volunteers who received a stipend than like professional employees who should be paid a just wage.

In addition, not only school teachers, but parish staff members, whether secretaries or pastoral associates, have often been treated in unjust ways. The clerical culture has played a role in this. If a new pastor comes in, he often feels no obligation, in the name of justice, to the people who have been faithful and competent employees for years. He often feels that he is in charge, and what he says, or what the bishop wants, goes. In the Catholic Church, a diocesan priest's assignment to a particular parish does not depend on a call from the community because of a match between that person's competencies and the parish's needs. Instead, the priest is assigned by the bishop, to whom he has promised obedience. Priests, and even bishops, sometimes function as loyal middle managers, not as shepherds of the flock. Their first concern is loyalty to the hierarchy and to their fellow priests, not the needs of a particular community of faith.

ONE DIOCESE'S STORY

The following is the story of what happened in one diocese. This story is told, not because it is unique, but because it is not unique. Many dioceses around the United States have had similar experiences.

Some twenty-five years after the Second Vatican Council, a diocesan bishop did everything he could to see that the Catholic Church's teachings on social justice were implemented at every level: the diocesan level, the parish level, and the school level.

This bishop was not only asking those accountable to him to teach Catholic social justice to others, but to integrate these teachings into policies that would ensure that the diocese was practicing what it teaches. The diocesan staff was delegated the responsibility to develop and implement policies whose goal was that the diocese would teach social justice, not only by word but by example. The bishop received advice from a number of sources and implemented the following policies:

- All employees were to have a written job description.
- All employees were to have a performance evaluation once a year, based on the job description, using a process approved by the diocese. An employee had to be given the opportunity to discuss and sign the performance evaluation. The evaluation was to become part of the employee's personnel file.
- All employees were to have a contract or a letter of employment that included, among other things, that person's salary and the name of the person to whom that person was accountable. This information was to be forwarded to the Diocesan Finance Office. Employees were to be paid according to a diocesan salary scale that required the payment of a just wage.
- An employee could be dismissed only for sufficient cause. If an employee believed that he or she had been treated unjustly, that person could appeal the dismissal through a grievance procedure.
- Full-time educational employees would earn a minimum of six sick days per year and could accumulate sixty days. When necessary, a sick day could be used to care for a family member.
- Employees were entitled to family and medical leave. This leave would be without pay unless the employee had unused sick days, personal days, or vacation days, in which case those days would be used.

All of these policies were well publicized so that not just priests and administrators, but all employees, knew how employees were to be treated.

If an educational employee had a grievance, it was the responsibility of the secretary of educational ministries to decide the matter. The grievance process was designed to facilitate reconciliation and to maintain unity. Grievances were to be settled as close to the problem as possible. This requirement was based on the principle of subsidiarity that is taught in the encyclical *Quadragesimo Anno* (*On the Reconstruction of the Social Order*, 1931).

The secretary of educational ministries would not get involved in a grievance unless the aggrieved person had first spoken to the person who had offended him or her, and had then moved on up the line of authority with the grievance. This requirement was based on Matthew's Gospel, which says, "If another member of the church sins against you, go and point out the fault, when the two of you are alone" (Matt 18:15–17).

Once a grievance was filed, the secretary of educational ministries was to ask each of the people involved whether or not diocesan policies had been followed. All priests and administrators knew that they could not arbitrarily dismiss people without cause. Personnel evaluations showing that the employee had received feedback and had been offered an opportunity to improve his or her performance were necessary in order for an employee's dismissal to be upheld.

When the bishop who designed and implemented these policies was succeeded by another bishop, actions that many in the diocese thought were not compatible with the Catholic Church's teachings on social justice or with diocesan policy took place. Diocesan employees were not evaluated in the light of their job descriptions. Five lay employees were dismissed, based not on performance but on a "restructuring." The dismissed employees were offered severance packages that demanded secrecy. The confidential release and severance agreement stated that the agreement was confidential and that the employee could not disclose its existence, terms, or provisions. Four of the five dismissed employees were unwilling to agree to secrecy. (This was after the detrimental role that secrecy had played in the child abuse scandals was known by all.)

The original severance agreement demanded that the employee immediately return all information and properties of the employer. Are underlined books, notes, and presentations developed to teach classes the property of the teacher or the employer? If the teacher has no access to them, he or she is at a distinct disadvantage when it comes to teaching in other settings.

The original agreement informed the employee that references would be limited to the job title at the time of termination and the dates of employment. If one has spent one's whole professional life working for one diocese, the diocese dismisses that person without cause, and the diocese then refuses to write that person a letter of recommendation, how is the employee to apply for another job?

The diocese said that sick days used to take care of family members could no longer be used that way. Therefore, the employee's paid, unused vacation days would be reduced to cover the sick days used to take care of family members.

When challenged on these unjust actions that were contrary to diocesan policies, the diocese backed down. However, the process took several months, received both local and national publicity, and severely undercut the Catholic Church's ability to teach social justice.

One might well ask: "Why bring all this up? Why not just move on?" It is true that this experience is over for those five employees who were originally dismissed, but it is not over for many others. The same kind of behavior continues in the diocese described and in other dioceses. Individual people are being let go without cause and without just treatment. Those who have been served by these individuals and those who love them continue to be scandalized and to be very angry. The result is not unity and peace, but division.

The bishops themselves explain why we should not remain silent about injustice in their document *Economic Justice for All*: "The Church cannot redeem the world from the deadening effects of sin and injustice unless it is working to remove sin and injustice in its own life and institutions. All of us must help the Church to practice in its own life what it preaches to others about economic justice and cooperation."[2]

Naming this systemic problem is one way of helping the Catholic Church practice in its own life what it preaches to others.

One of the social justice themes that the bishops want Catholics to emphasize is solidarity. As mentioned earlier, in describing this theme the bishops state:

> Learning to practice the virtue of solidarity means learning that "loving our neighbor" has global dimensions in an interdependent world. This virtue is described by John Paul II as "a firm and persevering determination to commit oneself to the common good; that is to say to the good of all and of each

individual, because we are all really responsible for all." (*Sollicitudo Rei Socialis*, no. 38)[3]

When the diocesan restructuring described in this chapter took place, the diocesan coordinator for peace and justice practiced the virtue of solidarity. Those who called him on the day after the dismissals and heard his voice mail message were told that he was "standing in solidarity with the diocesan employees who have been dismissed. Please leave a message."

By leaving this voice mail on his answering machine, the coordinator for peace and justice was himself leaving a message. That message is that those who love the Catholic Church and want the Church to have a credible teaching voice for themselves, their children, and their grandchildren, must speak up when they see their beloved Catholic Church undercutting the Church's teaching voice by the way in which it treats its own lay employees.

CONTINUING THE CONVERSATION

1. What experience do you have to bring to bear on the Catholic Church's teaching on social justice, either from the inside or the outside?
2. Are the Catholic Church's teachings on social justice well integrated into the educational programs in your diocese? In your parish?
3. Are you involved in living out some of the seven themes of Catholic social justice teaching? How are you involved? If not, how could you become involved?
4. Do the policies and practices in your diocese and in your parish integrate Catholic social justice teachings? How? How not?
5. Do you believe that it is a duty to bring systemic injustices to light? Why or why not?

Chapter Ten

Unity in the Body of Christ

The unity of all divided humanity is the will of God.

—John Paul II, *Encyclical on Commitment to
Ecumenism, Ut Unum Sint,* par. 6

"[Division] openly contradicts the will of Christ, provides a stumbling block to the world and inflicts damage on the most holy cause of proclaiming the good news to every creature."

—John Paul II, *Encyclical on Commitment to Ecumenism,
Ut Unum Sint,* par. 6, quoting the *Decree on Ecumenism,* 1

For all who eat and drink without discerning the body, eat and drink judgment against themselves.

—1 Cor 11:29

I tell you, keep away from these men and let them alone; because if this plan or this undertaking is of human origin, it will fail; but if it is of God, you will not be able to overthrow them—in that case you may even be found fighting against God.

—Gamaliel's advice to the Sanhedrin about what to do
regarding the apostles' preaching about Jesus; Acts 5:38b–39a

Love is patient; love is kind; love is not envious or boastful or arrogant or rude. It does not insist on its own way; it is not irritable or resentful; it does not rejoice in wrongdoing, but rejoices in the truth. It bears all things, believes all things, hopes all things, endures all things. Love never ends.

—Paul to the Corinthians; 1 Cor 13:4–8a

I therefore . . . beg you to lead a life worthy of the calling to which you have been called, with all humility and gentleness, with patience, bearing with one another in love, making every effort to maintain the unity of the Spirit in the bond of peace. There is one body and one Spirit, just as you were called to the one hope of your calling, one Lord, one faith, one baptism, one God and Father of all, who is above all and through all and in all.

—Eph 4:1–6

Divisions in the body of Christ are a scandal and a stumbling block to Christians becoming the witnesses to Jesus Christ and to the Gospel that they are called to be. In this chapter we will discuss two of these divisions: the division between Catholics and other Christians, and the division within the Catholic Church itself. After examining what Scripture has to say and what the Church teaches, we will offer guidelines for how to heal our divisions: reimage truths for a twenty-first-century Church, invite others to Catholic Eucharist, and engage in respectful dialogue.

DIVISIONS BETWEEN ROMAN CATHOLICS AND OTHER CHRISTIANS

For the first millennium of Christianity, some visible degree of unity among Christians existed. The first split in the body of Christ that still exists today was between the Church in the East and the Church in the West in the eleventh century. The second split in the body of Christ that is painfully evident in the United States is the split within Western Christianity, a split that began during the Reformation in the sixteenth century and continues with ever more fragmentation in our own time. Although each of these divisions occurred long after the canon of Scripture reached its present form, what Scripture has to say in relation to divisions among Christians is still extremely relevant.

WHAT DOES SCRIPTURE HAVE TO SAY?

Lack of unity was a problem in the early Church, too, and the New Testament has a good deal to say about it. For instance, Paul, in his first letter to the Corinthians, begs the Corinthians to stop fighting with each other. Paul says: "Now I appeal to you, brothers and sisters, by the name of our Lord Jesus Christ, that all of you be in agreement and that there be no divisions among you, but that you be united in the same mind and the same purpose. For it has been reported to me by Chloe's people that there are quarrels among you" (1 Cor 1:10–11).

Paul reminds the Corinthians that they are already one in Jesus Christ and that Christ is the source of their unity. He says: "The cup of blessing that we bless, is it not a sharing in the blood of Christ? The bread that we break, is it not a sharing in the body of Christ? Because there is one bread, we who are many are one body, for we all partake of the one bread" (1 Cor 10:16–17).

Paul is particularly distressed that the divisions among the Corinthians are evident when the community gathers for Eucharist. Paul says, "For, to begin with, when you come together as a church, I hear that there are divisions among you; and to some extent I believe it. . . . When you come together, it is not really to eat the Lord's supper. For when the time comes to eat, each of you goes ahead with your own supper, and one goes hungry and another becomes drunk" (1 Cor 11:19, 20–21). Paul is outraged that at the very time when the Corinthians are celebrating Eucharist they are failing to take care of the poor in their midst.

After describing Jesus's actions in instituting Eucharist on the night before he died, Paul teaches the Corinthians the significance of receiving the body and blood of Christ: "Whoever, therefore, eats the bread or drinks the cup of the Lord in an unworthy manner will be answerable for the body and blood of the Lord. Examine yourselves, and only then eat of the bread and drink of the cup. For all who eat and drink without discerning the body, eat and drink judgment against themselves" (1 Cor 11:27–29).

When Catholics read this passage, they often understand the words, "without discerning the body" as affirming the Catholic Church's teaching about Christ's actual presence in Eucharist. The bread and wine are not simply symbols; they become the body and blood of Christ. However, Scripture scholars point out that Paul is concerned that people are failing to discern the body of Christ, not in the sacramental elements of bread and wine, but in the living, breathing Church, the Church that has become a reality through baptism and Eucharist. Paul is correcting the Corinthians because the poor in their midst are part of the body of Christ, and the Corinthians are simply ignoring this fact by ignoring the needs of the poor.

The Corinthians were blind to the fact that the poor are part of the body of Christ just as many Catholics have been blind to the fact that those whom Catholics often call "non-Catholics" are part of the body of Christ. Paul is horrified that this blindness should exhibit itself at Eucharist, of all places, the sacrament celebrated in Christ's name to effect and affirm the very unity to which the Corinthians were blind, as revealed by their behavior. Today's divisions between Catholics and other Christians, who Catholics now acknowledge are part of the body of Christ, also exhibit themselves at Eucharist: Catholics do not ordinarily invite these "non-Catholics" to the table. Would Paul be outraged with us, too? (More about this later.)

In 1 Corinthians, Paul then goes on to compare the unity of Christ's body, the Church, to the unity of a physical body. Paul says, "Now there are varieties of gifts, but the same Spirit; and there are varieties of services, but the same Lord; and there are varieties of activities, but it is the same God who activates all of them in everyone. To each is given the manifestation of the Spirit for the common good" (1 Cor 12:4–7).

The diversity of members in the body is a necessary part of God's plan: "But as it is, God arranged the members in the body, each one of them as he chose. If all were a single member, where would the body be? As it is, there are many members, yet one body. The eye cannot say to the hand, 'I have no need of you'" (1 Cor 12:18–21a).

Paul assures the Corinthians that they "are the body of Christ and individually members of it" (1 Cor 12:27). While their gifts differ, one from another, all are for the common good. At the same time, each person should strive for the greatest gift of all: love. "Love is patient; love is kind; love is not envious or boastful or arrogant or rude. It does not insist on its own way" (1 Cor 13:4–5a). Paul is teaching the Corinthians that the unity that is already a fact in their lives because they are all part of the body of Christ is lived out and experienced through love, not through agreement on everything.

The essential importance of unity is also taught in John's Gospel. On the evening before Jesus dies, John pictures Jesus praying not only for his disciples but for "those who will believe in me through their word" (John 17:20b). In other words, John pictures Jesus praying for twenty-first-century Christians. Jesus prays that Christians may all be one.

> As you, Father, are in me and I am in you, may they also be in us, so that the world may believe that you have sent me. The glory that you have given me I have given them, so that they may be one, as we are one, I in them and you in me, that they may become completely one, so that the world may know that you have sent me and have loved them even as you have loved me. (John 17:21–23)

Just as Jesus is one with God, so are we to be one with each other, rooted in the love between Jesus and his Father. Why? John tells us that the reason is "so that the world may know that you have sent me and have loved them even as you have loved me." Christians cannot reveal God's love for God's people, nor be faithful witnesses to Jesus Christ, unless they are one, unless they learn to love one another. They cannot be who they are called to be as Church, the body of Christ giving witness to Christ and to his teaching, if they remain divided.

WHAT DOES THE CATHOLIC CHURCH TEACH?

In chapter 3, "Can Catholic Church Teaching Change?" we discussed how Catholic Church teaching has changed in regard to Catholics' stance toward other Christians. The sea change came in the Second Vatican Council's document *Decree on Ecumenism* (1964) in which the Magisterium acknowledged that "the Spirit of Christ has not refrained from using them [i.e., separated brethren, whether considered as individuals or as communities and churches] as means of salvation."[1]

In addition, Pope John Paul II wrote a prophetic encyclical on ecumenism titled *Ut Unum Sint* ("That All May Be One"), in which he renewed the call to Christian unity. John Paul states that "the commitment to ecumenism must be based upon the conversion of hearts and upon prayer, which will also lead to the necessary purification of past memories."[2] Not only non-Catholics, but "all," including Catholics, are called "to acknowledge with sincere and total objectivity the mistakes made and the contingent factors at work at the origins of [our] deplorable divisions."[3]

The stated goal of ecumenism is that we all be able once more to gather around one Eucharistic table. We are to pray that "the Lord increase the unity of all Christians until they reach full communion."[4] John Paul II goes on to say that "the mission of the bishop of Rome is particularly directed to recalling the need for full communion among Christ's disciples."[5]

The Catholic Church must be committed to ecumenism because "the unity of all divided humanity is the will of God."[6] Quoting the Decree on Ecumenism, John Paul stresses that division "openly contradicts the will of Christ, provides a stumbling block to the world and inflicts damage on the most holy cause of proclaiming the good news to every creature."[7]

The pope then acknowledges that ecumenical discussion may lead to a reform in the way we formulate doctrine. In explaining this point the pope says:

> The unity willed by God can be attained only by the adherence of all to the content of revealed faith in its entirety. In matters of faith, compromise is in contradiction with God, who is truth. In the body of Christ, "the way, and the truth, and the life" (John 14:6), who could consider legitimate a reconciliation brought about at the expense of the truth (par. 18)? . . . Even so, doctrine needs to be presented in a way that makes it understandable to those for whom God himself intends it. . . . The expressions of truth can take different forms. The

renewal of these forms of expression becomes necessary for the sake of trans-
mitting to the people of today the Gospel message in its unchanging meaning. [8]

After explaining the importance of dialogue in the ecumenical movement and
describing some of the progress that has been made, the pope emphasizes the
importance of this progress being received by the whole people of God:

> A new task lies before us: that of receiving the results already achieved. . . .
> We are in fact dealing with issues which frequently are matters of faith, and
> these require universal consent, extending from the Bishops to the lay faithful,
> all of whom have received the anointing of the Holy Spirit. It is the same Spirit
> who assists the Magisterium and awakens the *sensus fidei.* [9]

As he concludes *Ut Unum Sint*, John Paul discusses the role of the papacy in
the ecumenical movement. He says:

> I am convinced that I have a particular responsibility in this regard, above all
> in acknowledging the ecumenical aspirations of the majority of the Christian
> communities and in heeding the request made of me to find a way of exercis-
> ing the primacy which, while in no way renouncing what is essential to its
> mission, is nonetheless open to a new situation. [10]

He prays for himself and for "the pastors and theologians of our churches,
that we may seek the forms in which this ministry may accomplish a service
of love recognized by all concerned."[11]

   In other words, the pope calls Christians to be open to a new understanding, a new way of expressing revealed truth so that it is understandable to the
present age, and a new way of exercising the Petrine role, all in order to
promote and accomplish God's will for God's people: *ut unum sint*—that
Christians may be one.

PROBING THE MYSTERY OF EUCHARIST

When the pope calls Christians to "a new understanding, a new way of
expressing revealed truth," he is not calling upon Christians to change their
basic beliefs. He has already clearly stated that "in matters of faith, compro-
mise is in contradiction with God, who is truth."[12] Rather, the pope is calling
upon Christians to reimage revealed truth so that it is more understandable to
people of our century.

In order to illustrate just what the pope called Christians to do, it may be helpful to discuss just how Catholics have imaged the Catholic belief that Christ is truly present in Eucharist. After we discuss various ways of imaging Christ's presence in Eucharist, we will see if such reimaging might make it possible for the Catholic Church to consider inviting other Christians to the Eucharistic table.

Most Catholics learned to express their beliefs about Eucharist using Greek philosophical categories of thought to define doctrine rather than using the narrative language of Scripture. For instance, the *Baltimore Catechism* for second grade, used to educate Catholic children around the United States for many years in the twentieth century, teaches the following in a question-and-answer format:

Question: When did Christ institute the Holy Eucharist?

Answer: Christ instituted the Holy Eucharist at the Last Supper, the night before He died.

Question: What happened at the Last Supper when Our Lord said: "This is My body . . . this is My blood?"

Answer: When Our Lord said, "This is My body," the bread was changed into His body; and when He said, "This is My blood," the wine was changed into His blood.

Question: Did anything of the bread and wine remain after they had been changed into Our Lord's body and blood?

Answer: After the bread and wine had been changed into Our Lord's body and blood, there remained only the appearances of bread and wine.

Question: What do we mean by the appearances of bread and wine?

Answer: By the appearances of bread and wine we mean their color, taste, weight, and shape. [13]

Baltimore Catechism No. 3 goes on to teach:

Question: What is the change of the entire substance of the bread and wine into the body and blood of Christ called?

Answer: The change of the entire substance of the bread and wine into the body and blood of Christ is called Transubstantiation. [14]

The word *transubstantiation* has been traditionally used by Roman Catholics to express the belief that Jesus Christ is truly present in Eucharist. However, that word did not become a part of the way the Catholic Church passed on its belief in Christ's actual presence until the Fourth Lateran Council in 1215. The word causes ecumenical problems even with other Christians who share the Catholic belief in the real presence because the word is often misunderstood. The categories of thought *substance* and *accident*, which are crucial to an understanding of the word *transubstantiation*, are unknown to many people in the pews. Some think that when Catholics claim that Christ is truly present in the bread and wine they are making a scientific claim. Scientifically, the bread is no longer bread and the wine is no longer wine. This, of course, is not what is being claimed.

Using the word *transubstantiation* to teach Christ's real presence in Eucharist was a reimaging of how to teach the truth behind the words, a moving away from biblical imagery. That was appropriate and helpful in the thirteenth century. In the twenty-first century, such categories of thought may be less helpful.

According to a study by CARA, the Center for Applied Research in the Apostolate at Georgetown University, the number of Catholics who agree that "Jesus Christ is really present in the bread and wine of the Eucharist" has declined. In 2001, 63 percent of Catholics agreed with this statement. By 2008, the number who agreed had dropped to 57 percent. [15] These figures illustrate the ineffectiveness for many in the way the Catholic Church teaches that Christ is truly present in Eucharist.

SCRIPTURE AND EUCHARIST

Instead of using Greek philosophical categories of thought to probe the mystery of Eucharist, the Bible uses a variety of narrative forms. We have already noted Paul's account of Eucharist in his letter to the Corinthians. It is clear that Paul had taught the Corinthians about Christ's real presence when he was with them, because Paul assumes that they have this knowledge. Paul asks: "The cup of blessing that we bless, is it not a sharing in the blood of Christ? The bread that we break, is it not a sharing in the body of Christ?" (1 Cor 10:16). Paul is confident that the answer all will give is yes. Based on this underlying understanding, Paul challenges the Corinthians on their divisive behavior at Eucharist.

Luke's Gospel probes the mystery of Christ's presence in Eucharist from the beginning of his Gospel to the end. As Luke begins, he tells an infancy story in which he pictures Jesus being placed in a manger (Luke 2:7). A manger is, of course, the place where one puts the food for the flock. Luke is teaching that Jesus is food for his flock.[16]

Later, Luke recounts Jesus's last meal with his disciples before he dies, which, in all three synoptic Gospels (Mark, Matthew, and Luke), is the Passover meal. Luke tells us that Jesus "took a loaf of bread, and when he had given thanks, he broke it and gave it to them, saying, 'This is my body, which is given for you. Do this in remembrance of me.' And he did the same with the cup after supper, saying, 'This cup that is poured out for you is the new covenant in my blood'" (Luke 22:19–20).

Finally, Luke tells the story of the two disciples on the road to Emmaus (Luke 24:13–35). The disciples fail to recognize the presence of Christ in the stranger on the road and in the word proclaimed, but they do recognize Jesus in the breaking of the bread.

In John's Gospel, Jesus's last meal with his disciples is not the Passover meal (see John 13:1–20), and John does not recount the story of Jesus instituting Eucharist on that occasion. Rather, in order to teach Jesus's true presence in Eucharist, John pictures Jesus giving his "I Am the Bread of Life" discourse (John 6:22–65). In this discourse Jesus says:

> Very truly I tell you, unless you eat the flesh of the Son of Man and drink his blood, you have no life in you. Those who eat my flesh and drink my blood have eternal life, and I will raise them up on the last day; for my flesh is true food and my blood is true drink. Those who eat my flesh and drink my blood abide in me, and I in them. (John 6:53–56)

We see, then, that inspired biblical authors use many different images and narrative forms to teach a mystery that is beyond our comprehension: the risen Christ is truly present in Eucharist. The concept of transubstantiation is one way to teach the same truth, but certainly not the only way.

THE QUESTION OF INTERCOMMUNION

As stated earlier, today's divisions among Christians, all of whom are members of the body of Christ, are evident at Eucharist. The present position of the Catholic Church is that because Eucharist is a celebration of unity in faith, worship, and ecclesial life, it must not be shared with other Christian churches and ecclesial communities on a regular basis until that unity is achieved.

The Catholic Church's present ecumenical posture in regard to intercommunion is spelled out in the *Directory for the Application of Principles and Norms on Ecumenism* put out by the Pontifical Council for Promoting Christian Unity (1993). This Directory, which is the basis for regional directories, addresses the question of "Sharing Sacramental Life with Christians of Other Churches and Ecclesial Communities." The *Directory* explains that two basic principles must be balanced with each other. The first is:

> A sacrament is an act of Christ and of the Church through the Spirit. Its celebration in a concrete community is the sign of the reality of its unity in faith, worship and community life. As well as being signs, sacraments—most specially the Eucharist—are sources of the unity of the Christian community and of spiritual life, and are means for building them up. Thus Eucharistic communion is inseparably linked to full ecclesial communion and its visible expression. [17]

The second basic principle is:

> The Catholic Church teaches that by baptism members of other Churches and ecclesial communities are brought into a real, even if imperfect communion, with the Catholic Church and that "baptism, which constitutes the sacramental bond of unity existing among all who through it are reborn . . . is wholly directed toward the acquiring of fullness of life in Christ." The Eucharist is, for the baptized, a spiritual food which enables them to overcome sin and to live the very life of Christ, to be incorporated more profoundly in Him and share more intensely in the whole economy of the Mystery of Christ. [18]

Based on these two principles, the Catholic Church teaches that "in general the Catholic Church permits access to its Eucharistic communion . . . only to those who share its oneness in faith, worship, and ecclesial life." At the same time, the Catholic Church "recognizes that in certain circumstances, by way of exception, and under certain conditions, access to these sacraments may be permitted, or even commended, for Christians of other Churches and ecclesial Communities." [19]

A Catholic who agrees with both principles, that the sacrament of Eucharist celebrates unity and effects unity, might well ask: Must sharing Eucharist with other Christians celebrate unity that has already been accomplished, or could it not be a prayer for, and an expression of longing for full unity among Christians who have grown to love one another? Is not love, rather than agreement, the bond of unity? Could not Christians celebrate Eucharist together as a step toward full unity rather than as a celebration of accomplished unity? A basis for such shared Eucharist can be found in Scripture, in the Catholic understanding of sacrament, and in the Eucharistic liturgy itself.

WHAT DOES SCRIPTURE HAVE TO SAY?

As we read the Gospel stories in which Jesus celebrates the first Eucharist with his disciples, we can readily see that the celebration was not one of accomplished unity. In Matthew's account, before Jesus celebrates that first Eucharist, he says to the twelve: "Truly I tell you, one of you will betray me" (Matt 26:21). . . . "Judas, who will betray him, said, 'Surely not I, Rabbi?' He replied, 'You have said so'" (Matt 26:25). It is after this exchange that "Jesus took a loaf of bread, and after blessing it he broke it, gave it to the disciples, and said, 'Take, eat; this is my body'" (Matt 26:26). It appears that Jesus offered Judas Eucharist, knowing that Judas was going to betray him.

Judas was not the only person whom Jesus knew would betray him. After the dinner, when they were at the Mount of Olives, Jesus tells the disciples: "You will all become deserters because of me this night" (Matt 26:31). Peter is positive that he will never desert Jesus. Jesus tells Peter, "Truly I tell you, this very night, before the cock crows, you will deny me three times" (Matt 26:34). It seems that Jesus offered the whole group his body and blood, knowing that the whole group would desert him. Jesus's love for his disciples and his invitation to the disciples did not depend on their worthiness or their agreement. It was freely offered, completely unearned, and without strings. It was a gift offered in love by Christ, not a reward for right thinking or right behavior.

When the Catholic Church celebrates Eucharist in remembrance of Christ, why does it not model itself on Christ? Why does the Catholic Church not invite to Eucharist all who have gathered for worship and who feel called to accept the invitation? To invite only those who agree with the Magisterium, who are already acting and thinking as the Magisterium would have them act and think, seems to be using Eucharist as a tool to manipulate or judge people, not as a gift offered in love by Christ to saint and sinner alike.

THE CATHOLIC UNDERSTANDING OF SACRAMENT

As we mentioned when defining the two principles upon which the Catholic Church's present practice rests, Catholics believe that sacraments effect what they symbolize. As the *Directory for the Application of Principles and Norms on Ecumenism* says, "As well as being signs, sacraments—most specially the Eucharist—are sources of the unity of the Christian community and of spiritual life, and are means for building them up."[20] In addition, "The Eucharist is, for the baptized, a spiritual food which enables them to overcome sin and to live the very life of Christ, to be incorporated more profoundly in Him and share more intensely in the whole economy of the Mystery of Christ."[21]

Given these beliefs, how can Catholics, in Christ's name, exclude from the Eucharistic celebration baptized people who want to receive Eucharist? Does the Catholic Church want to deprive them of the very food they need in order to become more faithful disciples of Jesus Christ? If Eucharist were simply an ineffective sign, the present practice could be supported. But since Catholics believe that Eucharist is an effective sign, are Catholics not defeating their own purpose by denying Eucharist to some who desire it?

THE EUCHARISTIC CELEBRATION

The words of consecration at a Catholic mass add to the argument that Christians who are not Catholic should not be excluded from receiving Eucharist. While presiding at Eucharist, the priest says: "Take this, *all of you*, and eat it. . . . Take this, *all of you*, and drink from it. . . ." The Catholic Church always says "all of you" at the consecration, but the present practice of the Catholic Church does not conform with the words of the prayer. The "all of you" called to Eucharist are not all of those who have gathered to worship together. The Catholic Church un-invites those who do not agree with the Magisterium on some issues, such as the way they explain Christ's presence in Eucharist. The Catholic Church un-invites those who have behaved in ways that the Magisterium does not accept, such as marrying a Catholic without benefit of an annulment. As it now stands, the Catholic Church's liturgical celebration and its present practice are not consistent with each other.

DIVISIONS AMONG ROMAN CATHOLICS

Perhaps even more painful than the divisions among Catholics and other Christians are the divisions among Roman Catholics themselves. These divisions exhibit themselves in actions that are diametrically opposed to the ways in which the Gospel teaches us to treat each other. Examples are threats and intimidation, public disruption of speakers or refusing to allow them to speak at all, misrepresentation of another's thinking, outright lying, even offering money to those in power if one's wishes prevail.

WHAT DOES SCRIPTURE SAY?

During our discussion of the divisions between Catholics and other Christians we quoted many scriptural passages that emphasize the importance of unity among Jesus's disciples. The unity is to be rooted in love. In John's Gospel, Jesus says that love for one another is the preeminent sign that a person is his disciple: "I give you a new commandment, that you love one another. Just as I have loved you, you also should love one another. By this everyone will know that you are my disciples, if you have love for one another" (John 13:34–35).

As we pointed out earlier, Paul, in 1 Corinthians, describes the qualities of love that affect a person's behavior: "Love is patient; love is kind; love is not envious or boastful or arrogant or rude. It does not insist on its own way; it is not irritable or resentful; it does not rejoice in wrongdoing, but rejoices in the truth. It bears all things, believes all things, hopes all things, endures all things. Love never ends" (1 Cor 13:4–8a).

Catholics who intend to act as disciples of Jesus Christ and in service to the truth would do well to compare their tactics to this description of the qualities of love. It is arrogant to think that a person with whom one disagrees has nothing to say that would be helpful to us or to anyone else. We should let the person speak and take Gameliel's advice.

We read Gameliel's wise advice in the Acts of the Apostles. Gameliel was a Pharisee and a member of the Sanhedrin in the earliest days of Christianity when the apostles were preaching about Jesus, much to the Sanhedrin's dismay. The question before the Sanhedrin was what to do about the apostles. Should they be imprisoned again? Gameliel advises the Sanhedrin to leave the apostles alone and not to try to silence them. He says: "I tell you, keep away from these men and let them alone; because if this plan or this undertaking is of human origin, it will fail; but if it is of God, you will not be able to overthrow them—in that case you may even be found fighting against God" (Acts 5:38b–39a). If Catholics take Gameliel's advice they will refrain from using deception or rude and arrogant behavior to stop another person from being heard.

However, Gameliel's advice does not help Catholics bring some sort of healing to a painful division in the Catholic Church. To leave someone alone is not to be reconciled. When people who live in the same community or worship in the same parish are at odds over their beliefs, the divisions are painful not only for the those involved, but for the community as a whole. How are such divisions to be healed?

Matthew, who was writing to settled communities, addresses this question. He pictures Jesus telling the disciples what steps to take when a person believes that he or she has been sinned against:

> If another member of the church sins against you, go and point out the fault when the two of you are alone. If the member listens to you, you have regained that one. But if you are not listened to, take one or two others along with you, so that every word may be confirmed by the evidence of two or three witnesses. If the member refuses to listen to them, tell it to the church; and if the offender refuses to listen even to the church, let such a one be to you as a Gentile and a tax collector. (Matt 18:15–17)

This advice ends on an ironic note, because Jesus taught his fellow Jews to love even the Gentiles (people like most present-day Christians!) and the tax collectors. Matthew, in picturing Jesus speaking to his disciples in this way, is teaching his fellow Jews that if they do their best to reconcile with someone, and all their efforts fail, they have to simply accept the situation for the time being. No one can reconcile with a person who has no desire to be reconciled.

Jesus is pictured as saying something similar to the disciples when they are commissioned to teach in Jesus's name. Jesus says, "If anyone will not welcome you or listen to your words, shake off the dust from your feet as you leave that house or town" (Matt 10:14). In this passage Jesus is simply saying that people's time is not well spent beating their heads against a wall.

Christians are to do their best to reconcile. They are to do their best to teach what they understand to be the truth. If people do not accept it, they are to move on. They are not to spend their time arguing with, or trying to silence, those with whom they disagree.

DIALOGUE

If one person wants to reconcile or come to agreement and another does not, the person who wants to reconcile is wise to back off, pray for reconciliation, and be patient. However, if both people want to reconcile, but each passionately believes things with which the other passionately disagrees, even finds abhorrent, what can be done? One answer is dialogue.

Some very helpful guidelines for dialogue appear in Michael Kinnamon's book, *Truth and Community: Diversity and Its Limits in the Ecumenical Movement.*[22] His guidelines are helpful not only in ecumenical settings, but in Catholic settings. What follows is an adaptation of some of his ecumenical guidelines to a Catholic context.

- Dialogue must have a spiritual orientation. Each person must enter the dialogue open to new understanding and conversion. (If a person's attitude is "I am right and you are wrong," then dialogue cannot occur. A willingness to grow, to understand things to which one has previously been blind, is essential. The desired fruit of dialogue is mutual growth, not victory.)
- In dialogue each person must be given the right to define his or her own understanding. (People often misrepresent the thinking of those with whom they disagree and then argue against their own misunderstanding. They do not realize, or do not acknowledge, that they are misrepresenting the other person's views. Those who do understand the other person's point of view know that the critics are arguing against a straw man [straw person?] of their own construction.)
- Be willing to separate essentials from nonessentials. (Catholics tend to divide over nonessential issues. The essentials are the beliefs that we profess in the Creed. Examples of nonessentials are: Who washes the chalices after Eucharist? What role does Eucharistic adoration have in the spirituality of this parish? Differences over nonessentials need not cause division.)
- Interpret the faith of the person with whom one disagrees in the best light, not the worst light. (In order to do this, one may find Paul's analogy of the body very helpful [see 1 Cor 12:12–27]. For instance, when one person encounters another who appears to be ruled by law [inflexible], not love [flexible], and who rails against the pilgrim Church's growing into a new way of understanding eternal truths in the light of new knowledge, that person can remind himself or herself that the body needs both bones

[inflexible] and skin [flexible]. The skin cannot say to the bones: "I do not need you.")

- While Catholics are trying to reach agreement, or at least mutual understanding on issues, they should strive to find ways to be faithful disciples in action together. (People do not have to agree intellectually on the Catholic approach to Scripture in order to pray together or to feed the hungry together.)

Dialogue is difficult, and it takes patience. However, if people persevere, if they refuse to leave the table and continue to remind themselves that they are called to love one another, dialogue can be the stepping-stone to new understanding and visible unity.

Dialogue will help Catholics respond to this plea in Ephesians:

> I therefore . . . beg you to lead a life worthy of the calling to which you have been called, with all humility and gentleness, with patience, bearing with one another in love, making every effort to maintain the unity of the Spirit in the bond of peace. There is one body and one Spirit, just as you were called to the one hope of your calling, one Lord, one faith, one baptism, one God and Father of all, who is above all and through all and in all. (Eph 4:1–6)

Catholics are not called to bully and misrepresent their adversaries, even if they think they are doing so in the service of truth. Rather, Catholics are called to speak the truth in love. As Ephesians says: "But speaking the truth in love, we must grow up in every way into him who is the head, into Christ, from whom the whole body, joined and knit together by every ligament with which it is equipped, as each part is working properly, promotes the body's growth in building itself up in love" (Eph 4:15–16).

How are Catholics to grow ecumenically and in union with each other? Perhaps thinking of themselves as one family of faith might be helpful. Jesus called God *Abba* ("Father, Daddy"), not to say that God is male, but to say that his (and his followers') relationship with God is intimate and loving, like that between a parent and a child. Jesus taught us that we are all God's children, we are all brothers and sisters to each other. We do not have to agree on everything, but we do have to love one another.

Any parent would find it very distressing if his or her children disagreed so much that they wouldn't talk to each other, honor each other, cooperate with each other, and celebrate family unity at family meals together. After all, the children are brothers and sisters, children of the same parents, whether they admit it or not. They are one family. They need to find ways to live in fidelity to that unity.

The same is true of the divisions within the body of Christ. Christians are already children of the same God and, by baptism, members of the one body of Christ, the Church. Christians are called to overcome their divisions and to love one another. Only when Christians have accomplished this can they be faithful disciples of Christ and witnesses of God's love to the world.

CONTINUING THE CONVERSATION

1. When you use the word *Church*, to what are you referring? An individual congregation? The Catholic Church? The whole body of Christ? Explain.
2. Do you think the divisions within Christianity are a stumbling block to our fulfilling our mission as a Church? Explain.
3. Have you experienced divisions within the Catholic Church? If so, what caused the divisions? Were the divisions over essentials? Explain.
4. Have you ever followed the advice in Matthew (see Matt 18:15–17) about what to do if someone has sinned against you? If so, what happened? If not, why not?
5. Do you have any experience with dialogue as a way of healing divisions? What behaviors on the part of each person do you think are necessary for dialogue to be successful?

Conclusion

As we conclude *Why the Catholic Church Must Change*, we return to the question that we posed in the introduction: What can the Catholic Church do "to restore the luster, the credibility, the beauty of the [Catholic] Church 'ever ancient, ever new?'"[1] Remember, the United States Conference of Catholic Bishops is asking itself this same question. The answer to the question is of utmost importance because it will affect not only the future of the institutional Catholic Church, but also the lives of millions of Christians who seek to know God's will, and who listen to what the Catholic Church teaches as part of discerning God's will.

Having posed this question and having suggested changes in three areas of teaching (contraception, women's ordination, and homosexuality) and in four areas of practice (strategies to abolish abortion, annulments, unjust treatment of lay employees, and divisive actions in the body of Christ), we will conclude by looking for root causes of the Catholic Church's present loss of credibility in the minds and hearts of at least one-third of those who were raised Catholic (see the introduction). What are the underlying attitudes and behaviors in the leadership of the Catholic Church that are contributing to the Catholic Church's present loss of credibility? I believe there are six characteristics of present Catholic Church culture that need to be named and discussed, all of which have surfaced in our previous discussions on specific topics.

THE ORDAINED'S RESISTANCE TO LEARNING FROM THE NONORDAINED

First, there appears to be a resistance on the part of ordained Catholic leaders, including the Magisterium, to listen and learn from nonordained people. This behavior was definitely operative in the debate about contraception that preceded the publication of *Humanae Vitae*. One pope put a commission in place for the purpose of seeking the wisdom of the laity, and another pope changed the commission's membership, changed the role of the commission, and rejected the commission's advice (see chapter 4).

This resistance seems to be operative in the question of whether or not homosexuality is a disorder. Psychiatrists claim it is not a mental illness. A homosexual orientation is not a physical illness. If a person can live, love, and flourish once that person's sexual orientation is accepted, why does learning this information based on experience not affect the teaching of the Catholic Church (see chapter 6)?

The Magisterium's apparent unwillingness to listen and learn from nonordained people is also evident in other settings. For instance, in the United States, when the nation was discussing the Affordable Care Act, the Catholic Health Association and the United States Conference of Catholic Bishops (USCCB) were not in agreement on whether or not to support the legislation. The Catholic Health Association did support it; the bishops did not. The disagreement was not about Catholic Church teaching, but about prioritizing various teachings and gauging the effect of the legislation once it was implemented. Following the disagreement, the president of the USCCB criticized the Catholic Health Association for its public position. Are only the bishops to advise Catholics on public policy in a pluralistic society? Since the topic was not about teaching faith or morals, but about how to remain faithful to Catholic teaching in a legislative matter, why were Catholics not encouraged to hear both voices?

The name often given to this sense of superiority on the part of the ordained is *clericalism*. It seems that many ordained people believe, precisely because they are ordained, that they have more access to truth than do those who are not ordained. They regard access to truth as a grace of the sacrament of ordination. They view their ordained state as a privileged class.

This exalted view of priesthood appeared in a column in a diocesan newspaper as the Year of the Priest (2009–2010) came to a close. The author of the article, referring to the Curé of Ars (St. John Vianney [d. 1859], a French parish priest), said:

> Explaining to his parishioners the importance of the sacraments, he [the Curé of Ars] would preach: "Without the Sacrament of Holy Orders we would not have the Lord. Without the priest the passion and death of our Lord would be of no avail. Who put Christ there in the tabernacle? The priest. Who welcomed your soul at the beginning of your life? The priest. Who feeds your soul and gives it strength for its journey? The priest. Who will prepare it to appear before God, bathing it one last time in the blood of Christ? The priest. And if the soul should happen to die as a result of sin, who will raise it up? The priest. After God, the priest is everything. Only in heaven will he fully realize what he is."[2]

The author went on to comment:

> To some ears the Curé's words might sound excessively pietistic. I believe his words reveal his supreme awe before the sacraments, especially the Most Holy Eucharist. He was not bragging before his congregation about his priesthood: he was begging them to accept the truth. This is not shameful clericalism; this is unashamed Catholicism.[3]

While the author of the article claims that the focus of the Curé of Ars was on the sacraments, particularly the Eucharist, the article itself was addressing the importance of priesthood. In that context, the ideas expressed are not pietistic but blatantly clerical.

To say that "without the Sacrament of Holy Orders we would not have the Lord" is simply untrue. Did Christians in the first two centuries not have the Lord because they did not have ordained priests? Do only those Christians who celebrate the Sacrament of Ordination have the Lord? The Catholic Church certainly does not teach that this is the case. In Matthew, does not Jesus say: "For where two or three are gathered in my name, I am there among them" (Matt 18:20)?

To say that without the priest the passion and death of our Lord would be of no avail is also untrue. Paul, in his letter to the Galatians, talks about what circumstances might make Jesus's death of no avail. Paul says: "If justification comes through the law, then Christ died for nothing" (Gal 2:21b). Paul is teaching the Galatians that people are not saved by their own works, but by faith in Jesus Christ: "We ourselves are Jews by birth and not Gentile sinners; yet we know that a person is justified not by the works of the law but through faith in Jesus Christ" (Gal 2:15–16). It is faith in Jesus Christ, not the presence of a priest, that makes Jesus's passion and death efficacious in a person's life.

In addition, the Catholic Church teaches that Christ's saving actions can be effective in the life of a person who is not Christian. The Second Vatican Council's *Declaration on the Relation of the Church to Non-Christian Religions* (*Nostra Aetate*, 1965), states: "All men form but one community. This is so because all stem from the one stock which God created to people the entire earth (cf. Acts 17:26), and also because all share a common destiny, namely God. His providence, evident goodness, and saving design extend to all men."[4]

The document then refers us to several biblical passages, including Romans 2:6–7: "For he [God] will repay according to each one's deeds: to those who by patiently doing good seek for glory and honor and immortality, he will give eternal life" (Rom 2:6–7).

Neither Paul nor the Second Vatican Council would agree that God's saving power through Christ is ineffective, is "of no avail," without a priest. If a priest really believes that next to God, he is everything, it is no wonder that he doesn't expect to learn anything from people who are not ordained.

How very different this clerical vision of Church is from the vision that Paul gives us. Comparing the Church to a human body, Paul says:

> For just as the body is one and has many members, and all the members of the body, though many, are one body, so it is with Christ. For in the one Spirit we were all baptized into one body—Jews or Greeks, slaves or free—and we were all made to drink of one Spirit.
>
> Indeed, the body does not consist of one member but of many. If the foot would say, "Because I am not a hand, I do not belong to the body," that would not make it any less a part of the body. And if the ear would say, "Because I am not an eye, I do not belong to the body," that would not make it any less a part of the body. If the whole body were an eye, where would the hearing be? If the whole body were hearing, where would the sense of smell be? But as it is, God arranged the members in the body each one of them, as he chose. If all were a single member, where would the body be? As it is, there are many members, yet one body. The eye cannot say to the hand, "I have no need of you," nor again the head to the feet, "I have no need of you." . . .
>
> Now you are the body of Christ and individually members of it. (1 Cor 12:12–21, 27)

The view of the Church that Paul gives us is neither hierarchical nor clerical. Rather, it is collaborative and service oriented. Gifts are given to all for the good of all. No role is so unique or important that without someone in that role the gathered community, the body of Christ, would be separated from the Lord. Nobody in any role can say to someone in a different role, "I do not need you."

This resistance on the part of the present Magisterium to be in a mutually enriching dialogue with the nonordained is in contradiction to Scripture and is in contradiction to what the Catholic Church believes and teaches. In Catholic teaching, part of the process of discerning truth involves the *sensus fidei*, the sense of the faithful (see chapter 1). To refuse to listen to advice from people who have knowledge that has been gained from experience, particularly that experience to which the Magisterium has had no personal access, is to open the Magisterium up to significant error.

PROTECTING THE AUTHORITY AND REPUTATION OF THE INSTITUTION

Also present in the leadership of today's Catholic Church is a pattern of behavior aimed at protecting the authority and reputation of the institution before giving witness to the truth or protecting the well-being of an individual person. A desire to protect the authority of the institution seems to be behind the Magisterium's resistance to changing a present teaching in the light of new knowledge, such as the teaching on contraception. In this instance, priests who disagreed with the teaching were called to act in obedience no matter what they personally believed, thus placing loyalty to the institution above serving those whom God had placed in their care (see chapter 4).

Obedience is stressed more than truth speaking at every level of the institution. Bishops are not to break their unity by publicly disagreeing. Priests and deacons promise to obey their bishops. To speak up if one sincerely disagrees is greatly discouraged, even punished. In fact, in 2011, a bishop in Australia, William Morris, was forced to resign, evidently because he had suggested that one solution to the priest shortage might be to consider the possibility of ordaining women.

Another sad example of these efforts to protect the authority and reputation of the institution over all else is the reaction of those in leadership to the child sex abuse scandal in the Catholic Church. The responsibility for this tragedy's becoming as pervasive as it has been rests not just on the misdeeds of the abusers but on the misdeeds of the administrators who kept the crimes secret and reassigned abusive priests to other locations. It seems undeniable that in this instance, the reputation of the institution and the reputation of the priests were more important than the welfare of the children.

This choice to protect the institution rather than the marginalized and perhaps powerless person flies in the face of the Gospel. As we have discussed over and over, the core of Jesus's teaching is love of God and love of individual people, who, Christians believe, are of great dignity because each has been made in the image of God. It is against Catholic teaching to consider the reputation of the institutional Catholic Church more important than the truth and more important than the welfare of those whom the Church is called to serve.

EXERTING AUTHORITY OVER INDIVIDUAL CONSCIENCES

A third type of behavior that has become evident in this *necessary conversation* is the attempt on the part of some in authority to try to impose their will on others and, in doing so, to trample on the consciences of those whom they are supposed to be teaching and serving. We see this in *Humanae Vitae*, when couples and priests are asked to obey the teaching authority of the Magisterium even if they personally disagree with the teaching (see chapter 4). We see it in the advice given to the parents of homosexual children (see chapter 6). We see it in the Magisterium's strategies to abolish abortion when individual bishops threaten to deprive Eucharist to politicians who do not support that bishop's political agenda (see chapter 7).

This behavior shows up in other aspects of Catholic parish life as well. For instance, despite canons 748 and 752 (discussed in our introduction), some bishops and some parish priests conduct themselves as if Catholics are required to submit both their wills and their intellects to teachings, even if the Magisterium cannot claim that the teachings have been taught as infallible and even if the person, in good conscience, cannot assent. Some of these ordained leaders are trying to enforce their will on their flock by requiring lay people to take a fidelity oath or make a promise of orthodoxy in order to serve in various roles in their parishes. These actions are coercive. They do not respect the consciences of the people involved.

According to the *National Catholic Reporter*, one diocesan bishop, in order to assure himself that "those who serve in official capacities hold interior positions consistent with church teachings,"[5] required those who served at mass to sign an Affirmation of Personal Faith. If a person was unable or unwilling to sign this affirmation, saying that he or she agrees on issues such as homosexuality and contraception, that person was no longer invited to participate in parish ministries.

If a person in the privacy of his or her heart disagrees with a noninfallible teaching, and if that person feels called to serve the Catholic Church as a lector or Eucharistic minister, why can the person not do so? Such roles offer no opportunity for public dissent. Nor does fulfilling those roles call into question the integrity of that person. It is not Christ's presence in the Word proclaimed or in the Eucharist that they doubt.

These fidelity oaths are, on occasion, being required of volunteer catechists. Obviously, a volunteer catechist should not use the position entrusted to him or her by the Catholic Church to teach anything contrary to what the Catholic Church teaches. To have a policy stating this, and to enforce this policy, is a wise and responsible thing to do. Parents do not send their children to parish religious education programs to learn the personal opinions of the teacher, but to learn the teachings and traditions of the Catholic Church.

However, to have such a policy is quite different than to ask a person to adhere with religious submission of will and intellect to noninfallible teachings. If a person disagrees with the Catholic Church's teaching on contraception, and at the same time feels called to teach a grade school religious education class, where is the danger of contradiction? Obviously, the topic of contraception will not be part of the curriculum. To have a policy that protects the integrity of a catechetical program is appropriate. To require a fidelity oath that violates the integrity of the catechist is not.

In addition, to encourage people to submit intellect and will to noninfallible teachings with which they disagree is to ask them to do something against Catholic Church teaching. This is a similar tactic to the one used in the twentieth century when all who were being ordained were required to take the Oath Against Modernism (see chapter 3). Such tactics exert authority rather than employ persuasive teaching. To use coercive authority is not conducive to giving witness to Jesus Christ or to his good news.

When it comes to faith, the Catholic Church teaches adults to be truth seekers, not to remain unquestioning, obedient children for their entire lives (see the introduction). In order to treat people with dignity and in a manner that will bear good fruit, those in authority must remember the characteristics of adult learners. Neither coercion nor the imposition of authority aids a self-directed adult learner. Rather, those who hope to serve adults in an effective manner must honor the experiences and competencies of their adult parishioners and must encourage, rather than discourage, questions and dialogue.

PREJUDICE AGAINST WOMEN

Also undercutting the credibility of the teaching voice of the Catholic Church is a manifest but unacknowledged discomfort with, and suspicion of, women. The most obvious example is the Magisterium's refusal to consider ordaining women, despite the evidence from Scripture that women served the early Church as deacons. This deep-seated preference to have men in ministerial roles reappears as male deacons take over roles that women have held for years, the roles having been duly delegated by a local bishop (see chapter 5).

This prejudice against women in Church leadership roles appears not only in Catholic documents like *Inter Insigniores* but in the way women are routinely treated in Catholic Church settings. One can't but think of the Vatican's actions to gain more control over the Leadership Conference of Women Religious, a group that represents about 80 percent of the women religious in the United States.

Instead of engaging the women religious in dialogue, the Magisterium simply announced corrective measures. It seems that women in ministry in the Catholic Church are always to function at the direction of ordained men. Their own life experiences, their own responses to the call of the Spirit, are suspect if their actions are not an extension of the decisions and the agenda of the Magisterium. The Sacred Congregation for the Doctrine of the Faith made this clear in its "Doctrinal Assessment of the Leadership Conference of Women Religious." The assessment says:

> Some speakers claim that dissent from the doctrine of the Church is justified as an exercise of the prophetic office. But this is based upon a mistaken understanding of the dynamic of prophecy in the Church: it justifies dissent by positing the possibility of divergence between the Church's Magisterium and a "legitimate" theological intuition of some of the faithful. "Prophecy," as a methodological principle, is here directed *at* the Magisterium and the Church's pastors, whereas true prophecy is a grace which accompanies the exercise of the responsibilities of the Christian life and ministries within the Church regulated and verified by the Church's faith and teaching office. [6]

In other words, the Magisterium does not see itself as the proper object of a prophetic voice but only as the speaker of a prophetic voice. Such a statement, addressed to the Leadership Conference of Women Religious, reveals an unwillingness to be open to change in some Catholic teachings, and particularly to be challenged to change by women.

As we have discussed, the exclusion of women from ordained roles is not supported by Scripture (see chapter 5). Scripture cannot legitimately be used to proof text that women cannot be ordained. Neither can the refusal of those with duly delegated authority to accept the charismatic gifts of others be supported by Scripture (see chapter 1). Peter accepted Paul, whom he did not initially appoint, and learned from Paul's life experience. Peter (authority) and Paul (charismatic gifts) engaged in dialogue.

It seems that the Catholic Church is still in the process of learning what Paul meant when he said that in Christ we are no longer male or female: "As many of you as were baptized into Christ have clothed yourselves with Christ. There is no longer Jew or Greek, there is no longer slave or free, there is no longer male and female; for all of you are one in Christ Jesus" (Gal 3:27–28). This profound insight has eventually had a bearing on Christians' view of other races and Christians' view of slavery, but it has not yet affected the way in which the Magisterium regards women and their God-given gifts.

A HESITANCY TO REIMAGE TRUTHS IN THE LIGHT OF NEW KNOWLEDGE

Another behavior that is causing the Catholic Church to lose credibility in the eyes of many is its slowness to reimage truths in the light of new knowledge, both new scientific knowledge and new knowledge based on the work of Catholic biblical scholars. In this book we have discussed the necessity to reimage truths in relation to what we teach about human beings' origin and what we mean by "original sin," based on the story of Adam and Eve (see chapter 3). We have also discussed how, as we probe the mystery of Christ's true presence in Eucharist, we might more effectively use biblical images than Greek philosophical categories of thought, like transubstantiation (see chapter 10).

This need to reimage truths in the light of new knowledge is part of the process of revelation. Wisdom literature performed this indispensable role for the Jews of the diaspora. Thomas Aquinas reimaged truths using Greek philosophical categories of thought. The Catholic Church must participate in this process in the twenty-first century. Heaven and hell may have to be reimaged as descriptions of relationships rather than of places. The resurrection of the body may have to be reimaged so that "body" is not equated with "flesh" (see chapter 7). The Magisterium must not ignore Pope John Paul II's admonition to keep "informed of scientific advances in order to examine if such be necessary, whether or not there are reasons for taking them into account" in the Catholic Church's teaching (see chapter 3).[7]

A HESITANCY TO ADMIT THAT THE CATHOLIC CHURCH IS NOT A FINISHED PRODUCT

Finally, in order to maintain credibility in the twenty-first century, the Magisterium must not resist or try to hide the fact that the Catholic Church is a pilgrim Church. Catholics express this belief at mass in Eucharistic Prayer III when they pray: "Be pleased to confirm in faith and charity your pilgrim Church on earth." It seems that to think of the Catholic Church and its teachings as a pilgrim Church, as people on a journey, is a great paradigm shift for many Catholics. Not knowing Church history and being resistant to change, they deny the possibility that the Catholic Church could change a long-standing teaching.

It is true that core teachings will never change, although the expressions of those teachings may change. However, many moral teachings are applications of core concepts to particular social settings. The core teaching is Christ's command that we always act lovingly toward others. However, the answer to the question, "What is the loving thing to do in this particular situation?" can change over time, given new circumstances.

Vatican II's *Dogmatic Constitution on the Church* (*Lumen Gentium*), says the following about the pilgrim Church:

> The Church, to which we are all called in Christ Jesus, and in which by the grace of God we acquire holiness, will receive its perfection only in the glory of heaven, when will come the time of the renewal of all things (Acts 3:21). . . . Already the final age of the world is with us (cf. 1 Cor. 10:11) and the renewal of the world is irrevocably under way; it is even now anticipated in a certain real way, for the Church on earth is endowed already with a sanctity that is real though imperfect. However, until there be realized new heavens and a new earth in which justice dwells (cf. 2 Pet. 3:13), the pilgrim church, in its sacraments and institutions, which belong to this present age, carries the mark of this world which will pass, and she herself takes her place among the

creatures which groan and travail yet and await the revelation of the sons of God. (cf. Rom. 8:19–22)[8]

There has never been a time when God's people were not in a growth process in regard to understanding God's will for God's people. Both the Old and New Testaments model a growth process (see chapter 2). Church history over the centuries models a growth process. Today's Catholic Church is involved in a growth process. To resist growth, to resist new understandings, is to resist the Holy Spirit.

Since the Catholic Church is a pilgrim Church it must continue to remain open to change, to growth, in some of its teachings and in some of its practices. Only then will the Catholic Church become the Church that God is calling it to be in the twenty-first century.

Come, Holy Spirit, come.

Acknowledgments

A number of people have helped me in the preparation of this manuscript by reading one or all of the chapters and offering valuable feedback, by helping with formatting footnotes and bibliography, or by helping with technical problems. To each of you I offer a heartfelt thank-you:

Don Ralph
Tony Ralph
Debbie Warren Ralph
Sister Helen Garvey
Beth Rompf
Barbara Murray
Nancy de Flon
Barbara Pfeifle
Ben Wyatt

To each of you I say: "I thank my God every time I remember you, constantly praying with joy in every one of my prayers for all of you, because of your sharing in the gospel from the first day until now" (Phil 1:3–5).

Notes

INTRODUCTION

1. Thomas Reese, "The Hidden Exodus: Catholics Becoming Protestant," *National Catholic Reporter*, April 18, 2011, http://ncronline.org/news/faith-parish/hidden-exodus-catholics-becoming-protestants (accessed July 2, 2012).

2. Timothy M. Dolan, "Archbishop Dolan Presidential Speech to USCCB Fall Meeting," November 14, 2011, Unapologetically Catholic, http://rootofjesse2.wordpress.com/2011/11/18/archbishop-dolan-presidential-speech-to-usccb-fall-meeting (accessed July 2, 2012).

3. Reese, "The Hidden Exodus."

4. Catholics United for the Faith, "No Bull: Papal Authority and Our Response," Faith Facts, http://www.cuf.org/faithfacts/details_view.asp?ffid=115 (accessed February 14, 2011).

5. Richard P. McBrien, *Catholicism* (Minneapolis: Winston Press, 1970), 995.

6. Richard M. Gula, *Reason Informed by Faith: Foundations of Catholic Morality* (Mahwah, NJ: Paulist Press, 1989), 226.

7. Gula, *Reason Informed by Faith*, 241.

8. Code of Canon Law, c748, in *The Code of Canon Law: A Text and Commentary*, ed. James A. Coriden et al. (Mahwah, NJ: Paulist Press, 1985), 547.

9. James A. Coriden, "Book III: The Teaching Office of the Church," in *The Code of Canon Law*, ed. James A. Coriden et al.

10. Code of Canon Law, c752 in *The Code of Canon Law*, ed. James A. Coriden et al., 548.

11. Coriden, *The Code of Canon Law*, 548.

12. Code of Canon Law, c750, in *The Code of Canon Law*, ed. James A. Coriden et al., 547.

13. Coriden, *The Code of Canon Law*, 547.

1. THE ROLE OF THE TEACHING CATHOLIC CHURCH IN OUR SEARCH TO KNOW GOD AND GOD'S WILL

1. Vatican Council II, *Dogmatic Constitution on the Church, Lumen Gentium* (November 21, 1964), par. 12, in *Vatican Council II: The Conciliar and Post Conciliar Documents*, vol. 1, ed. Austin Flannery et al., rev. ed. (Collegeville, MN: Liturgical Press, 1992), 363.

2. Vatican Council II, *Dogmatic Constitution on the Church, Lumen Gentium*, par. 25, in Flannery et al., *Vatican Council II*, 380.

3. Vatican Council II, *Dogmatic Constitution on the Church, Lumen Gentium*, par. 25, in Flannery et al., *Vatican Council II*, 380.

4. Sacred Congregation for the Doctrine of the Faith, *Declaration in Defense of the Catholic Doctrine on the Church against Certain Errors of the Present Day, Mysterium Ecclesiae* (June 24, 1973), sec. 5, http://www.saint-mike.org/library/curia/congregations/faith/mysterium_ecclesiae.html (accessed August 14, 2012).

5. Vatican Council II, *Pastoral Constitution on the Church in the Modern World, Gaudium et Spes* (December 7, 1965), par. 16, in Flannery et al., *Vatican Council II*, 916.

6. Vatican Council II, *Pastoral Constitution on the Church in the Modern World, Gaudium et Spes*, par. 17, in Flannery et al., *Vatican Council II*, 917.

7. Tertullian, *Prescription against Heretics*, quoted in Elaine Pagels, *The Origin of Satan* (New York: Random House, 1995), 164.

2. THE ROLE OF EXPERIENCE AND THE ROLE OF SCRIPTURE IN OUR SEARCH TO KNOW GOD AND GOD'S WILL

1. Vatican Council II, *Dogmatic Constitution on Divine Revelation, Dei Verbum* (November 18, 1965), par. 21, in *Vatican Council II: The Conciliar and Post Conciliar Documents*, vol. 1, rev. ed., ed. Austin Flannery et al. (Collegeville, MN: Liturgical Press, 1992), 762.

2. *Catechism of the Catholic Church* (Washington, DC: United States Catholic Conference, 1994), 110.

3. CAN CATHOLIC CHURCH TEACHING CHANGE?

1. A. J. Wilwerding, *Examination of Conscience for Boys and Girls* (Saint Louis, MO: The Queen's Work, 1927), 2.

2. Aloysius J. Heeg, *The Illustrated Catechism: A Practical Presentation of the Official Text of the Baltimore Catechism No. 1* (St. Louis, MO: The Queen's Work, 1958), 15.

3. Heeg, *The Illustrated Catechism*, 45.

4. Heeg, *The Illustrated Catechism*, 46.

5. Boniface XIII, Papal Bull *Unam Sanctam* (November 18, 1302), quoted in Richard P. McBrien, *Catholicism* (Minneapolis: Winston Press, 1970), 626.

6. Vatican Council II, *Decree on Ecumenism, Unitatis Redintegratio* (November 21, 1964), par. 3, in *Vatican Council II: The Conciliar and Post Conciliar Documents*, vol. 1, ed. Austin Flannery et al. (Collegeville, MN: Liturgical Press, 1992), 455.

7. Vatican Council II, *Decree on Ecumenism, Unitatis Redintegratio*, in Flannery et al., *Vatican Council II*, 456.

8. Vatican Council II, *Decree on Ecumenism, Unitatis Redintegratio*, par. 4, in Flannery et al., *Vatican Council II*, 457.

9. Vatican Council II, *Decree on Ecumenism, Unitatis Redintegratio*, par. 4, in Flannery et al., *Vatican Council II*, 457.

10. Pius X, *Encyclical on the Doctrines of the Modernists, Pascendi Dominici Gregis* (August 9, 1907), http://www.vatican.va/holy_father/pius_x/encyclicals/documents/hf_p-x_enc_19070908_pascendi-dominici-gregis_en.html (accessed April 16, 2009).

11. Pius X, *Encyclical on the Doctrines of the Modernists, Pascendi Dominici Gregis*, par. 28.

12. Pius X, *Encyclical on the Doctrines of the Modernists, Pascendi Dominici Gregis*, par. 13.

13. Pius X, *Encyclical on the Doctrines of the Modernists, Pascendi Dominici Gregis*, par. 13.

14. Pius X, *Encyclical on the Doctrines of the Modernists, Pascendi Dominici* Gregis, par. 28.

15. Pius X, *Encyclical on the Doctrines of the Modernists, Pascendi Dominici Gregis*, par. 34.

16. Pius X, *Encyclical on the Doctrines of the Modernists, Pascendi Dominici Gregis*, par. 34.

17. Pius X, "Oath against Modernism" (September 1, 1910), http://www.papal encyclicals.net/Pius10/p10moath.htm (accessed December 6, 2004).

18. Pius X, Oath against Modernism.

19. *Baltimore Catechism No. 2* (New York: Sadlier, 1945), 29.

20. Pius XII, *Encyclical on Promoting Biblical Studies, Divino Afflante Spiritu* (September 30, 1943), par. 17, http://www.vatican.va/holy_father/pius_xii/encyclicals/documents/hf_p-xii_enc_30091943_divino-afflante-spiritu_en.html (accessed May 18, 2009).

21. Pius XII, *Encyclical on Promoting Biblical Studies, Divino Afflante Spiritu*, par. 38.

22. Pius XII, *Encyclical on Promoting Biblical Studies, Divino Afflante Spiritu*, par. 44.

23. Pius XII, *Encyclical on Promoting Biblical Studies, Divino Afflante Spiritu*, par. 48.

24. Pius XII, *Encyclical Concerning Some False Opinions Threatening to Undermine the Foundations of Catholic Doctrine, Humani Generis* (12 August 1950), par. 37, http://www.vatican.va/holy_father/pius_xii/encyclicals/documents/hf_p-xii_enc_12081950_humani-generis_en.htm (accessed April 17, 2009).

25. *Catechism of the Catholic Church* (Washington, DC: United States Catholic Conference, 1994), 390.

26. John Paul II, "Faith Can Never Conflict with Reason," speech to the Pontifical Academy of Sciences (October 31, 1992), reported in *L'Osservatore Romano* (November 4, 1992), par. 4, http://unigre.it/cssf/comuni/documenti/chiesa/Galilei.html (accessed May 18, 2009).

27. John Paul II, "Faith Can Never Conflict with Reason," par. 5.

28. John Paul II, "Faith Can Never Conflict with Reason," par. 6.

29. John Paul II, "Faith Can Never Conflict with Reason," par. 8.

30. John Paul II, "Faith Can Never Conflict with Reason," par. 9.

4. CONTRACEPTION

1. Pius XI, *Encyclical on Christian Marriage, Casti Connubii* (December 31, 1930), n. 55, www.vatican.va/holy_father/pius_xi/encyclicals/documents/hf_p-xi_enc_31121930_casti-connubii_en.html (accessed July 6, 2009).

2. Pius XI, *Encyclical on Christian Marriage, Casti Connubii*, n. 125.

3. Robert McClory, *Turning Point: The Inside Story of the Papal Birth Control Commission* (New York: Crossroad, 1995), 1.

4. McClory, *Turning Point*, 1.

5. John T. Noonan, Jr., *Contraception: A History of Its Treatment by the Catholic Theologians and Canonists* (Cambridge, MA: Harvard University Press, 1966), 28.

6. Noonan, *Contraception*, 28.

7. Vatican Council II, *Pastoral Constitution on the Church in the Modern World, Gaudium et Spes* (December 7, 1965), n. 50, in *Vatican Council II: The Conciliar and Post Conciliar Documents*, vol. 1, rev. ed., ed. Austin Flannery et al. (Collegeville, MN: Liturgical Press, 1992), 953.

8. Vatican Council II, *Pastoral Constitution on the Church in the Modern World, Gaudium et Spes*, n. 51, in Flannery et al., *Vatican Council II*, 955.

9. Vatican Council II, *Pastoral Constitution on the Church in the Modern World, Gaudium et Spes*, n. 51, in Flannery et al., *Vatican Council II*, 955.

10. Paul VI, *Encyclical Letter on the Regulation of Birth, Humanae Vitae* (July 25, 1968), n. 2, http://www.vatican.va/holy_father/paul_vi/encyclicals/documents/hf_p-vi_enc_25071968_humanae-vitae_en.html (accessed August 16, 2012).

11. Paul VI, *Encyclical Letter on the Regulation of Birth, Humanae Vitae*, n. 3.

12. Paul VI, *Encyclical Letter on the Regulation of Birth, Humanae Vitae*, n. 4.

13. Paul VI, *Encyclical Letter on the Regulation of Birth, Humanae Vitae*, n. 11.

14. Paul VI, *Encyclical Letter on the Regulation of Birth, Humanae Vitae*, n. 12.

15. Paul VI, *Encyclical Letter on the Regulation of Birth, Humanae Vitae*, n. 14.

16. Paul VI, *Encyclical Letter on the Regulation of Birth, Humanae Vitae*, n. 14.

17. Paul VI, *Encyclical Letter on the Regulation of Birth, Humanae Vitae*, n. 28.

18. Richard P. McBrien, *Catholicism* (Minneapolis: Winston Press, 1970), 1025.

19. Paul VI, *Encyclical Letter on the Regulation of Birth, Humanae Vitae*, n. 6.

20. McBrien, *Catholicism,* 1020.

21. Garry Wills, *Papal Sin: Structures of Deceit* (New York: Doubleday, 2000), 78.

22. Pius XI, *Encyclical on Christian Marriage, Casti Connubii*, n. 57, quoted in Wills, *Papal Sin*, 78–79.

23. Paul VI, *Encyclical Letter on the Regulation of Birth, Humanae Vita*e, n. 4.

5. ORDINATION AND WOMEN'S ROLE IN THE CHURCH

1. Aristotle, *Generation of Animals*, 1, 728a, trans. A. L. Peck (Cambridge, MA: Harvard University Press, 1942), 103.

2. Aristotle, *Politics,* 1254 b-12, trans. H. Rackkham, in *Aristotle in Twenty-Three Volumes*, vol. 21 (Cambridge, MA: Harvard University Press, 1932), 21.

3. Thomas Aquinas, *Summa Theologica*, 1 q. 92, art. 1, reply to obj. 1, trans. Fathers of the English Dominican Province (New York: Benziger Brothers, 1946), 466.

4. Edward Schillebeeckx, *The Church with a Human Face: A New and Expanded Theology of Ministry* (New York: Crossroad, 1987), 144, quoted in Ray R. Noll, *Sacraments: A New Understanding for a New Generation* (Mystic, CT: Twenty-Third Publications, 1999), 103.

5. Pius XI, *Encyclical on Christian Marriage, Casti Connubii* (December 31, 1930), n. 29, http://www.vatican.va/holy_father/pius_xi/encyclicals/documents/hf_p-xi_enc_31121930 _casti-connubii_en.html (accessed July 6, 2009).

6. Vatican Council II, *Pastoral Constitution on the Church in the Modern World, Gaudium et Spes* (December 7, 1965), n. 29, in *Vatican Council II: The Conciliar and Post Conciliar Documents*, vol. 1, rev. ed., ed. Austin Flannery et al. (Collegeville, MN: Liturgical Press, 1992), 929.

7. Sacred Congregation for the Doctrine of the Faith, *Declaration on the Question of Admission of Women to the Ministerial Priesthood, Inter Insigniores* (October 15, 1976), introduction, http://www.ewtn.com/library/curia/cdfinsig.htm (accessed August 17, 2012).

8. Sacred Congregation for the Doctrine of the Faith, *Declaration on the Question of Admission of Women to the Ministerial Priesthood*, n. 1.

9. Sacred Congregation for the Doctrine of the Faith, *Declaration on the Question of Admission of Women to the Ministerial Priesthood*, n. 5.

10. Sacred Congregation for the Doctrine of the Faith, *Declaration on the Question of Admission of Women to the Ministerial Priesthood*.

11. Sacred Congregation for the Doctrine of the Faith, *Declaration on the Question of Admission of Women to the Ministerial Priesthood*.

12. Sacred Congregation for the Doctrine of the Faith, *Declaration on the Question of Admission of Women to the Ministerial Priesthood*, n. 6.

13. John Paul II, *Apostolic Letter on Reserving Priestly Ordination to Men Alone, Ordinatio Sacerdotalis* (May 22, 1994), n. 4, http://www.vatican.va/holy_father/john_paul_ii/apost _letters/documents/hf_jp-ii_apl_22051994_ordinatio-sacerdotalis_en.html (accessed July 7, 2009).

14. John Wright, "Patristic Testimony on Women's Ordination in *Inter Insigniores*," *Theological Studies* 58 (1997), 516.

15. Wright, "Patristic Testimony on Women's Ordination in *Inter Insigniores*," 526.

16. Sacred Congregation for the Doctrine of the Faith, *Declaration on the Question of Admission of Women to the Ministerial Priesthood, Inter Insigniores*, n. 5.

17. Sacred Congregation for the Doctrine of the Faith, *Declaration on the Question of Admission of Women to the Ministerial Priesthood, Inter Insigniores*, n. 5.

18. Sacred Congregation for the Doctrine of the Faith, *Declaration on the Question of Admission of Women to the Ministerial Priesthood, Inter Insigniores*, n. 1.

19. Sacred Congregation for the Doctrine of the Faith, *Declaration on the Question of Admission of Women to the Ministerial Priesthood, Inter Insigniores*.

20. Mountain East Region Report, "Issues and Concerns," *Cross Roads* (Lexington: Diocese of Lexington, 1997), iv.

21. "Lexington Diocese . . . Moves Full Speed Ahead on Lay Run Church," *The Wanderer*, January 22, 1998.

22. Code of Canon Law, c 129, in *The Code of Canon Law: A Text and Commentary*, ed. James Coriden et al. (Mahwah, NJ: Paulist Press, 1958), 93.

23. Ladislas Orsy, "Book I: General Norms," in Coriden et al., *The Code of Canon Law*.

6. HOMOSEXUALITY

1. *Catechism of the Catholic Church* (Washington, DC: United States Catholic Conference, 1994), 2357–59.

2. *Catechism of the Catholic Church*, 2357.

3. *Catechism of the Catholic Church*, 2357.

4. *Catechism of the Catholic Church*, 2357.

5. American Psychiatric Association, policy statement, taken from the American Psychological Association "Fact Sheet on Gay, Lesbian, and Bisexual Issues" (May 2000) at The Center for Lesbian and Gay Studies in Religion and Ministry, http://www.clgs.org/official-statement-concerning-homosexuality-american-psychiatric-associatio (accessed August 4, 2012).

6. American Psychiatric Association, position statement on "Psychiatric Treatment and Sexual Orientation," (1998), taken from the American Psychological Association "Just the Facts about Sexual Orientation and Youth: A Primer for Principals, Educators, and School Personnel," http://www.apa.org/pi/lgbt/resources/just-the-facts.aspx.

7. U.S. Bishops' Committee on Marriage and Family, *Always Our Children: A Pastoral Message to Parents of Homosexual Children and Suggestions for Pastoral Ministers*, 1991, http://old.usccb.org/laity/always.shtml (accessed August 4, 2012).

8. U.S. Bishops' Committee on Marriage and Family, *Always Our Children*.

9. *Catechism of the Catholic Church*, par. 2333.

10. United States Catholic Conference. Office of Counsel; Secretariat for Doctrine and Pastoral Practices; Secretariat for Family, Laity, Women, and Youth, *Same-Sex Unions and Marriage: A Legal, Social, and Theological Analysis* (Washington DC: United States Catholic Conference, 1997), 4–5.

11. United States Catholic Conference, *Same-Sex Unions and Marriage*, 6–7.

12. Vatican Council II, *Pastoral Constitution on the Church in the Modern World, Gaudium et Spes* (December 7, 1965), n. 35, in *Vatican Council II: The Conciliar and Post Conciliar Documents*, vol. 1, rev. ed., ed. Austin Flannery et al. (Collegeville, MN: Liturgical Press, 1992), 934–35.

7. ABORTION: CHURCH, STATE, CONSCIENCE, AND EFFECTIVE WITNESS

1. Congregation for the Doctrine of the Faith, "Instruction on Respect for Human Life in Its Origin and on the Dignity of Procreation: Replies to Certain Questions of the Day" (February 22, 1987), sec. I, 1, http://www.vatican.va/roman_curia/congregations/cfaith/documents/rc_con_cfaith_doc_19870222_respect-for-human-life_en.html (accessed June 24, 2009).

2. Congregation for the Doctrine of the Faith, "Instruction on Respect for Human Life," introduction, 5.

3. Congregation for the Doctrine of the Faith, "Instruction on Respect for Human Life," sec. I, 4.

4. Congregation for the Doctrine of the Faith, "Instruction on Respect for Human Life, sec. II, b, 4.

5. Congregation for the Doctrine of the Faith, "Instruction on Respect for Human Life, introduction, 3.

6. *Baltimore Catechism No. 2* (New York: Sadlier, 1945), 27.

7. "Abortion," *Dictionary of Canon Law*, http://canonlawdictionary.blogspot.com/2008/10/abortion.html (accessed August 17, 2012).

8. *Catechism of the Catholic Church* (Washington, DC: United States Catholic Conference, 1994), 1778.

9. *Catechism of the Catholic Church*, 1782.

10. United States Conference of Catholic Bishops, *Catholics in Political Life*, par. 4, http://www.old.usccb.org/bishops/catholicsinpoliticallife.shtml (accessed July 1, 2009).

11. United States Conference of Catholic Bishops, *Catholics in Political Life*, p. 8.

12. Paul VI, *Evangelization in the Modern World, Evangelii Nuntiandi* (December 8, 1975), par. 41, in *Vatican Council II: The Conciliar and Post Conciliar Documents*, vol. 2, rev. ed., ed. Austin Flannery et al. (Collegeville, MN: Liturgical Press, 1992), 728.

8. MARRIAGE AND ANNULMENTS

1. *Catechism of the Catholic Church* (Washington, DC: United States Catholic Conference, 1994), 1612.

2. International Committee on English in the Liturgy, *Rite of Marriage: Introduction* (1969), par. 1–2, htpp://www.liturgyoffice.org.uk/Resources/Rites/Marriage.pdf (accessed August 20, 2012).

3. International Committee on English in the Liturgy, *Rite of Marriage:*, par. 3.

4. International Committee on English in the Liturgy, *Rite of Marriage:*, par. 4.

5. International Committee on English in the Liturgy, *Rite of Marriage:*, par. 7.

6. W. Becket Soule, *The Catholic Teaching on Annulment: Preserving the Sanctity of Marriage* (New Haven, CT: Catholic Information Service, Knights of Columbus Supreme Council, 1997), 11.

7. Soule, *The Catholic Teaching on Annulment*, 11–12.

8. Soule, *The Catholic Teaching on Annulment*, 12–18.

9. Nathaniel Reeves, Presentation on Marriage and Nullity (Continuing Education Day, Catholic Diocese of Lexington, handouts distributed on September 27, 2000), 3.

9. TEACHING SOCIAL JUSTICE AND TREATING EMPLOYEES JUSTLY

1. United States Conference of Catholic Bishops, *Sharing Catholic Social Teaching: Challenges and Directions* (Washington, DC: United States Conference of Catholic Bishops, 1998), 3, http://www.usccb.org/beliefs-and-teachings/what-we-believe/catholic-social-teaching/sharing-catholic-social-teaching-challenges-and-directions.cfm (accessed May 21, 2009). Unless otherwise noted, all subsequent quotations in this chapter are from this document.

2. United States Catholic Bishops, *Economic Justice for All: Pastoral Letter on Catholic Social Teaching and the U.S. Economy* (Washington, DC: United States Conference of Catho-

lic Bishops, 1986), par. 24, http//www.usccb.org/upload/economic_justice_for_all.pdf (accessed August 21, 2012).

3. United States Conference of Catholic Bishops, *Sharing Catholic Social Teaching*, 4.

10. UNITY IN THE BODY OF CHRIST

1. Vatican Council II, *Decree on Ecumenism, Unitatis Redintegratio* (November 21, 1964), par. 3, in *Vatican Council II: The Conciliar and Post Conciliar Documents*, vol. 1, rev. ed., ed. Austin Flannery et al. (Collegeville, MN: Liturgical Press, 1992), 455.

2. John Paul II, *Encyclical on Commitment to Ecumenism, Ut Unum Sint* (May 25, 1995), par. 2, *Origins* 25, no. 4 (1995), sec. 2.

3. John Paul II, *Encyclical on Commitment to Ecumenism, Ut Unum Sint*, sec. 2.

4. John Paul II, *Encyclical on Commitment to Ecumenism, Ut Unum Sint*, sec. 3.

5. John Paul II, *Encyclical on Commitment to Ecumenism, Ut Unum Sint*, sec. 4.

6. John Paul II, *Encyclical on Commitment to Ecumenism, Ut Unum Sint*, sec. 6.

7. John Paul II, *Encyclical on Commitment to Ecumenism, Ut Unum Sint*.

8. John Paul II, *Encyclical on Commitment to Ecumenism, Ut Unum Sint*, sec. 19.

9. John Paul II, *Encyclical on Commitment to Ecumenism, Ut Unum Sint*, sec. 80.

10. John Paul II, *Encyclical on Commitment to Ecumenism, Ut Unum Sint*, sec. 95.

11. John Paul II, *Encyclical on Commitment to Ecumenism, Ut Unum Sint*.

12. John Paul II, *Encyclical on Commitment to Ecumenism, Ut Unum Sint*, sec. 19.

13. *Baltimore Catechism No. 2* (New York: Sadlier, 1945), 131–32.

14. *Catechism of Christian Doctrine No. 3* (New York: Benziger, 1921), 189.

15. Center for Applied Research in the Apostolate, "Sacraments Today: Belief and Practice among U.S. Catholics" (2008), 54, http://cara.georgetown.edu/sacramentsreport.pdf (accessed August 21, 2012).

16. Margaret Nutting Ralph, *And God Said What? An Introduction to Biblical Literary Forms* (Mahwah, NJ: Paulist Press, 2003), 189.

17. Pontifical Council for Promoting Christian Unity, *Directory for the Application of Principles and Norms on Ecumenism* (March 25, 1993), par. 129, www.vatican.va/roman_curia/pontifical_councils/chrstuni/general-docs/rc_pc_chrstuni_doc_19930325_directory_en.html.

18. Pontifical Council for Promoting Christian Unity, *Directory*.

19. Pontifical Council for Promoting Christian Unity, *Directory*.

20. Pontifical Council for Promoting Christian Unity, *Directory*.

21. Pontifical Council for Promoting Christian Unity, *Directory*.

22. Michael Kinnamon, *Truth and Community: Diversity and Its Limits in the Ecumenical Movement* (Grand Rapids, MI: Eerdmans, 1988).

CONCLUSION

1. Timothy M. Dolan, "Archbishop Dolan Presidential Speech to USCCB Fall Meeting," November 14, 2011, Unapologetically Catholic, http://rootofjesse2.wordpress.com/2011/11/18/archbishop-dolan-presidential-speech-to-usccb-fall-meeting (accessed July 2, 2012).

2. *Cross Roads* (Lexington: Diocese of Lexington, July 4, 2010), 4.

3. *Cross Roads*, 4.

4. Vatican Council II, *Declaration on the Relation of the Church to Non-Christian Religions, Nostra Aetate* (October 28, 1965), sec. 1, in *Vatican Council II: The Conciliar and Post Conciliar Documents*, vol. 1, rev. ed., ed. Austin Flannery et al. (Collegeville, MN: Liturgical Press, 1992), 738.

5. Dan Morris-Young, "Bishop Requires Lay Ministers to Sign Orthodoxy Affirmation," *National Catholic Reporter* (July 2, 2004), 4.

6. Sacred Congregation for the Doctrine of the Faith, "Doctrinal Assessment of the Leadership Conference of Women Religious" (April 18, 2012), III, 1, http://www.usccb.org/upload/Doctrinal_Assessment_Leadership_Conference_Women_Religious.pdf (accessed August 21, 2012), 5.

7. John Paul II, "Faith Can Never Conflict with Reason," speech to the Pontifical Academy of Sciences (October 31, 1992), *L'Osservatore Romano* (November 4, 1992), http://unigre.it/cssf/comuni/documenti/chiesa/Galilei.html (accessed May 18, 2009).

8. Vatican Council II, *Dogmatic Constitution on the Church, Lumen Gentium* (November 21, 1964), par. 48, in *Vatican Council II: The Conciliar and Post Conciliar Documents*, 407.

Bibliography

"Abortion." *Dictionary of Canon Law*. October 25, 2008. http://canonlawdictionary .blogspot.com/2008/10/abortion.html.

American Psychiatric Association. "Position Statement on Psychiatric Treatment and Sexual Orientation." 1998. http://www.psychiatry.org/advocacy--newsroom/position-statements.

Aquinas, Thomas. *Summa Theologica*, vol. 1. Translated by Fathers of the English Dominican Province. New York: Benziger, 1946.

Aristotle. *Politics*. In *Aristotle in Twenty-Three Volumes*, vol. 21. Translated by H. Rackham. Cambridge, MA: Harvard University Press, 1932.

————. *Generation of Animals*. Translated by A. L. Peck. Cambridge, MA: Harvard University Press, 1942.

Baltimore Catechism No. 2. New York: Sadlier, 1945.

Catechism of Christian Doctrine No. 3. New York: Benziger, 1921.

Catechism of the Catholic Church. Washington, DC: United States Catholic Conference, 1994.

Catholics United for the Faith. "No Bull: Papal Authority and Our Response." Faith Facts. http://www.cuf.org/faithfacts/details_view.asp?ffid=115.

Center for Applied Research in the Apostolate. "Sacraments Today: Belief and Practice among U.S. Catholics." 2008. http://cara.georgetown.edu/sacramentsreport.pdf.

Congregation for the Doctrine of the Faith. "Instruction on Respect for Human Life in Its Origin and on the Dignity of Procreation: Replies to Certain Questions of the Day." February 22, 1987. http://www.vatican.va/roman_curia/congregations/cfaith/documents/rc_con _cfaith_doc_19870222_respect-for-human-life_en.html.

Coriden, James A., et al., eds. *The Code of Canon Law: A Text and Commentary*. Mahwah, NJ: Paulist Press, 1985.

Dolan, Timothy M. "Archbishop Dolan Presidential Speech to USCCB Fall Meeting." November 14, 2011. Unapologetically Catholic. http://rootofjesse2.wordpress.com/2011/11/18/ archbishop-dolan-presidential-speech-to-usccb-fall-meeting.

Gula, Richard M. *Reason Informed by Faith: Foundations of Catholic Morality*. Mahwah, NJ: Paulist Press, 1989.

Heeg, Aloysius J. *The Illustrated Catechism: A Practical Presentation of the Official Text of the Baltimore Catechism No. 1*. St. Louis, MO: The Queen's Work, 1958.

International Committee on English in the Liturgy. *Rite of Marriage: Introduction.* 1969. http://www.liturgyoffice.org.uk/Resources/Rites/Marriage.pdf.

John Paul II. *Apostolic Letter on Reserving Priestly Ordination to Men Alone. Ordinatio Sacerdotalis* (May 22, 1994). http://www.vatican.va/holy_father/john_paul_ii/apost_letters/documents/hf_jp-ii_apl_22051994_ordinatio-sacerdotalis_en.html.

———. *Encyclical on Commitment to Ecumenism. Ut Unum Sint* (May 25, 1995). *Origins* 25, no. 4 (1995).

———. "Faith Can Never Conflict with Reason." Speech to the Pontifical Academy of Sciences (October 31, 1992). *L'Osservatore Romano* (November 4, 1992). http://www.unigre.it/cssf/comuni/documenti/chiesa/Galilei.html.

Kinnamon, Michael. *Truth and Community: Diversity and Its Limits in the Ecumenical Movement.* Grand Rapids, MI: Eerdmans, 1988.

McBrien, Richard P. *Catholicism.* Minneapolis: Winston Press, 1970.

McClory, Robert. *Turning Point: The Inside Story of the Papal Birth Control Commission.* New York: Crossroad, 1995.

Morris-Young, Dan. "Bishop Requires Lay Ministers to Sign Orthodoxy Affirmation." *National Catholic Reporter*, July 2, 2004.

Noll, Ray R. *Sacraments: A New Understanding for a New Generation.* Mystic, CT: Twenty-Third Publications, 1999.

Noonan, John T., Jr. *Contraception: A History of Its Treatment by the Catholic Theologians and Canonists.* Cambridge, MA: Harvard University Press, 1966.

Pagels, Elaine. *The Origin of Satan.* New York: Random House, 1995.

Paul VI. *Encyclical Letter on the Regulation of Birth. Humanae Vitae* (July 25, 1968). http://www.vatican.va/holy_father/paul_vi/encyclicals/documents/hf_p-vi_enc_25071968_humanae-vitae_en.html.

———. *Evangelization in the Modern World. Evangelii Nuntiandi* (December 8, 1975). In *Vatican Council II: The Conciliar and Post Conciliar Documents*, vol. 2. Edited by Austin Flannery et al. Collegeville, MN: Liturgical Press, 1992.

Pius X. *Encyclical on the Doctrines of the Modernists. Pascendi Dominici Gregis* (August 9, 1907). http://www.vatican.va/holy_father/pius_x/encyclicals/documents/hf_p-x_enc_19070908_pascendi-dominici-gregis_en.html.

———. "Oath against Modernism" (September 1, 1910). http://www.papalencyclicals.net/Pius10/p10moath.htm.

Pius XI. *Encyclical on Christian Marriage. Casti Connubii* (December 31, 1930). http://www.vatican.va/holy_father/pius_xi/encyclicals/documents/hf_p-xi_enc_31121930_casti-connubii_en.html.

Pius XII. *Encyclical on Promoting Biblical Studies. Divino Afflante Spiritu* (September 30, 1943). http://www.vatican.va/holy_father/pius_xii/encyclicals/documents/hf_p-xii_enc_30091943_divino-afflante-spiritu_en.html.

———. *Encyclical Concerning Some False Opinions Threatening to Undermine the Foundations of Catholic Doctrine. Humani Generis* (August 12, 1950). http://www.vatican.va/holy_father/pius_xii/encyclicals/documents/hf_p-xii_enc_12081950_humani-generis_en.html.

Pontifical Council for Promoting Christian Unity. *Directory for the Application of Principles and Norms on Ecumenism.* March 25, 1993. http://www.vatican.va/roman_curia/pontifical_councils/chrstuni/general-docs/rc_pc_chrstuni_doc_19930325_directory_en.html.

Ralph, Margaret Nutting. *And God Said What? An Introduction to Biblical Literary Forms.* Mahwah, NJ: Paulist Press, 2003.

Reese, Thomas. "The Hidden Exodus: Catholics Becoming Protestant." *National Catholic Reporter*, April 18, 2011. http://ncronline.org/news/faith-parish/hidden-exodus-catholics-becoming-protestants.

Sacred Congregation for the Doctrine of the Faith. *Declaration in Defense of the Catholic Doctrine on the Church against Certain Errors of the Present Day. Mysterium Ecclesiae.* June 24, 1973. http://www.vatican.va/roman_curia/congregations/cfaith/documents/rc_con_cfaith_doc_19730705_mysterium-ecclesiae_en.html.

———. *Declaration on the Question of Admission of Women to the Ministerial Priesthood. Inter Insigniores* (October 15, 1976). http:www.ewtn.com/library/curia/cdfinsig.htm.

———. "Doctrinal Assessment of the Leadership Conference of Women Religious." April 18, 2012. http://www.usccb.org/upload/Doctrinal_Assessment_Leadership_Conference_Women_Religious.pdf.

Soule, W. Becket. *The Catholic Teaching on Annulment: Preserving the Sanctity of Marriage.* New Haven, CT: Catholic Information Service, Knights of Columbus Supreme Council, 1997.

U.S. Bishops' Committee on Marriage and Family. *Always Our Children: A Pastoral Message to Parents of Homosexual Children and Suggestions for Pastoral Ministers.* 1991. http://old.usccb.org/laity/always.shtml.

United States Catholic Bishops. *Economic Justice for All: A Pastoral Letter on Catholic Teaching and the U.S. Economy.* Washington, DC: United States Conference of Catholic Bishops, 1986. http://www.usccb.org/upload/economic_justice_for_all.pdf.

United States Catholic Conference. Office of Counsel; Secretariat for Doctrine and Pastoral Practices; Secretariat for Family, Laity, Women, and Youth. *Same-Sex Unions and Marriage: A Legal, Social, and Theological Analysis.* Washington, DC: United States Catholic Conference, 1997.

United States Conference of Catholic Bishops. *Catholics in Political Life.* htpp://old.usccb.org/bishops/catholicsinpoliticallife.shtml.

———. *Sharing Catholic Social Teaching: Challenges and Directions.* Washington, DC: United States Conference of Catholic Bishops, 1998. http://www.usccb.org/beliefs-and-teachings/what-we-believe/catholic-social-teaching/sharing-catholic-social-teaching-challenges-and-directions.cfm.

Vatican Council II. *Declaration on the Relation of the Church to Non-Christian Religions. Nostra Aetate* (October 28, 1965). In *Vatican Council II: The Conciliar and Post Conciliar Documents*, vol. 1. Rev. ed. Edited by Austin Flannery et al. Collegeville, MN: Liturgical Press, 1992.

———. *Decree on Ecumenism. Unitatis Redintegratio* (November 21, 1964). In Flannery, *Vatican Council II.*

———. *Dogmatic Constitution on the Church. Lumen Gentium* (November 21, 1964). In Flannery, *Vatican Council II.*

———. *Dogmatic Constitution on Divine Revelation. Dei Verbum* (November 18, 1965). In Flannery, *Vatican Council II.*

———. *Pastoral Constitution on the Church in the Modern World. Gaudium et Spes* (December 7, 1965). In Flannery, *Vatican Council II.*

Wills, Garry. *Papal Sin: Structures of Deceit.* New York: Doubleday, 2000.

Wilwerding, A. J. *Examination of Conscience for Boys and Girls.* Saint Louis, MO: The Queen's Work, 1927.

Wright, John. "Patristic Testimony on Women's Ordination in *Inter Insignores.*" *Theological Studies* 58 (1997): 516–26.

Index

About the Author

Margaret Nutting Ralph, PhD, is a teacher with forty years of experience in both church and academic settings. She is a thirty-year diocesan retiree, having served in a variety of roles: high school teacher, adult education consultant, director of RCIA and evangelization, and finally as secretary of educational ministries in the Diocese of Lexington for sixteen years. Since 1988 she has served on the faculty at Lexington Theological Seminary as director of the Master of Arts in Pastoral Studies degree for Roman Catholics. Dr. Ralph has authored thirteen books on Scripture. Her work has been translated into Spanish, Italian, Portuguese, and Korean, with special editions in English for the Philippines and India. She and her husband, Don, have four adult children and fourteen grandchildren.